EUROPE AT THE DAWN OF THE MILLENNIUM

Europe at the Dawn of the Millennium

Enrique Barón
Member of the European Parliament
Brussels

Forewords by

Paul Preston
and
Carlos Fuentes

First published in Great Britain 1997 by
MACMILLAN PRESS LTD
Houndmills, Basingstoke, Hampshire RG21 6XS and London
Companies and representatives throughout the world

A catalogue record for this book is available from the British Library.

ISBN 0–333–65050–6 hardcover
ISBN 0–333–65051–4 paperback

 First published in the United States of America 1997 by
ST. MARTIN'S PRESS, INC.,
Scholarly and Reference Division,
175 Fifth Avenue, New York, N.Y. 10010

ISBN 0–312–16575–7

Library of Congress Cataloging-in-Publication Data
Barón, Enrique.
Europe at the dawn of the millennium / Enrique Barón ; forewords by
Paul Preston and Carlos Fuentes.
p. cm.
Includes bibliographical references and index.
ISBN 0–312–16575–7
1. European federation.   I. Title.
D1060.B27   1996
341.24'2—dc20   96–41004
                                                              CIP

This book is printed on paper suitable for recycling and made from fully managed and
sustained forest sources.

10   9   8   7   6   5   4   3   2   1
06   05   04   03   02   01   00   99   98   97

Printed in Great Britain by
The Ipswich Book Company Ltd
Ipswich, Suffolk

Contents

List of Abbreviations

ACP	Lomé Agreement beween the EC and 69 African, Caribbean and Pacific countries
APEC	Asian – Pacific Economic Cooperation
CAP	Common Agricultural Policy
CECA (or EAEC)	European Atomic Energy Community
CEDEFOP	European Centre for Development of Vocational Training
CFSP	Common Foreign and Security Policy
CIS	Commonwealth of Independent States
COMECON	Council for Mutual Economic Assistance
COREPER	Committee of the Permanent Representatives (of the governments of the countries)
CSCE	Conference on Security and Cooperation in Europe
DG	Directorate-General (of the Commission)
EAGGF	European Agricultural Guideline and Guarantee Fund
EBRD	European Bank for Reconstruction and Development
EC	European Community
ECB	European Central Bank
ECHO	European Emergency Humanitarian Aid Office
ECOFIN	Council of Economic and Finance Ministers
ECSC	European Coal and Steel Community
ECU	European Currency Unit

EDC	European Defence Community
EDF	European Development Fund
EEA	European Economic Area
EEC	European Economic Community
EFMC	European Fund for Monetary Cooperation
EFTA	European Free Trade Association
EIB	European Investment Bank
EMI	European Monetary Institute
EMS	European Monetary System
EMU	Economic and Monetary Union
EP	European Parliament
EPC	European Political Cooperation
ERDF	European Regional Development Fund
ESC	Economic and Social Committee
ESCB	European System of Central Banks
ESF	European Social Fund
EU	European Union
EURATOM (or EAEC)	European Atomic Energy Community
EUROPOL	European Police Office
FAO	Food and Agriculture Organization (UN)
FIR	Air Traffic Control Centre
G7	Group of the world's seven most industrialised and wealthy Countries (Canada, France, Germany, Italy, Japan, UK and USA)
GATT	General Agreement on Trade and Tariffs
GDP	Gross Domestic Product
IBRD	International Bank for Reconstruction and Development
IGC	Intergovernmental Conference
ILO	International Labour Organization (UN)
IMF	International Monetary Fund
MIT	Massachusetts Institute of Technology

NAFTA	North American Free Trade Area
NATO	North Atlantic Treaty Organization
NGO	Non-governmental Organisation
OECD	Organization for Economic Cooperation and Development
OPEC	Organization of Petroleum Exporting Countries
PES	Party of European Socialists
PHARE	Assistance for the Restructuring of the Hungarian and Polish Economies (extended in 1991 to other Eastern European Countries)
PIC	Preparatory Interinstitutional Conference
PPE	European People's Party
SEA	Single European Act
SMUs	Small and Medium-sized Undertakings
STABEX	System of Stabilisation of Export Earnings
Sysmin	System of aid to mining products
TACIS	Technical Assistance to the Commonwealth of Independent States and Georgia
TEU	Treaty on European Union
UN	United Nations Organization
UNCTAD	United Nations Conference on Trade and Development
UNDP	United Nations Development Programme
UNHCR	United Nations High Commissariat for Refugees
VAT	Value-added Tax
WEU	Western European Union
WTO	World Trade Organization

Foreword

Mrs Thatcher and the majority of the Conservative Party were once enthusiasts for Europe as a single market. The recent change in her personal views and the emergence of a malcontent group of so-called 'Eurosceptics' with which she sympathizes has its basis in the fact that a united Europe is about more than a single market. Their opposition derives in part from the fact that European Union stands as a more humane alternative to the low wage, free-for-all which, in Britain under Margaret Thatcher, spread insecurity as it brought down industries that with a little help might have survived.

It is to be wondered what Mrs Thatcher would make of Winston Churchill's ambition, described in a letter to Stafford Cripps in 1948, 'to make a real brotherhood of Europe, overriding all national, class and Party frontiers'. Three months later, speaking as President of Honour at the Congress of Europe held at the Hague in May 1948, Churchill declared

> We shall only save ourselves from the perils which draw near by forgetting the hatreds of the past, by letting national rancours and revenges die, by progressively effacing frontiers and barriers which aggravate and congeal our divisions, and by rejoicing together in that glorious treasure of literature, of romance, of ethics, of thought and toleration belonging to all, which is the true inheritance of Europe, the expression of its genius and honour, but which by our quarrels, our follies, by our fearful wars and the cruel and awful deeds that spring from war and tyrants, we have almost cast away.

The perceived totalitarian threats which inspired Winston Churchill in the late 1940s may have receded. Nevertheless, the ideals which inspired him are all the more necessary in a Europe which has known the savagery of the Balkan civil war and the short-sighted inanity which permitted a British government to attempt to hide its own regulatory deficiencies and its responsibility in the generation of the BSE crisis behind an artificially generated 'Beef War' with their European partners.

Enrique Barón shares Churchill's vision. He makes no bones

about seeing as 'courageous and opportune' the decisions taken
at Maastricht, turning the European Community into the
European Union with its commitment to both political union
based on common citizenship and economic and monetary
union based on a single currency. The central metaphor of his
book is that Europe is a half-built cathedral, the foundations
laid long ago but the walls still under construction, the roof
still no more than a future prospect. However, he has no doubt
of the need to complete the task or of the fact that the creation of good things takes time.

He writes from a position of authority, having been President of the European Parliament of which he is still a member. This is not a collection of personal anecdotes – although
it is a book uniquely enriched by its author's long experience
at the heart of Europe – but a contribution to a debate which
is of significance to every citizen of the European Union. It is
an especially crucial debate to citizens of Great Britain who
are not sure whether the concentration of power in Brussels is
a real threat to liberty or merely a device used by beleaguered
governments to create a spurious national unity. The Conservative government feels able to play on the idea of Europe
as a threat because the attitude of the British towards European unity differs so much from that of Continental Europeans and of the Spaniards in particular.

For most Europeans, the twentieth century has seen levels
of war and devastation far beyond anything experienced on
a British soil which has escaped the scourge of German or
Russian occupation. Europe as a project to absorb and channel
German strength means more to the French, the Dutch and
the Belgians than it does to the British who still live, falsely, on
their memories of triumphs over Germany (triumphs to which,
it is conveniently forgotten, American industrial strength made
such an important contribution). For Spaniards, neutrality in
both world wars meant that they did not suffer German or
Russian occupation. However, while Britain knew imperial glory
between the seventeenth and nineteenth centuries, Spain has
experienced a history of decline, of international humiliation
culminating in the final loss of empire at the hands of the
United States in 1898, and of intense domestic strife. The Civil
War of 1936–1939 was the third within a century and Spain's
modern experiences, until the rebirth of democracy in 1977,

have been dominated by bloodshed and repressive dictatorship. The experience of Portugal has been comparable. Accordingly, it is hardly surprising that Spaniards, Portuguese and Greeks have embraced the European idea with such enthusiasm.

In other words, for Continental Europeans, whether out of memories of world wars or of civil wars, a united Europe represents an escape from an unwanted past. In the depths of the Second World War, and hoping for a better aftermath, Jean Monnet sought the nucleus of a united Europe in the quest for a lasting future peace through Franco-German collaboration. Europe represents an institutionalization of the free society denied by Hitler, by Mussolini, by Franco, by Salazar, by the Greek colonels. It represents a prospect for peace because it signifies the taming of Germany and some renunciation of the national sovereignty which required armed forces to defend and lay at the heart of centuries of war. For Britain, it is different. However, in an apposite quotation, Enrique Barón cites the phrase of Joaquín Costa, the Spanish social thinker and inspiration of the regenerationism to the effect that to face the future, Spain needed to lock the tomb of El Cid with seven keys, in other words, as he says, 'we do not have the option of living off our memories'.

Of course, some British scepticism about Europe is entirely healthy. The discrepancy between the rhetoric and the reality of Euro-enthusiasm in some member states is highlighted by Enrique Barón when he says 'It is no coincidence that both Denmark and the UK head the list in the translation of Community legislation into national law, whereas other partners, so enthusiastic that they are ready to achieve the final objective as of now, are late as far as the application of Community legislation is concerned.' The consequent resentments can easily be turned by politicians into issues of national pride.

In this context, Enrique Barón does well to remind us of other words of Winston Churchill who, as President of Honour at the Congress of Europe held at the Hague in May 1948, affirmed 'the urgent need for close and effective unity among the peoples of Europe'. Speaking of political unity, Churchill acknowledged that this involved some sacrifice of national sovereignty but said 'I prefer to regard it as the gradual assumption by all the nations concerned of that larger sovereignty, which alone can protect their diverse and distinctive customs and characteristics and their national traditions, all of which under totalitarian systems, whether Nazi, fascist or communist, would certainly be blotted out for ever.' Infuriated by the lack of official support for the idea of a united Europe, he had spoken on the radio three months earlier, saying

> We are asking the nations of Europe between whom rivers of blood have flowed, to forget the feuds of a thousand years and work for the larger harmonies on which the future depends: and yet we in this island, who have so much in common, who have no serious grievances or vendettas to repay, are unable to lay aside even for the sake of such a cause on which we are all agreed, party strife and party prejudice.

Enrique Barón is an optimist and an enthusiast for Europe. He is fully aware that things have changed since the positive mood of the late 1980s, when the creation of the single market stimulated economic activity and the revolutions in Eastern Europe seemed to herald, if not the end of history, at least progress towards a world of democratic consensus. The present recession and the surge of bloodthirsty nationalisms in the Balkans and in parts of the old Soviet empire do not diminish his enthusiasm for Europe. Enrique Barón has a long historical perspective. It is unlikely that his reflections on the precedents of the Carolinglan, Habsburg, Napoleonic and Hitlerian empires will generate much enthusiasm. However, his explanation of the both the ideals and the practical goals that have inspired the progress from the Schuman Plan to the European Union is both salutary and useful.

Indeed, it is difficult to imagine a more clearly structured and agreeably written history of the project of European unity and of the development from EEC to EC to EU. For that alone, this book will be of immense utility of students. It is every bit as important as a critical yet affectionate and often witty guide to the complex labyrinth that is the Union and its institutions. At the same time, however, it is significant contribution to the present debate especially as it is postulated in Great Britain. His remark that 'if the Community were to seek membership of the Community, it would be rejected because it is not democratic' will strike many a chord among the more critical British observers of Europe. Similarly, he notes Robert Schuman's comment on the dead weight of the Community officials 'The coalition of technicians is a fearful thing'. He is aware of the resentments that arise from the lack of consistency between member states in the implementation of European legislation or from the hunger of the Brussels bureaucracy for more regulatory powers. Enrique Barón's explanations will not convince every British Eurosceptic although he agrees with Jim Hackett that the British sausage is more than a tube full of emulsion. Nor will he please the autonomous nationalists of Catalonia, the Basque Country, Padania, Scotland or Britanny with practical pessimism about the progressive replacement of the member states or what de Gaulle called '*l'Europe des Patries*' by the Europe of the regions.

The question of the single currency is one of equal, if not greater, concern to all Europeans, albeit for different reasons. The possibility that having to follow the monetary disciplines of a currency which, whatever it happens to be called, Euro or écu, will in most respects resemble the Deutschmark, and renounce their armouries of devaluation, naturally seems to pose a threat to the peripheral economies of Europe, to Britain, to Spain and Italy alike. On this vexed question, Enrique Barón presents an informative, carefully nuanced account which is lightened by an amusing tour around European attitudes to local currencies.

This lively account of Europe at the dawn of the next millennium has certainly achieved Enrique Barón's goal of avoiding what he calls the EU 'obscuranto' made up of 'inferences, winks and acronyms'. I started this book with the prejudice that books on Europe and its institutions tend to be tedious and formulaic. To my delight, I found a virtuoso display of intelligence, wit and jucidity. Anyone who reads it, whether politician, teacher, journalist or just a citizen, cannot fail to be significantly better equipped for the debate on which all our futures depend.

Professor Paul Preston,
Chairman of the European Institute,
London School of Economics

Prologue

In an elegant paragraph in this elegant book, Enrique Barón compares the construction of Europe to the construction of a cathedral, the emblem of European civilization. He is right; as we Mexicans know very well, building a cathedral takes centuries. Ours, in the *Zócalo* in Mexico City, was begun in 1573 and not finished until 1813.

Political structures can also be a long time in the building, and that of Europe has been under construction, as Barón describes it, since the time of 'famous Itálica', the Roman city near Seville whose ruins were celebrated by the Baroque poet Rodrigo Caro. The loss of Roman unity pulverized Europe, and the ephemeral political unity of the Carolingian world was no match for religious unity, even though the struggles between Gregory VII and Henry IV, Boniface VIII and Philip the Fair created a healthy political tension between the temporal and spiritual power. Without that tension, as our professor of Theory of the State at the University of Mexico, the Sevillian Manuel Pedroso, said, there would be no democracy in Europe. Without that tension, Europe would have been like Russia, a preserve for a perpetual confrontation between 'Caesars' and 'Popes' which even now casts its political shadow over that contentious part of the world. Europe avoided fusing the sphere of Caesar with the sphere of the Pope, and in doing so created the concept of national jurisdictions, the subordination of all political actors to national law. Because the nation came into existence, Europe was able to give itself a penal code, modern democracy, education and industry.

It also gave itself another gift: when national law came into existence, so did international law. Five hundred years ago, the world experienced a gigantic expansion; the only way that world could understand itself was through unification.

During the Middle Ages, war was the norm and peace the exception. But the European internationalists of the 16th and 17th centuries made peace into the norm and war into the exception. In Holland, Grotius established the norms for relationships among 'civilized' nations. But in Spain, Vitoria and Suárez went even further: they consecrated both the rights of the aboriginal peoples and the way the men and women of the colonies were to be treated. It was at that moment that Europe and America truly united their destinies in politics and law, the moment when Victoria gave the Indians the same rank – legal subjects – possessed by the inhabitants of Seville, when his disciple Suárez declared the people to be the source of all authority, therereby declaring all peoples legally exempt from conquest.

Nothing exemplifies the positive influence of Europe in the world as much as that dispute between those, like Sepúlveda, who denied any rights to the colonized and those, like Victoria, who founded international law on the universality of rights inherent in every individual. The many ills of the colonial era could never eclipse the judicial goodness of a system which, even when practice made a mockery of it a thousand times over, maintained a modicum of humanity and legality for indigenous communities that we modern Latin Americans have reduced and violated to an even greater degree than the cruellest of the Pizarros.

'We respect the law but we don't carry it out.' That cruel maxim of the colonial authorities thwarted to a considerable extent what could have been a Hispanic community of nations, as the Count of Aranda proposed to King Charles III. The obstruction of that aspiration, which would have benefited all of us, Spaniards and Spanish Americans, meant for Spain a long century of decadence that culminated in the fatal year 1898; and for Spanish America, it meant the threat of anarchy, dictatorship, and two equally unpleasant alternatives: balkanization of the empire into small republics or a centralist dictatorship. The Nation, the State, ultimately became the compromise between those extremes. But then we lost our connection to Spain and Europe and were victimized too many times by the hegemonic power of the continent. Will we be able to recover our lost time with Spain through Europe, and with Europe through Spain?

European unity, therefore, has immense importance for Latin America. Along with Europe, we lived the *annus mirabilis* of 1989. The fall of the Berlin Wall, the end of Moscow's domination of central Europe, *perestroika*, the end of the cold war and the arms race. In Latin America, we celebrated the triumph of democracy and, prematurely, the market economy.

Today, with the publication of Enrique Barón's splendid
book, we can evoke the title of a novel by Balzac, *Lost Illusions*.
An anguished world contemplates Europe's political inability
to end the genocide of Sarajevo or to halt the process leading
fatally to another holocaust: xenophobia, racism, the pogrom
against Arabs, Jews, Africans, Turks raises its dark head once
again. Does the end of communism sanction the resurrection
of fascism?

In our Latin America, macroeconomic successes have not
translated into greater well-being for those who live in the
microeconomy: concrete men and women, workers. We have
already seen manifestations of discontent in Venezuela, Peru,
Brazil and Mexico; economic ills jeopardize political and democratic achievements. Democracy and security cannot tolerate a
situation of growing poverty.

We look toward Europe. First, because we know that the
economic models prevalent there are superior to the suppos-
edly universal model we in Latin America have been squeezed
into. Europe tells us that capitalist wisdom does not find its
last word in the trickle-down models – the voodoo economics
practised by Reagan and Bush – the kind we practised in Latin
America in the 19th century. The neoliberal model applied to
Latin America concentrates wealth at the top but does not
force it to reach the bottom.

Nor does it increase productivity from the base up. To do
that, we would need a model closer to that of the European
Community, which includes social legislation, workers' participation, collective negotiation, and the conviction that without
a close relationship between employment, salary and productivity, a community becomes unjust and, ultimately, grows poor.

In Latin America, we need balance between the public sector and private sectors, and only the social sector, civil society
and its organizations can create it. Once again, Europe gives
us the alternative to the narrow, egoistic models of monetarism.
Europe for us is a source of diversification, an anti-dogmatic
warning that the market is not an end in itself, but a means to
achieve well-being in both social and individual goals.

But there is something more that Enrique Barón highlights
and lucidly analyses – something intrinsic to the European
Community and essential to the political future of Latin
America. It is the theme of federalism as a pivot, or at least a

hinge for political and economic democracy. How well our author describes the modern relevance of the theme, starting with the debate in the Federalist Papers in the early years of the United States. The triumph of the arguments of Hamilton, Madison and Jay gave the young North American republic the enviable political flexibility it has enjoyed, renewed when the federal pact was broken by the second independence revolution, Lincoln's war against the southern slave owners. Beyond Rome and Charlemagne, beyond Christian unity and nationalist unity, federalism today is once again the basis for a democratic future. In Europe, local authority allows issues to be dealt with and resolved at the local level and only then to be passed on to the community level. The goodness and logic of this solution seem indisputable to me. The nation retains all it needs and hands over to the Community what is appropriate for all, including the nation. The possibilities of better common action with regard to matters that require it increase for that very reason.

It is important for the whole world, because Europe, as disconcerted as the rest of the world by the loss of the Manichean comforts of the cold war and the ideological sanctuary it offered, also finds itself abandoned and confused, ready to take refuge in its worst historical traditions: antisemitism, chauvinism and xenophobia. We Latin Americans, Europe's other face, the thing most like Europe outside Europe, want, as Jacques Derrida has written, to recall that Europe is what has been promised in the name of Europe: the best of Europe. But this implies first that Europe submit to the rule of law the evil humours born from the ruins of the cold war and, second, that it open itself up more and more to what is not Europe, to the world that does not want to see in Europe colonial or fascist residues but the shared responsibility for economic cooperation, cultural exchange and the creation of a juridical order for the new millennium.

The Community is working hard to achieve these goals. Until now, as Peter Drucker notes in his *Postcapitalist Society*, schemes for transcending the European nations and creating transnational systems have all failed because every imperial attempt to unify Europe (Philip II, Richelieu, Louis XIV, Napoleon, Wilhelm II, Hitler, Stalin) has lacked the power to integrate those nations and has ended up strengthening the nation, now seen as the means whereby the nation saves itself from conquest by another nation. Until now, the modern empire has lacked the power of integration reserved for the national state.

The European Union creates, finally, the possibility of joining forces without doing violence to the power of local integration and its cultural attributes. These, at the same time, will blossom because of their contact: cultures in isolation perish. But in another sense, the European Union will overcome one more conflict of our dangerous times: the struggle between transnational, international, regional, national, local and tribal jurisdictions which, devoid of a judicial framework to contain them, threatens to overflow into multiple and successive conflicts.

For us Latin Americans, the success of a European federal system is essential for democratic development. Our continent passes rapidly from the concept of population to that of citizenship, from power exercised from above and from the centre to powers demanded from the periphery and below. We are the heirs of the imperial and centralized empires of the Aztecs and the Incas, of the Spanish crown and of the independent republics that ceased to be centralist and Bourbon to become centralist and France. Today the accumulated problems of injustice, inequality and authoritarianism demand as a solution a federalism that would allow our rural, indigenous and provincial communities to choose freely their representatives in free elections monitored by the citizens themselves.

European federalism and Latin American federalism: perhaps, beginning with this parallel experience, we shall succeed in reuniting, in accord with Einstein's theory, at the point where parallel lines converge. Let us hope the European cathedral is finally completed. Enrique Barón is one of its architects. Today I salute him and his admirable European volume, praying that in the plazas surrounding the cathedral of Europe we will all have a place, that its avenues will be wide and that, better still, the cathedral will be for all of us.

After all, in the dawn of our common civilization, the first great mestizo writer of Iberoamerica, el Inca Garcilaso de la Vega, wrote these beautiful and prophetic words: 'There is only one world'.

Carlos Fuentes
San Jerónimo, México, 1994

Introduction

> It was the universal belief in the Middle Ages that the world was to come to an end in the year one thousand A.D. . . . This world beheld nothing but chaos within but it aspired to order and trusted to find it in death. . . . Trouble upon trouble, ruin upon ruin. There had to be something more to come, and the people waited for it. The captive waited in his black dungeon, in the sepulchral *in pace*; the serf waited in his furrow beneath the shadow of the hated keep; the monk waited, in the abstinence of the cloister, in the solitary tumults of the heart . . .
>
> Jules Michelet

This is a work written in a half-built house. It has neither the advantage of a historical account which tells the story of a birth whose outcome is already known, nor the blinding freedom enjoyed by the author who has a blank page in front of him on which he can limn his dreams.

Essentially, this is a collection of thoughts jotted down by a citizen who shares with many others the trades of stonemason and architect working on a large building site. Who does not know the tale of the pilgrim who, stopping in front of a cathedral under construction – that most emblematic of European buildings – asks some workmen 'What are you building?'. One answers, 'A wall'; another says 'A cathedral'.

In the case in question, we have already left the laying of the foundations far behind us. Not only is the building already there, but we are living in it and it has a name – the European Union. Now we are attempting to put the finishing touches to the building, get the roof on, and even increase the capacity of this cyclopean edifice. It is not an unheard-of challenge: the majority of cathedrals took centuries to build, and bear the traces of diverse masters, superimposing their styles.

The problem is knowing how to calculate and recalculate the equilibrium with the system of weights and counter-weights capable of supporting different forces and pressures which may even be contradictory of one another. Moreover, one has to know how to do it at a time when not only must one heed the opinions of the members of a select guild of master builders but when everybody has the right to speak in chapter when it comes to uniting our destinies: we are dealing with the purse and with life, i.e. the single currency and citizenship.

I would warn the reader, therefore, that this is not a collection of anecdotes about my experience in the European Parliament, including that of being President. Books of that kind, drawn up without the distance which memoirs allow the author, combine the very most gossiping tittle-tattle with self-praise, as well as displaying a certain tendency to denigrate most of the people whose names appear in heavy type. Often, such works become mere exercises in narcissism, with the author always in the right, if he is speaking in the first person, or violating his essential commitment to keep secrets, if he is a secretary. He never makes a mistake nor a fool of himself; in short, he is unreal. As Paco Fernández Ordóñez rightly said about a book of this kind written by a former colleague, 'It's the perfect way to make sure that people stop saying hello to you.'

This book links up with *El rapto del futuro*, published in 1989, a date as close as it is distant. At that time, the dominant concern was the completion of the internal market, with the tools of the Single Act, and how to organize a new *modus vivendi* with a new USSR in the throes of *perestroika*, which had finally decided to recognize the existence of the EEC with the Luxembourg Declaration of June 1988. Five years later, both the USSR and COMECON are lying on the scrap heap of history, while the EEC has turned into the European Union.

Following a phase of progress and consolidation accompanied by prosperity, we are now in a phase of difficulties, of crisis. It is not a terminal crisis, leading to break-up or divorce. We are living through a debate filled with questions as to the appropriateness and usefulness of going ahead and the efforts and sacrifices that will be asked of us.

For over 40 years, the Community has been taking shape. The pendulum has swung to and fro and the crises have been impassioned. But the revolutions have been palace ones. Today, for the first time, we have escaped from the gentle despotism of a group of bold politicians, high officials, motivated diplomats and indefatigable activists and find ourselves in the midst of an open democratic debate which is, for that very reason, unpredictable. Such is the greatness and the excess of democracy.

The great issue raised, therefore, is the nature and political scope of the Union, because the step taken raises as many questions as it answers. Why does the Union exist and what is it for? Is it an alliance or a federation? How are executive powers to be shared between the Commission and the Council? And how is the legislative power to be shared between the Council and Parliament? Should the legislative process be public? What will the single currency be like? Will it be worth more or less? These and many other questions are on the lips of the citizens of the Community countries. They cover everything, from the concentration of bureaucratic power in Brussels, feared by many UK citizens, to the exchanging of a solid D-mark for a currency whose name makes many Germans think of cows[1], the extension of the right of voting in local elections to Maghrebins feared by many French citizens, the effort required to achieve convergence demanded of and by many Spaniards, or the Italians' or Belgians' concern with tightening their belts and paying off their debts. These problems may be real or imaginary; what matters is that they exist in people's minds and influence their collective consciousness and, therefore, public opinion. In democracy, debates are very difficult to steer and cannot be limited to explanations, however much or little detail is supplied.

Moreover, the unjust if stable world order provided by North American tutelage in a bipolar world of two superpowers implicitly allied by the terror of nuclear weapons has come to an end. The thaw and the flood of events which in 1989 burst the Iron Curtain and its most famous symbol, the Berlin Wall, have not only changed the pace of history but, with German unification, they have put Community cohesion to the test in its most sensitive area, confronting it with its own responsibilities. In short, the time has arrived to come of age and set ourselves free, and we do not have the option of living off our memories. Each one of us, in his own house, is now obliged to lock the tomb of his own personal Cid with seven keys, as Joaquín Costa so wisely advised.

In the face of this flood of events, which has sometimes threatened to overwhelm us, it is more necessary than ever to encourage debate. Because the most reasonable criticism which may be levelled at the Treaty on European Union is not only its alienating and somewhat technocratic complexity, but, above all, its excessive boldness as far as certain smug forms of society (Galbraith's 'culture of contentment') are concerned.

Here, I regret that I cannot share Ralf Dahrendorf's assessment when he affirms that the Treaty is the work of a group of tired politicians, although I recommend that those who are interested in Germany's role in the Community read his letter to a Polish friend. I think, on the contrary, that this is one of the rare occasions on which we can claim that the political leaders of twelve countries, with very different approaches to life and society, had the clear-mindedness to take a step forward whose consequences are unpredictable, as is always the case when we emulate Zarathustra and say 'yes to life'.

From the prosperity generated by the wave of growth which accompanied the setting-up of the internal market during the period 1985–1992, we moved into the greatest economic crisis in Europe since the war. The hopes aroused by the spectacular affirmation of shared values in the democratic revolutions in Central and Eastern Europe have been overshadowed by the Yugoslavian tragedy, the complex break-up of the Soviet empire and the reappearance of demons from the past such as all-or-nothing nationalism, xenophobia and fratricidal intolerance.

In the political sphere, the framework of post-war political life has been blown to pieces. This has taken place more brusquely in countries where taking turns in office has been a de facto impossibility since the war – such as in Italy, which is undergoing a major revolution, or Japan, where the taboo of an eternal majority has also been broken. Electorates are more voluble and are tending to use revolt as a punishment, thus imparting a greater degree of uncertainty to political life. Over against the sway of the great decidedly pro-European families (Christian Democrats, Socialists and Liberals), the Greens, regionalists and extreme right are gaining strength, with their very different and even contradictory visions of the European Union. In three Community countries controversial plebiscites took place: in Denmark the referendum had to be held twice, following a clarificatory renegotiation and a change of majority without elections; in Ireland the 'yes' won comfortably, although the majority changed; in France, in due keeping with the Gallic tradition of splitting down the middle in to two camps, the 'yes' divided the political parties and won by a hair's breadth.

Despite the fact that at an early stage there was a certain temptation to go ahead with a purely rubber-stamp ratification, it has been necessary to amend various constitutions (in France, Spain, Belgium, Germany, Portugal, Ireland and Luxembourg). In the case of Belgium, a state whose very nature has changed, there has never been the slightest conflict about belonging to Europe. And to crown it all, cooperation structures such as the EMS have taken the brunt of the speculation of operators who took what was agreed at Maastricht literally.

Despite all these difficulties and the change of leaders – almost half the Prime Ministers changed in less than two years, compared with the stability of the 1980s – the Treaty has been ratified. The case of the UK merits a special mention. For years an existential debate has been taking place in accordance with its best traditions, both in the parliamentary arena and in the press. Despite the exhausting procedural guerrilla campaign in the House of Commons, ratification was finally voted for, a fact which has a decisive political implication, since it is an undertaking formalized in each country's decision-making body. Certainly, a sceptic could riposte with De Gaulle's observation, namely that treaties last as long as roses, but what is beyond question is that since 1950, with major steps forward followed by a 'long and steady decline' as Spinelli[2] said of solemn summonses and deadlines not met, the Community's approach has always been to review the situation and try again, even in areas as hypersensitive as defence: the European Defence Community (EDC), which was shipwrecked in 1954, makes a significant, if merely implicit, reappearance in the Treaty.

It is often advanced as an irrefutable argument that we have to go forward because there is no alternative. If this is meant to mean that we could go off home, doubtless the survival instinct prevents such an idiotic choice, whose only outcome would be a return to the self-destructive thinking of the past. Doubtless, there is another alternative, which has been made explicit in the debates that have taken (or are taking) place in various member states.

The clearest instances are the UK and Denmark, the two most awkward and inflexible countries in Community negotiations

and discussions. There are deep-seated historic reasons, which
in the case of the UK involve not merely the outcome of its
own ''98'[3], i.e. the orderly winding-up of its experience as an
imperial world power, but also its traditional, successful policy
of seeking a balance on the basis of playing off continental
divisions – not a difficult matter, I might add – by joining
alliance with those under threat. In the case of Denmark, the
reason is that they have their heart and mind in the Nordic
world, while their stomachs and their interests depend on the
Community. But there is something more: their deep-rooted
democratic traditions and, in particular, the predominance of
Parliament. That is the reason why in these countries the
debates are so hard-fought and the decision-making process
so agonizing right up until the moment of the vote. From that
moment on, they are bound by their decision – 'my word is my
bond' – and what has been adopted will be implemented at
all costs. It is no coincidence that both Denmark and the UK
head the list in the translation of Community legislation into
national law, whereas other partners, so enthusiastic that they
are ready to achieve the final objective as of now, are late as
far as the application of Community legislation is concerned.

In European integration, we have to take people as they are,
and respect their idiosyncrasies and characters as we go forward. This means that perseverance, with a certain dose of stub-
bornness, is the highest virtue of all. Such is the principal
lesson I drew from my work as an MEP and as chairman of the
committee which drew up the Socialist Election Manifesto in
1989, fighting inch by inch, amendment by amendment, asterisk by asterisk, and culminating in my Presidency, when I had
to fight for Parliament's participation in the debate surrounding the birth of the Maastricht Treaty.

Nonetheless, the details are what counts. The word 'more'
added to the expression 'we want a united Europe' does not
signify a final step, but something less, an intermediate stage.
As Professor Tierno used to say, when people quoted him
from memory, 'that phrase could not be his because there was
an adverb or an adjective missing'. Not to mention the virtuosity required by the handling of 'points of order' in debates,
points which almost always have more to do with the issue at
stake than with the application of the Rules of Procedure. In
the House of Commons, the first week of the Treaty of Rome

debate consisted of points of order; and in the Maastricht marathon, procedural details, arcane to the layman, were an ever-present feature.

It is undeniable that this way of doing things exasperates certain of my compatriots, trained in a world of orders and commands, whose earflaps mean that they can only see things in black and white, or that they confuse nuances and second thoughts with deceit and lies – although in their private, family, emotional or professional life they have no problem whatever in taking advantage of half-truths.

Getting back to the point, we have to be fully aware that there is an alternative proposal, namely for a community of 'cooperation' between states, whose content would be limited to a free trade zone, more plausible if the Community is enlarged rapidly – above all, if this is done with countries whose politics and economics are very close to ours but which are extremely reticent on subjects concerning not only alcohol monopolies or cod fishing but issues as crucial as external security or defence.

But this is not the only tension which exists. The scale of what is at stake has provoked in-depth debates in other countries and, particularly, in the continent's prototype of the nation-state, France, where the opposing camps cut right through the middle of the political spectrum and, spectacularly, the new conservative majority. This has produced a complex and restrictive debate on citizenship in the motherland of universalism. At this very moment, deep-seated currents of resistance are evident, which are not limited only to the traditional agricultural *Fronde* and are affecting fundamental choices involving commitments given with regard to trade liberalization, currency, external policy and asylum policy.

Since its very beginnings, European integration has enjoyed favouring winds during periods of growth; during periods of stagnation of recession, it acquires the cadences, almost, of a dying fall. Europe's status as a motherland is not a consolidated one, and people do not respond to it in the same way as they do to their own country. People do not question their Frenchness, Portugueseness or Germanness in terms of how the economy is doing, unless they choose to emigrate. The Community, on the other hand, has to show a profit year after year. Despite this and the poor marketing of the EC, attitudes to the

Community – if we may believe the Eurobarometer results – continue to be extremely positive and there are no credible political trends advocating diametrically opposed alternatives.

Nonetheless, this fact should not encourage demobilizing optimism. At best, with everything in our favour, there is heaps of work still to be tackled on a regular, steady basis before the year 2000. Here, the Teutonic approach of pulling out the diary after the great event and fixing the dates of future meetings and checks on results comes together with the French concern to fix deadlines involving the carrying out of specific commitments.

With this calendar in hand and taking account of the fact that, prudently, a new rendez-vous has been fixed for 1996 with the provisions made for calling an Intergovernmental Conference (IGC), I have written this book, which takes as its central thesis the fact that the European Union has, since the outset, been an undertaking whose motivation and objectives are political and whose route to taking concrete shape has been an economic one.

As currently constituted, the Community is a form of stable and cooperative union between the fifteen states, with Community elements functioning along federative lines. Far more progress has been made towards federalism in fact than in theory.

The Treaty on European Union represents a quantum leap, establishing the final goal of the process, namely a Community which shares a common destiny, with two vectors or driving forces: citizenship in the political sphere and currency in the economic sphere. Both are directed at people of flesh and blood, at their hearts and at their stomachs, and it is therefore unsurprising that their repercussions are immediate. Nonetheless, we are dealing with a double commitment – rigorously phased as far as the steps concerning the Economic and Monetary Union (EMU) is concerned, although its final goal, the single currency, is vague, while as far as Political Union is concerned, the commitment remains even more indeterminate and imprecise.

I have sought to avoid Europeanist apologetics when dealing with my subjects, because I believe European integration requires a more even-tempered frame of mind than that of blind faith.

For that reason, I begin the present work with a school-masterly 'ramble through historic Maastricht', an exercise from which conclusions of enormous relevance and interest to all Europeans, Union citizens or not, may be drawn.

The order of the chapters which follow reflects the major issues which face us. These are the problems which have to be solved in order to complete the building – and in order to formulate them, my itinerant labours both as a speaker and a thinker, throughout the length and breadth of the Community in universities, high schools, clubs, conferences, hustings and meetings have been hugely useful.

In particular, in order to set out the principal blocks, I have adopted the following scheme. Chapters 2 to 5 are devoted to the political process as an open-ended constitutional development, and to a description of the Community labyrinth, the gestation of the Treaty on European Union and its basic thrust, and the main issues for the ICG of 1996. Chapters 6 to 8 cover setting sail for a single currency, the EURO, convergence and the great issue of the future of employment and welfare. Chapter 9 deals with Europe and the world and covers foreign and security policy, Europe against the background of enlargement, and association, including transatlantic association.

I have attempted, as far as possible, to avoid that Community 'obscuranto' beloved of the initiated, a labyrinth of inferences, winks and acronyms. Although I doubt if I have succeeded, I hope that the reader's goodwill and interest will prevail. In any case, the important thing is to obtain a correct perspective and establish what steps have yet to be taken. Here, difficulties multiply. The Community bodies have not yet become an integral part of everyday life and stand apart from it: both the Commission, with its excessive self-sufficiency, and Parliament, whose voice is that of one crying in the wilderness.

As for the press, if faces two major problems. The first is that in order to make news out of Community affairs, they need to be dramatized with pepper and spice. Disaster is thus seen at every stage and at every obstacle. It does not matter that all the prophecies fail systematically to fulfil themselves. Who reads yesterday's papers? Another more complicated problem derives from the sheer market-strength of certain extremely influential British and Anglo-Saxon dailies and weeklies, whose point of departure is a philosophy which is the very antithesis of the Treaty, and against which all dailies and quality publications in French, let alone Dutch, Italian and Spanish (amongst others) can make little headway beyond their national readership. It is a pity that the German press, with all the importance it attaches to Community affairs, is read only by the initiated. A headline in Gothic type about EMU is no laughing matter!

Strange to tell, we Euro-initiates derive our nourishment from an extraordinary, almost home-made publication, the EUROPA bulletin.

This situation turns the road ahead into a Via Crucis winding its way between the epitaphs of commentators, the sceptical articles of intellectuals and the claims of the defenders of some 'other Europe' whose features and face nobody has ever seen. If only we could launch a debate such as featured in the Federalist Papers, where Alexander Hamilton, James Madison and John Jay pooled their writing skills under the pseudonym of 'Publius' to produce a total of 85 articles which constitute one of the most remarkable political texts in history, one which had a decisive effect on the final adoption of the Constitution of the USA.

The Federalist articles were written in 1787–1788, in the midst of the debates of the Philadelphia Constitutional Convention, which had rebelled against its own mandate and had called on the country to rebel against its Government, proposing that the Constitution be ratified by elected assemblies and that Congress should not have the final say. Against the undertaking that 'union shall be perpetual', it was argued that only nine states were necessary to form the Union, abandoning the other four to their fate. The toughest case was that of New York, whose delegates had not approved the draft: two of the three delegates had walked out of the discussions in protest, leaving Hamilton in the minority. At the same time, the state of New York had implemented a trade and customs policy which placed it in a privileged position. Hamilton decided that an intensive and ambitious propaganda campaign was required to convince voters, and he prepared a 'saturation bombing campaign' with articles appearing in four of the five New York dailies four times a week. Although the New York Convention abandoned its opposition to the Constitution, above all out of fear of finding itself alone following ratification by the ninth state (New Hampshire), the Federalist papers became the major authority for interpreting the Constitution of the United States[4].

In the terms used by the Federalists, the present European Union is already functioning as a 'compound Republic', in Madison's fine turn of phrase in Federalist Paper 51, whose division of powers provided 'double security for the rights of the people'. It would be highly desirable to foment controversy as rich as the aforementioned on the European front, over and above the internal debate within each member state. To date, the British lead the field here, since they were the first to debate the question of their own state and its legitimacy versus federalism, in terms which were on occasion Manichean and disproportionate, as befits the great British theatrical and democratic tradition.

Without doubt, this is quite clearly the responsibility of intellectuals, university teachers and students, politicians and social leaders who are concerned with the public good. Or of those artists who have voiced or sung their faith in the European cause, often to large audiences, such as the Irish group U2, the rock star Bob Geldof or, here at home, Miguel Ríos o Dyango. The basic thesis of the need to consolidate double democratic legitimacy as a priority goal needs to be complemented by the corollary requirement that the system should continue to develop in a federative manner, leading to what Delors has rightly called a federation of nation-states. Indeed, without seeking to provoke a debate about nomenclature, that is precisely the way the system, providing it continues to develop in accordance with its own logic, is headed. At a time when there has been so much speculation about the end of history, I would claim that we are at a stage in which history can be written more forcefully than ever, as a day-to-day revolution rather than the erecting of monuments commemorating victories and defeats. Mercifully, not one single monolith was raised to commemorate the entry into force of the Treaty on European Union.

Finally, I should like to expressly thank Sami Nair for his insistence that I write this book, Federico Mancini, Gil Carlos Rodríguez Iglesias, José Pons, Enrico Vinci, Geoff Harris, Francesca Ratti, Thérèse Lepoutre, Jacques Nancy, Marco

Aguiriano, Julio Bernárdez, Ton Orobitg for their kindness and patience in reading the manuscript and for their criticisms and observations. Javier Moreno proved a tireless helper. I am, however, entirely and personally responsible for all the opinions expressed in the book.

Foreword for the English Version

The appropriate Macmillan policy of publishing books on European affairs allows me to address the British public without intermediaries. I hope this moderate federalist European vision of a convinced European social democrat will contribute to the ongoing debate in the UK and on the continent. To favour it, I have tried to update the discussion with the latest developments and advances in the building process.

Beyond that, the role of English as the main 'lingua franca' of the current times opens the door to new audiences in Europe and overseas. I want to thank expressly Professor Alfred MacAdam for his brilliant translation of the Prologue of Carlos Fuentes and the dedicated team of translators, experts in 'Euroenglish', who have accomplished outstanding work which has only been possible with the the support of the Group of the PES in the European Parliament.

The advice of Gregg Orifici has been very positive for the last touches.

I want to express my gratitude to my agent and friend Nicolas de Santis, from Twelve Stars Communication, for all his endeavour, and to Marina Juan for her patient work of word-processing and correcting the text.

Madrid and Brussels, June 1996

1 A Ramble Round Historic Maastricht

- Where are we going? asked Lamme.
- Maastricht, answered Ulenspiegl.
- But my dear fellow, they say that it is surrounded by the Duke's army and that the Duke himself is in the city.

Charles de Coster,
The Glorious Adventures of Tyl Ulenspiegl

One of the fundamental causes of the 'post-Maastricht crisis' is without a doubt the jolt the Treaty has given to the world-views – *Weltanschauungen* – perpetuated by our education and value systems. To this we have to add the thaw initiated in 1989 in Central and Eastern Europe, which led to a veritable historical upheaval. Susan Sontag may well have been right in declaring that the 21st century began in 1991 with the collapse of the Soviet Union. She made this observation in Sarajevo, that tortured city which also saw the advent of the 20th century in 1914, with all that year implied for subsequent European history.

For this reason, the development of the 'European model' is, above all, a process of re-education. Our view of the world is based on the belief that the present set-up of nation-states is natural, each with an identity of its own and an eternal destiny. Exalted by French revolutionary nationalism and German romanticism, the State, the Fatherland and the Nation were identified in essence with an absolute destiny, handed down from father to son and carried to a destructive extreme through wars which were initially confined to Europe but which this century reached global dimensions. However, as Ortega rightly pointed out in *The Rebellion of the Masses*, if we were to take stock today of the contents of our minds, of our opinions, values, desires and assumptions, we would see that for the most part they do not derive from France for the French or from Spain for the Spanish, but from a common European background[1].

A study of the contents of the history books used in schools reveals a vision of reality in which the history of each people has been shaped in terms of manifest destiny, heroic deeds against its neighbours and assertion of a separate identity. E.L. Jones[2] hit the nail on the head when he noted that seen from the usual perspective of its national histories, Europe is a mosaic of different peoples who speak different languages, frequently governed by mutually hostile sovereigns, its nation-states laboriously hewn from a single variegated stem – and yet, on turning the kaleidoscope, a new image appears: that of a common culture. If we adopt the latter perspective, it is a revelation to see how many common or shared elements are mistakenly considered to be special and exclusive characteristics, or are simply looked at in isolation. A case in point is the fact that in the time of Christ there should have existed a Political, Economic and Monetary Union stretching from London to Jerusalem; and that many centuries later, the long branches linking the Visigothic kings and others, enriched by the Caliphate of Córdoba, to the luxuriant family tree of Queen Victoria, whose branches still extend throughout Europe, were never isolated growths. The policy of dynastic alliances through marriage has been a permanent and powerful mechanism in the continual drawing and redrawing of the map of Europe, dominated by patrimonial thinking which led to the pursuit of unions or divisions when it came to the apportioning of inheritances.

In saying that the 'eternal-national' is a concept which one should handle with care and that Europea history cannot be explained through national histories regarded as 'windowless monads' and immutable entities, because both Europe and the nations themselves are subject to change, Henri Brugmans gives a far better explanation of past events, and one which helps us to understand why there is an absolute need to seek a common system of coexistence and governance. It would be useful to adopt this perspective since, as José Antonio Maravall noted, a knowledge of history is a precondition for exercising autonomous thought and, therefore, for the building of liberty.

The Dutch city of Maastricht has, fortuitously, come to symbolize the 'wager against ourselves' of the Treaty on European Union (TEU); and as Maastricht's own history is a perfect microcosm of that of Europe, a short ramble through the city will prove enlightening.

A Crossroads

Maastricht lies almost on the Belgian border, a mere stone's throw from Germany and not far from Luxembourg. It is the seat of the FIR (regional air traffic control), the European Institute of Public Administration and has recently been named as seat of the World Journalism Centre.

The city grew around the Roman bridge built by Augustus over the Maas (Mosae Trajectum) linking Gaul and Germany. With the decline of the Empire and the increase in attacks by Germanic tribes, a fort was erected to protect this vital crossing. In the 4th century, the prevailing lawlessness and danger led St Servatius to seek refuge in the castle, founding the Church of 'Onze Lieve Vrouw' (Our Lady) in whose vicinity Bishop Monulphus built the Church and Chapterhouse of St Servatius. For centuries, these two churches became the rival centres of a city divided under the Prince-Bishop of Liège and the Duke of Brabant[3].

The rules governing the sharing of the divided city were established in the *Alde Caerte* (Old Charter) of 1284, which specified that the citizens were shared between both ruling houses. The Municipal Council was made up of an equal number of members from both parts, who had joint responsibility for the mint, the fortifications and the city gates but not the river, which upstream was under the control of the Bishop and under that of the Duke downstream. For two centuries the city prospered and new churches and monuments were built.

Maastricht has always been a crossing point, a meeting point but also a point of confrontation. It lies in the heart of the former region of Lotharingia, that overcrowded patch of land, laboriously and shrewdly tilled and exploited, which was a cradle of technological progress (the agricultural revolution and the textile industry in the Middle Ages) and saw the birth of the bourgeoisie and of bourgeois culture (especially painting and the decorative arts, a prime example of which is the Arnolfini Marriage by van Eyck) and of new political formulae (the first modern state with a parliament playing a leading role emerged from the Estates-General of the United Provinces). An unavoidable crossing and meeting point for the principal economic and trade flows and artistic currents from Italy and France – the *Caminus Francigenus*, with the trade fairs of Champagne, and later the Spanish Way[4] – Maastricht enjoyed some links with the British Isles, representing a port of entry to the European hinterland. The cross which the city's privileged location has forced it to bear is that it has always been a prize much desired both by its neighbours and by all who have wanted to rule and dominate Europe.

It is like living in the High Street. Successively it has seen Romans, Goths, Franks, Spaniards, Frenchmen, Austrians, Britons – not to mention Germans – pass through it. The Spanish public at large will no doubt have been surprised to find out that the city was destroyed by the *Tercios de Flandes* (Flemish regiments) under the command of Alessandro Farnese during the Reign of Philip II, or that Lope de Vega should have described its destruction in *El Asalto de Mastrique* (The Assault on Maastricht). Later, it was the French who on two occasions occupied the city. More recently, the city has been occupied twice this century.

Thus, for the people of Maastricht, peace does not merely represent one dream among many, but rather a vital necessity. The need to adapt to and to co-exist with the powers-that-be led them to adopt original approaches which allowed them, for example, to treat with equal consideration the two rulers who for centuries jointly governed the city, the Duke of Brabant and the Bishop of Liège. The ingenious solution was to build two symmetrical staircases in the Town Hall and to formulate a wise political proverb: 'One lord, oh my Lord! Two lords, heaven-sent!'.

Imperial footsteps: from Charlemagne . . .

Still, the history of the area has not only been that of its invasions. It has always been the cradle of projects of European scope. All the important attempts at European unity have left their mark on the city. This is true of the Carolingian, Habsburg, Napoleonic and Hitlerite empires. Much can be learned from a comparative study of these experiences.

Maastricht lies in the neighbourhood of Aachen at the centre of Charlemagne's empire. The city made good use of its position, with large donations coming into its churches and increased prosperity and influence. The King of the Franks was crowned Emperor of the Holy Roman Empire of the German Nation (the First Reich) by the Pope on Christmas Day in the year 800, in an attempt to restore the Roman Empire of Constantine the Great; an Emperor whose secular memory is reflected in the painting by Dürer, in which he is portrayed with the German eagle and the French fleur-de-lys. It was his wish to establish a kingdom in which the authority should be tied to unity and faith. For this purpose he created a network of Counts throughout the Empire, an ecclesiastical network which also played an administrative role, and a system of envoys (*missi dominici*) who travelled throughout the territory conveying his orders. As a conqueror he took Lombardy, partially ceding central Italy to the Pope after the latter had abased himself before him, and gaining the recognition of Byzantium, establishing the March of Friuli; in what was now Germany, he conducted his campaigns over a period of thirty years, establishing the frontier marches of Denmark, of Swabia and of the Avars to the North, East and South which stretched to the Slav world through alliances and vassalage; in Spain he created another march but failed in his expedition to Pamplona and Saragossa in 778. At Roncesvalles, his army's rearguard, led by Roland, Margrave of the March of Brittany, was crushed. There are two versions of the event, the 'Chanson de Roland' which ascribes the ambush to the Moorish King of Saragossa, and a traditional Basque poem, the 'Altabizaren Kantua', which ascribes it to the Basques[5]. (As can be seen, conflicting versions of battles have respectable antecedents!). In the Eastern Pyrenees, he succeeded in consolidating the March of Spain, a forerunner of present-day Catalonia, and later, in 798, he helped Alfonso II the Chaste, King of Asturias, in his campaign against the then Muslim city of Lisbon, even though a pretender to the Caliphate of Córdoba was at that time on his way to Aachen to seek his support.

However, the story of Charlemagne is not limited merely to military actions. In what has been called the Carolingian Renaissance – which according to the historian Robert López 'lit an altar candle in the darkness, whereas the Renaissance took a little light from heaven and gave it to mankind'[6] – Charlemagne pushed forward a policy to develop education, creating schools (following the updated Roman method of St Isidore of Seville) and the invention of Carolingian script (lower-case letters), accompanied by legislative and moral reforms, reflected in the capitularies, which combined spiritual and temporal considerations as well as intellectual reforms. For this purpose, he brought together a team of scholars, led by Alcuin of York, which included the Italians Peter of Pisa, Paul the Deacon and Paulinus of Aquileia, the German Hermann of Mainz and the Iberian Theodulf.

Strangely, in an age when communications were very difficult, it was quite normal (as has been the case throughout history) to form teams which we would now define as multinational.

The Carolingian Empire outlived its creator only for a short period. Only three years after his death, his son Louis the Pious (Ludovicus Pius) divided the empire among his own three sons through the *Divisio Imperii* Act which, while insisting on maintaining the 'imperial unity' identified with Christianity itself, in fact partitioned it. Whilst Lothair would receive the title of Emperor, Pepin retained Aquitaine and Louis the German the eastern dependencies. The situation quickly deteriorated.

To the internal attempts of the new rulers to consolidate their positions and the external pressures on the Empire's frontiers was added civil war. The spark that set this off was the Emperor's promise in 829 to concede Germany, Alsace and part of Burgundy to his new son Charles. The three elder brothers rebelled and, whilst Louis attempted to negotiate with his sons, they bribed his army at the 'Field of Lies' near Colmar, so that the Emperor was captured and deposed. On his death, Lothair proclaimed himself Emperor and Louis and Charles united against him with the oath of Strasbourg in 842, the first document written both in the French Romance and Germanic tongues. After defeating Lothair, they concluded the Treaty of Verdun, apportioning the western Frankish territories (west of the Rhône and the Garonne) to Charles, and the eastern Frankish territories (east of the Rhine) to Louis.

In between, from Frisia through to Provence and Lombardy, a narrow strip ran for almost 2000 km, constituting the main axis both of transport and wealth and almost impossible to defend.

Even since then, this area of passage and linguistic frontier between the Romance and Germanic linguistic worlds has seen the greatest amount of economic, commercial and, at the same

time, military activity in the Continent (and perhaps of all
time). Curiously, it now appears on the economic maps of
Europe as the 'crescent' of wealth, and it is the route taken by
the migratory Community institutions in their constant movement between Brussels, Luxembourg and Strasbourg.

... to the Universal Monarchy of Charles V

This was the Empire which Charles the Bold wanted to re-
create – the powerful Duke of Burgundy who, starting with an
industrialized and wealthy Flanders which had held back repeated French attempts to expand to the North[7], tried to re-
create the former Lotharingia. His defeat and death at the
hands of the soldiers of the emerging Swiss Confederation
changed the fate of Europe. But his dream would be realized
by his grandson, Charles I of Spain and V of Germany.

His Europe, too, left its mark on Maastricht, and it is rewarding to take a closer look at both the similarities and the
differences. What is surprising is, above all, the almost identical nature of the central nucleus and the geographic framework
of these two Europes.

That of Charles V had Lotharingia as its initial nucleus, i.e.
the centre of the Carolingian Empire. From this point, its
growth began with Charles's inheritances on both sides (that of
Burgundy and Austria on the paternal side and the Hispanic-
Italian-American dominions on the maternal side), forming a
Europe which essentially coincided with that of the Community, with the exception of France. As Braudel puts it, with his
accustomed exactitude: 'The Catholic Kings laid the groundwork for their grandson's fortune. Had they not, after all, moved
in all useful directions: England, Portugal, Austria, the Low
Countries, and time and again played the lottery of matri-
mony? The idea of surrounding France and dominating this
dangerous neighbour defined the curious empire of the
Habsburgs from the outset, as though it was hollow, with a
gaping hole at its very centre. Charles of Ghent was a calcu-
lated risk, for whom Spain had prepared and for whom it
longed[8].'

Spain's European policy combined with fate in a process
which has been best described by Ramón Carande: 'whole

dynasties came to an end upon offering him their thrones, and the world expanded before him as virgin lands emerged from the depths of mystery[9].' Charles was going to play at the table of European politics: he became increasingly Spanish only towards the end of his life. His political trail was a planned work of European Union which turned into a veritable Myth of Sisyphus.

The beginnings were stunning. To his rich inheritance, Charles added the crown of the King of the Romans at the age of 19 and a little later, following a hard-fought and costly electoral campaign against Francis I of France, the elected crown of Emperor of the Holy Roman Empire of the German Nation (the Reich). This once again brought the concept of European unity to the fore, the concept of the Universal Empire superseding the Roman and Carolingian Empire. This rebirth of the Reich was made possible by the impetus of the Renaissance and its rediscovery of classical antiquity, and was subject to a systematic public relations exercise which would put present-day marketing to shame. The sovereign once again came to be known as the Holy Roman Emperor, whose portrayal even in coins was that of a true Roman Emperor, wearing a cuirass and a laurel wreath. Constantine and Charlemagne were proclaimed examples worthy of all emulation. The Pillars of Hercules were added with the proud motto 'Plus Ultra', thus expressing a global ambition which for the first time had been made possible by the discovery of America, a symbol which was to dominate the period. Strong tells us that, following the defeat of the Armada, Queen Elizabeth of England was portrayed, in a clear allusion, standing on the Pillars of Hercules and that in the triumphal arch built to welcome Henry IV in Avignon the same Pillars were included, along with the French Crown and the Papal Tiara, above the motto 'Duo Protegit Unus'[10].

The myth of the Universal Empire, created around the figure of the Emperor Charles, gained wide currency and left its mark on the mythologies then springing up around all the traditional monarchies. In addition to iconography, protocol permitted the fusion of Burgundian and Roman etiquette, transforming Imperial feasts into 'great compilations of all the suitable elements for expanding the Imperial myth' with 'a systematic cult of the House through visual and literary panegyrics'. Strong winds up by saying that 'the feasts were an important element of the alliance between humanism and sovereignty, whose aim was systematically to spread the dynastic myth'[11].

The ideological basis was also decisive. The Imperial Court was characterized by its cosmopolitanism, bringing together the most brilliant intellectuals of the age, notably the theoricians of the 'Imperial idea' such as Gattinara, Antonio de Guevara with his 'Diall of Princes' or Alfonso de Valdés, who after the infamous 'Sacco di Roma' wrote a Dialogue in which he portrayed the sacking as an act of divine destiny. However, the most important argument without a doubt was that of Erasmus, who in 1516 dedicated his work *Institutio Principis Christiani* to the then Prince, in which he brought up to date the medieval idea of the *speculum principis*, according to which the ideal prince should unite Christian education with a humanist education and the study of classical models; this, it was thought, would enable him to act spontaneously to achieve universal peace. The work enjoyed an extraordinary success in its day.

Moreover, Charles directly encountered the most important scholars of the time. In the text of the Edict against Luther, written in his own hand at the Diet of Worms, the Emperor explained his defence of the faith in terms of dynastic obligation. For his part, Bartolomé de las Casas was successful in forcing the Empire to reconsider the basis of the legitimacy of its conquest: strangely enough, that of an Emperor in whose names two unsuspected Empires – Montezuma's Mexico and Atahualpa's Peru – had been conquered in less than ten years, and who had defeated and taken prisoner his arch-rival, Francis I of France. Nevertheless, the illusion of universality did not last long; Erasmus himself spoke of an 'Empire' which was but a 'mere shadow of a great glory'.

In fact the Empire only existed in the person of the Emperor, elected in Frankfurt following a complex, dirty and costly campaign by the great Electors; in his person he brought together an inheritance run by a Directorate which at the same time was a family council. There was no centralising drive, as we would find in the case of a single state with a monolithic administration. Some progress in that direction was made – for example, in the Low Countries, where the first steps were taken towards a common legislation, establishing the 'Burgundian Circle'.

Charles's conception of the European Union and of the universal monarchy was based on what his biographer Karl Brandi described as 'the dynasty as a force for unity'. The unifying links and the common denominator of such a rich and diverse mosaic of peoples, languages and cultures were his person and Roman Catholicism. In the words of Fernández Alvarez: 'He projected himself as a Master of many States: a Burgundian amongst the Burgundians, a Spaniard in Castille and Aragon and an Italian amongst Italians'[12].

He is not merely a distant memory, relegated to history books. Just as the prestigious Charlemagne Prize, organized by the city council of Aachen, is the fruit of a popular initiative, there is a celebration in commemoration of Charles V which the people of Brussels, Community capital par excellence, repeat every year: the *Ommegang*, held in the first week in July to commemorate the ceremonial entry of the Emperor to the city in 1549, when he introduced his son Philip II into society. It is a magnificent spectacle, uniting the splendour of the Court of Burgundy with the most picturesque of Flemish traditions. The original objective of the ceremony was the swearing of an oath of allegiance by the assemblies of the provinces and cities to the future King as they ratified the uniform regulation of succession by means of the Pragmatic Sanctions.

Against the incomparable backdrop of the Grand-Place, hung with period decorations, the Emperor and his son appear, accompanied by a glittering company comprising his sisters Mary of Hungary, the regent, Eleanor of France and Isabel of Denmark, the knights of the Order of the Golden Fleece, with Maurice of Orange, the Counts of Egmont and Horn, and the Duke of Alba, followed by a motley procession of guilds, peasants and jokers on stilts, creating a picture worthy of Brueghel. The procession is crowned by horsemen carrying the standards of the Universal Empire, including those of the Low Countries, the Iberian kingdoms, Austria, Hungary, Jerusalem and the Indies. It is not an official event. The organization of the *Ommegang* is entirely private.

In 1987, the Kingdom of Belgium, for its part, minted ECU1 coins in commemoration of the 30th anniversary of the Community. The coin is a reproduction of the Spanish ducat of the time, and the legend reads 'C.F. CAROLUS D.G. ROM. IMP.HISP.REX.DUX.BURG' (Caesar Charles by the Grace of

God Emperor of the Romans, King of the Spaniards and Duke of Burgundy).

These two examples, one private and one public, show just how long-lived has been the figure of the Emperor and his symbolic value in the very heart of modern Europe. One could mention other examples which show how deeply rooted certain internal divisive lines in Europe which also stem from that period continue to be, such as the almost reflex-like division of the Members of the European Parliament along the frontier between the Reformation and the Counter-Reformation laws when it came to voting on a sitting in Rome to commemorate the thirtieth anniversary of the Treaty of 1957.

Or beyond the seas (*plus ultra*), where we find in the awe-inspiring desolation of the Bolivian *puna* the Imperial City of Potosí, on which the Emperor conferred his symbols which appear on his coat of arms, from the Golden Fleece to the Pillars of Hercules, in addition to its own legend[13] – a mark of the importance of what was a great city, whose mountain came to be in no small measure the source of European prosperity, supplying the hard cash which, after a fleeting stay through Spain, was endlessly consumed by Imperial policies and ultimately enriched the Low Countries.

The actual exercise of government was exhausting. Those currently in power who complain of constant European shutting would do well to remember that Charles spent his life travelling, as he himself noted in his moving speech of abdication: ten journeys to the Low Countries, nine to Germany, seven to Italy, six to Spain, four journeys across France, two to England and two to Africa. A considerable record even now, but all the more so under the conditions of the time and with the weakened health of a prematurely aged man. The fact that he was accompanied by an exceptional eyewitness, Titian, enables us to follow with startling immediacy his personality, character and evolution.

In short, he attempted what Maravall has described as the transformation of traditional family relationships into a modern instrument of power in his attempts to create a 'universal monarchy'. The result of this attempt at hegemony by the Habsburgs was that for a century and a half, in the words of Paul Kennedy, 'a continent-wide combination of kingdoms, duchies and provinces ruled by the Spanish and Austrian members of the Habsburg family threatened to become the predominant political and religious influence in Europe[14].'

The combination exhibited a certain bipolarity almost from the beginning, since Charles V himself quickly conceded administration and sovereignty of the hereditary Austrian lands to his brother Ferdinand in 1520, forming a union superbly symbolized by the double eagle of his coat of arms, with Madrid and Vienna as the heads, one facing west and the other east. Still, the patrimonialist concept prevailed, as was shown by the brief liaison between Philip II and Mary Tudor, who made him King Consort of England, or by the disappearance of Dom Sebastian which gave him the Portuguese throne. The Empire increasingly came to rely on the Kingdom of Spain, with Castile as the milch-cow supplying human and fiscal resources, and periodic 'allowances' from the Indies enabling it to bear the continuous strain of conducting campaigns on all fronts over a period of almost 150 years, with two gaping wounds which consumed every resource: the defence of Catholicism in the central European front, and the challenge of Islam, particularly of the Ottoman Empire, in the Mediterranean basin. It was during this period – which was characterized by even faster technological and scientific developments, accompanied by a revolution in military technology and the emergence of modern industrial and mercantile capitalism – that the modern nation-states began to consolidate their positions. Europe increasingly took the form of a single system of states in which changes in one cell had an effect on all others. France was set on breaching its encirclement; the Low Countries were immersed in a revolt which laid the foundations of their independence, albeit with religious and political fissures which would later help the emergence of Belgium; England was strengthening its strategic position; Germany was the central arena of the religious conflict, which was resolved with the application of the principle *cuius regio, cuius religio*, according to which one's denomination, Catholic or Protestant, was determined by that of the local ruler – even though the country continued to be a mosaic of tiny states until the beginning of the 19th century, whilst divided Italy was the object of all desires due to its riches and culture. One should not forget the considerable military power of Sweden under Gustavus Adolphus which had a significant presence in the Germanic world. The confrontation spread to global dimensions with the growth of the Dutch and English fleets and the attacks on the bases and communication and transport links of the Spanish and Portugese colonial empires. The result was the opposite of what had been expected. Though the wish had been to achieve a universal peace, the harsh reality was one of continuous military conflict, and desire for prosperity contrasted sharply with the need to finance the military efforts which proved to be an endless drain on resources.

Although methods used to collect taxes at the time were rather expeditious, such as those applied by Charles himself in the communal revolt in Castile (the scaffold), or to his own countrymen of Ghent (whom he subjugated by means of the hangman's rope), revenue was not forthcoming. Towards the end of the 1540s, 65% of normal revenue was used to pay debts, leading to the confiscation of the treasure of the Indies and to bankruptcy in 1557. The only consolation was that France also declared itself bankrupt. Ramón Carande has rightly spoken of the 'ruin of this symbiosis' between Charles and his bankers[15].

On average, military expenditure in Elizabeth Tudor's England or Philip II's Spain accounted for three-quarters of the budget, going both on current military expenditure and the debts amassed by previous wars[16]. This money was earmarked for the Spanish Infantry, considered by Peter F. Drucker to be the first modern organization. Counteracting this threat was the explicit motivation of the father of the nation-state, the French lawyer Jean Bodin, author of the six-volume *De la République*, who wrote that the 'day will arrive in which Germans and Gaulois, realising that they are blood brothers, will join in a perpetual alliance and friendship'[17].

However, the attempts made during the period to build a united Europe were not limited to the schemes of the house of Austria. The Protestant Henri of Navarre, who became the Catholic Henri IV of France after recognizing that 'Paris is well worth a mass', worked with his minister Sully between 1600 and 1607 on his 'Grand Dessein' whose aim was to create a directorate of the fifteen principal European kingdoms in order to resolve religious, border and internal conflicts and to present a united front against the Eastern threat personified, at that time, by the Turks.

The Birth of the Low Countries

This era has been indelibly etched into the history and the stones of Maastricht. International events once again decided the fate of the city when religious conflict combined with an uprising against Spanish domination. During the long revolt of the Low Countries (1555–1649), which led to the emergence of Holland as a nation, Maastricht was besieged, sacked and destroyed twice in succession (in 1576 and 1579) by the *Tercios de Flandes* (Flemish Regiments) under Alessandro Farnese, Duke of Parma and ruler of the Low Countries. The siege of 1579 ended with the destruction and sacking of the city known as the 'Spanish Fury'. The Estates-General made two fruitless attempts to regain control of the city (1592 and 1594). During these assaults, new techniques of attack and defence were employed, such as the undermining of the fortifications and the building of underground galleries.

What started as a deeply felt acceptance of the solemn abdication of the Emperor in his 'patrimonial provinces', in 1555, rapidly developed into open insurrection. There already was what the Dutch historian Pieter Geyl described as a deep-seated 'distrust of governing authorities', which proved to be a real obstacle to the development of a national consciousness and state in what was a community of wealthy cities: 'Always, behind the governments tireless admonitions to get closer together in order to be better able to render mutual assistance in case of foreign danger, the subjects suspected that the intention was to extort more money and to encroach on provincial autonomy.'

Geyl concludes that 'when the conflict with the monarchy erupted, a strong national consciousness was suddenly created. For the authors of the Beggars' Songs (*Geuzenliederen*), the Netherlands were the land of the seventeen provinces; the new emergent North-east as well as the Walloon area were comprehended in the patriotic enthusiasm of the first stage'[18].

However, independence did not bring an end to the misfortunes of the people of Maastricht. The Low Countries, due to their strategic situation and their wealth, made a very desirable prize. The thirty years following the Peace of Westphalia, in which Spain recognized the independence of Holland, saw no fewer than three wars between England and Holland, one of them involving France. Louis XIV personally led the attack and capture of Maastricht, the siege of which is well remembered since D'Artagnan died in it. France occupied the city for six years, doing so again 70 years later, in 1748, during the War of the Austrian Succession – extending the concept of the 'retaining wall' to the whole of the Lotharingian border, where the Rhine-Meuse axis attained a primary importance. With a continuity stemming from its strength as a State and the pursuit of an active policy of assimilation, France sustained a campaign of integration of the northern frontier regions, particularly evident in the case of Alsace-Lorraine, the bone of Franco-German contention over a long period of time.

The French Revolution and Napoleon

At the end of the 18th century, Maastricht was caught in the crossfire of the Belgian and Dutch revolutions, contemporaries of the French revolution, in which the 'French patriots' – petits bourgeois, craftsmen and peasants, who favoured annexation – were in conflict with the 'Dutch patriots', the grand bourgeois and merchants, who wanted a Republic. The decisive battles of the French revolution took place in the region (Valmy and Jemappes).

In 1792, the National Convention adopted the principle of 'revolutionary expansion' to bring 'fraternity and assistance to the peoples wishing to regain their liberty'. This was the beginning of a new war, this time encompassing the whole of the continent, where the idea of helping the people was replaced by a new attempt to unify Europe – a plan which, as far as economic matters were concerned, was embodied in a mercantilist thrust in which France was the dominant economy, whilst the economies of the vassals were dominated and supplied the raw materials and the finance necessary for the war effort. The picture was completed with the continental embargo on Britain and the systematic pillaging of works of art and treasures, which were sent to Paris. These included the first dinosaur jaw-bones found in the quarries near the city in 1770, thus rendering Maastricht of topical interest in our age of 'Jurassic Park'. In short, it was an attempt to make the economy to 'set the beat' which increased the unpopularity of the Empire.

The city was occupied in 1794 by General Kléber, who swept aside the old traditions and the dual authority and incorporated the city into the Department of the Lower Meuse. The Batavian Republic was created, compelled to be an ally of France, followed by the re-establishment of the Monarchy with the proclamation of Louis Napoleon, brother of the Emperor, as the King of Holland. The plan was to establish a Europe of vassal states, where the Emperor distributed crowns among the members of his family with a brazenness which made previous attempts look modest. Napoleon considered that the Dutch people had supported his draft Constitution in a plebiscite, in which 16 000 votes where cast in favour and 25 000 against, by simply counting the 347 000 abstentions as 'yes' votes[19].

This, however, did not prevent him from dethroning his own brother, considering him to be insufficiently stringent in the implementation of the blockade of Britain. This was the European project which Napoleon recounted to Las Cases in St Helena:

> Peace in Moscow was to complete and finish my military expeditions. It was to be, as regards the great cause, the end to risk-taking and the beginning of security. A new horizon and new tasks were to develop, full of welfare and prosperity for all. The European system had been founded; all that remained to be done was to organize it.
>
> Satisfied on these major heads, and at peace everywhere, I would also have had my Congress and my Holy Alliance. These ideas were stolen from me. In this council of all sovereigns we would have been able to manage our affairs within the family circle, and to count on the support of the whole populace.
>
> I would have wanted to have the same principles, the same system everywhere. A European Code, a European Court of Cassation, giving redress to all for any miscarriages of justice, just as our court of appeal which redresses the errors of the courts. A single currency with different coinages; the same weights, the same measures, the same laws, etc., etc.

Europe, he said, would thus have been destined to become nothing more than a single people, and when travelling one would have always been 'in the common fatherland'.

This universal project, based on French revolutionary nationalism, which considered that what was true for one man was true for all others, never came to fruition. It did, however, have direct consequences for Europe, in that it gave the initial impetus to German romantic nationalism and to Consolidation of Nation States in the Continent. The 'Executions of the 3rd of May' by Goya, express this contrast in a dramatic way.

This process directly affected Maastricht, which saw the strengthening of its character as an enclave, with the consolidation of the border of new States mere kilometres away. On the one hand, there was the independence of Belgium in 1830, which segregated the Low Countries of the South for political and religious reasons – although, geographically, Maastricht should have been incorporated into Belgium, the garrison remained loyal to the House of Orange, and when in 1839 the Province of Limburg was divided, it remained in Holland – whilst on the other, the survival of the Grand-Duchy of Luxembourg was consolidated, starting with the Holy Alliance, through which Metternich dominated the European scene in what Kissinger has termed 'a world restored'.

German Unification

However, the most decisive consequence of the Enlightenment and of the French Revolution was the impetus given to the birth of romantic nationalism, which took a tremendous toll on a Holy Roman Empire consisting of over 1800 autonomous countries united by the figure of the Emperor, his Legal Council, the Perpetual Diet and the Supreme Tribunal, and by a postal system of acknowledged efficiency. The Reich was a confederation of mini-states in which princes and lords ruled with absolute power, with primogeniture disputed by the two leading powers, Prussia and Austria. Social organization was rigid and subject to a medieval class structure.

Slowly a national consciousness began to take hold in a process evoked thus by Schiller: 'Whilst the Empire has been growing weaker politically, it has continued to grow in strength and to perfect itself spiritually'. It was the concept which Herder termed the '*Volkgeist*', the national spirit based on the common mother tongue, customs and the spirit, which following the occupation and defeat of Prussia led to a fight for freedom based on the notion of belonging to the 'German nation'. Fichte, in his 'Discourse for the German Nation', and Jahn, a prime mover of the physical education movement, gave a great stimulus to the fight for liberation and to the creation of a spirit of confrontation with large, powerful France, which dominated the continent. The consolidation of the nation-states, pushed forward by the mighty industrial development and the creation of internal markets (the '*Binnenmarkt*' was a decisive element in the configuration of the German unification process, in that it created the foremost demographic and economic power of the continent, in search of its own hegemony to exercise), would lead to a situation of immense power tied to disunity. The result of this was the struggle for hegemony and the spiralling conflicts between France and Germany, where the battlefields time and again followed the central axis of Lotharingia. The wars of 1870 and 1914–18 filled the peaceful landscapes of Alsace, Lorraine, Belgium and Luxembourg with military cemeteries.

Worse still was the progressive exaltation of German culture and its destructive confrontation with the prestige of Revolutionary and Napoleonic France, which had guaranteed the supremacy of that country on the continent (even though, globally, the 19th century was dominated by the British Empire), humiliating German aspirations. As Maurizio Serra rightly noted, 'the discord between both nations and cultures had become the basis of a latent conflict in Europe', starting with the growth of the myth of decadence and the regeneration by fire and sword of the younger nation with the exaltation of the '*Sedan Feste*' and the '*Heroenkult*' of Germany under Kaiser Wilhelm[20]. This provocation was to continue with the myth of the reciprocal 'revenge', a descendant of the phobias of decadence, whose embodiment in the confrontation of the two greatest continental powers produced the greater disasters in Western Europe in the first 50 years of this century[21].

The organized labour movement and social democracy, which from the middle of the 19th century onwards reaffirmed the ideals of a world without frontiers and of the freedom of the peoples (the First International grew out of an act of solidarity with the Polish struggle for independence), clashed head-on with these nationalist excesses. During the First World War, the vote by the German Social Democrats in the Reichstag and by the French Socialists in the Assembly in favour of war credits resulted in the break-up of the Second International.

The current conflict which we are witnessing between Serbs and Croats is a pathetic caricature-like repetition of the extremes that can be reached by the hatred generated by the 'culture of revenge' amongst neighbouring and kindred peoples.

Hitler's New Europe

The most recent attempt at imposing a unification of Europe which the citizens of Maastricht have had to endure was the terrifying 'New Europe' of Hitler. Even when he called his regime The Third Reich – the new Holy Roman Empire – , the dictator, consistent in his racist obsession, based his claim on the aspirations of the Saxon Widukind, enemy of Charlemagne, considering the latter not to have been a true German. The centre of the Empire was the 'Greater Germany' with approximately 100 million inhabitants, stretching from Luxembourg to Alsace-Lorraine in the west, through to Memel (now the Lithuanian port of Klaipeda) to the east, and from Schleswig in the north through to Slovenia (which was considered as the territory of an unfortunate German people which had lost its language) to the south. The Third Reich came to be surrounded by a buffer of protectorates, ruled directly by Nazi dignitaries (Bohemia-Moravia, Poland, Ukraine and the East) which formed the embryo of its *Lebensraum*, and by occupied territories under military rule such as Norway, Denmark, Belgium, the Netherlands, Yugoslavia, Greece and part of France. In addition, there were the countries which were 'allied' by virtue of the Tripartite Pact of 1940 between Germany, Italy and Japan on the 'new European order'. Hungary, Slovakia and Romania joined the Pact in 1940 and Bulgaria and Croatia in 1941, progressively turning into satellite states with autonomous Nazi parties for the German minorities, fascist parties in power and the re-issuing of German anti-semitic legislation.

Economic organization complemented the political hierarchy: both were to Germany's advantage. The system led to the specialization of countries, with the Centre as an industrial

emporium, and was complemented with 'compensatory' mechanisms: compensation for the occupying forces, requisitioning
of workers, expropriation of assets and an embargo on precious
metals, or authorizations to carry out black market operations.
The system of pillaging (whose uniqueness owes more to the
scale of operations than to its basic idea) allowed the war
effort to be maintained without having a commensurate effect
on the standard of living in Germany.

Community versus Empire

Despite the length of time and the different circumstances
which separate all of these unification processes, they do have
certain elements in common: the extraordinary initial success
of a man, who, on a new impulse, makes Europe his own
thanks to a combination of politics and chance and, once in
power, attempts to subjugate and shape the continent according to his will, albeit with the intention of bringing prosperity
and happiness to his subjects. Since 'the road to hell is paved
with good intentions', the history of emperors, kings and dic-
tators has been one of continuous warring and fighting in a
desperate attempt to realize their dreams. Without a doubt,
Charlemagne was the most fortunate, since he did not witness
the end: it was his grandchildren who destroyed his achievements. After staging his own death, Charles V ended up mend-
ing clocks in the rural solitude of Yuste; Napoleon similarly
finished up reliving past victories in his imagination on St
Helena.

There is a 'crescendo' in the tragic fate of these omnipotent
leaders which almost runs parallel to the level of violence and
to the development of the technology of tyrannization and
collective oppression. For in all these cases, the role which the
different European peoples were meant to accept was to obey
and cooperate with the designs of the Divinely Chosen.

Another shared feature was the excessive commitment or
'over-stretching', in the words of Paul Kennedy, of one's own
forces. Kennedy also notes that 'like the British Empire three
centuries later, the Habsburg bloc was a conglomeration of
widely scattered territories, a political and dynastic *tour de force*
which required enormous and sustained resources of material

and ingenuity to keep going'[22]. Kennedy is referring to the
capacity of one's forces to resist and 'stretch'; the common denominator is to force the subjugated peoples to bear the greatest burdens, if not the brunt of downright sytematic pillaging.

Confrontations aimed at achieving hegemony grew increasingly global and more destructive as wealth and economic
capacity increased and military technology developed. It was
military and economic might coupled with political disunity
which led the continent to destruction and to the brink of
annihilation.

The current process to establish a European Union shares
some of the objectives of previous attempts: to achieve both
union and peace. The substantive difference lies in the means.
In this respect, the interview between Professor Paul Reuter
and Jean Monnet on 12 April 1950, i.e. less than a month
before the Schuman Declaration, is of great interest: 'Following some pessimistic reflections on the current situation,
Monnet handed me a newspaper where one of Adenauer's
proposals for Franco-German cooperation was marked in red
and asked me: "What do you think of this?" I told him how
much I favoured the idea and how much I regretted the indif-
ferent silence on the part of France. His mind was already
made up; he searched for some time along these lines and
then, in an increasingly lively manner, counterposed certain
thoughts which were going around his mind. What do you
think of a Franco-German Parliament? I signalled my opposition: To do what? Isn't there the Council of Europe already?
Then a very strange idea emerged. Monnet listed the following in succession: The Dutch, the Belgians, Luxembourgers,
the people of Lorraine, the Saar, the Alsace and the Swiss and
said: "All of these people are not really German or French;
what if we are to rebuild something akin to the former
Lotharingia in this great Rhine Valley? Would it not be easier
to build Europe?" I reacted in a clearly hostile manner, expressing a number of opinions which were too obvious to repeat
here, except that Europe had to be built on a Franco-German
reconciliation but that the frontier communities had suffered
too much to be able to accept a loosening of the bonds which
united them with their respective fatherlands. Since Monnet
stuck to his position, I continued: "In any case, you should
leave their political status alone; you should do something in

the area of economics. Why not a Monnet Plan for the border regions?" From there it was easy enough to go on to the idea of limited sectoral action, since the Ruhr, the Saar and the Lorraine only have heavy industry, i.e. coal and steel; . . . we met twice more that week. Hirsch and Uri had also taken part in the last interviews and it wasn't until Sunday that we reached the conclusion that the project should cover the whole of the industry, not just France and Germany. I left Monnet late in the afternoon with a mandate to draw up a brief note. Across the top of the note three words were written in bold: Peace, France-Germany'[23].

Without a doubt, the most valuable aspect of Franco-German reconciliation is its role as catalyst. This role is now shared with all the other countries, since the Community is the achievement of all its members. It is therefore significant that the Treaty on European Union should in essence correspond to the draft by the Luxembourgish Presidency. Curiously, the ratification of the Treaty did not give rise to existentialist debate or heated arguments in the Benelux countries. This may be because they simply need Europe to survive.

The final text is undeniably uneven, daring in certain respects and deficient in others. Nevertheless, as in the cooperation between Reuter and Monnet, it is the fruit of a positive experience which arose as a result of seemingly wild proposals – as is usually the case with new, untested ideas, particularly when they go against current thinking.

In 1950, the idea of creating the ECSC was far more utopian. Nevertheless, that idea proved capable of triggering a unique process in which nation-states are creating a new political entity, the Union, without denying their own existence; instead of a process of conquests and domination, the method chosen is one of free and consensual association and the sharing of certain elements of sovereignty.

If any criticism can be justifiably levelled against this collective process aimed at reshaping history and avoiding a return to the bad old ways, it is that concerning the length of time that separates initial impulse from implementation. If any charge can be directed against our leaders, it is that they have taken so long to adopt these decisions. However, now that they have done so, it is surprising to hear from the sidelines the chorus of oracalar and sceptical comment on the hasty and impossible nature of the project. And I am not referring to the legitimate concerns and requests for information of many of our citizens, but to the pedantic and pretentious attitude of those who disdain that which they do not even know. Perhaps it would be helpful for the enlightenment of sceptics to remember that when Charles V bade farewell to his sister Mary of Hungary at Maastricht on 6 March 1546, he did so imploring that peace should reign: 'There is nothing in life that I desire and want more than peace and serenity in the world.' A few years later, under the reign of his son, the city was destroyed by the *Tercios de Flandes*. It was not to be the last sacking of the city . . .

2 An Open-Ended Constitutional Process

> The world, the being and the history have their own tempo, on which we can undoubtedly exercise a creative influence, but which nobody can dominate completely. The world and the being do not blindly obey the orders of a technocrat or a political engineer, and they are not there in order to fulfil their forecasts.
>
> Vaclav Havel

To look at the constitutional aspect of European integration we need to go back to the original, unfinished debate on its principles, organizations and objectives. At present, the ratification of the Treaty on European Union (TEU) – a truly Janus-like deity – has reopened the debate about the tension which exists between the intergovernmental and federal approaches.

The Treaty provides both camps with arguments; those who favour the intergovernmental alliance point to its 'pillar' structure, within which Justice and Home Affairs are intergovernmental and the Common Foreign and Security Policy (CFSP) both intergovernmental and federal, with the European Council as the supreme arbiter; supporters of federalism can point to European citizenship, the investiture of the Commission by the European Parliament and the co-decision procedure.

Those who are anxious to know when this debate will finally end should read the 1787 Federalist Papers and compare then with the USA as currently constituted. In comparative terms, Europe has made more progress in 40 years than the USA in its first hundred.

The history of the Community has been a slow crescendo, within which the tension intrinsic to this debate has been and continues to be a driving force. The Community's political goal and its democratic expression have remained merely implicit right up until the present in what has never, since its beginnings, been anything other than an ongoing constitutional process whose final goal is the European Union – which, in actual fact, is taking a federative form.

However, in order to defend this claim, we need to go back to the beginning.

Setting History to Rights

It is standard practice to say that the history of the Community began with the Treaty of Rome or, at most, with the Declaration of 9 May 1950 which gave birth to the ECSC. However, an examination of the gestation of the ideas which led certain clear-minded Europeans make a break with a fatalistic approach to history and to set it to rights is very revealing, as it allows us to understand both the underlying motivation and the final goal of an undertaking which has never been limited to the purely economic sphere. The horizon was much vaster, and we are only now beginning to glimpse it.

Whenever the motivation behind the Community is discussed, Jean Monnet's pragmatic personality is referred to as the motor driving an economic process. Without wishing to fall into a posthumous cult of the personality, we might with benefit recall, nonetheless, some of his wartime reflections, written at a desperate moment, when that 'free society' which we appreciate so little when its benefits are available to all simply did not exist. In a note written on 5 September 1943 in Algeria, Monnet observed that 'the objectives to be attained are the re-establishment or the establishment of a democratic regime in Europe and the economic and political organization of a "European entity"'. Both of these were essential to create conditions which would ensure that the normal state of Europe was one of peace.

There would be no peace in Europe if Europe contained regimes which did not respect the right of opposition and in which there were no free elections. Both conditions were essential if all the essential freedoms – freedom of speech, freedom to hold meetings, freedom of association, etc. – which constitute the very basis of the development of western civilization were to be re-established and upheld. There would be no peace in Europe if its states were to be reconstituted on the basis of national sovereignty, with everything that it implied as far as prestige and economic protection policies were concerned. If the countries of Europe were to start protecting themselves against each other once again, large armies would once again be necessary. The prosperity and social development Europe needs would be impossible unless the states of Europe form a federation or a 'European entity' which would convert them into a common economic body[1].

This thinking was shared by many Europeans and North Americans involved in the liberation of Europe. Its first element, the need to re-establish or establish democracy in Europe, was perfectly clear. Robert Schuman explained it with crystal clearness to the Council of Europe, when he said that the point of departure was far more political than economic: the need to take the poison out of relations between France and Germany, ensure peace, and create a climate of cooperation in Europe: 'This above all was our objective'[2].

The second element, the urgent need to take a major leap and organize a European federal body forthwith, had been advocated by an enthusiastic minority since Briand's 1926 proposal that links and a certain degree of federation should exist between the peoples of Europe, and that they should be working towards a common market and a European community, through the Ventotene Manifesto of that stubborn precursor of European federalism, Altiero Spinelli, to the 1944 Geneva Declaration by the fighters of the resistance.

The boundaries between these approaches were not hard and fast. Although the fact is usually ignored in accounts of the development of the Community, what Schuman and Monnet were bidding for was much more daring: even before the ECSC Treaty had been signed, the French Government proposed the setting-up of the European Defence Community (EDC) with a view to a common organization of European defence which would obviate the need to create a new German army. The urgency was justified by the outbreak of the Korean war and the worsening of the cold war. The EDC was set up in 1951, its Treaty was signed by the six founding members and ratified by five of them. In one of the ironies of history, the Treaty was sunk at its point of departure, namely France, where a furious debate raged for three years. The Mendès-France government vainly attempted to renegotiate the Treaty, whose ratification was rejected by the National Assembly in 1954 when the Socialist vote was divided as, to a lesser extent, was the Gaullist vote. The Western European Union (WEU) replaced the defunct EDC. For a long time, this organization simply vegetated; as Adenauer used to say, European integration is like a tree, and the dry branches produce buds in due season . . .

The Congress of Europe

The first public debate at the Congress of Europe in May 1948, held in a Hague still half in ruins, was organized by the International Coordinating Committee of the Movements for European Unity[3].

Amongst the names of those who called the Congress we find figures who had won enormous prestige in the fight to liberate Europe. Firstly, the President of Honour of the Congress was Sir Winston Churchill, the British Premier who, after winning the war, had embarked on an active pro-European Union campaign in which he made his historic Zurich and Strasbourg speeches. Alongside him, as chairman of the Congress's committees, we find the former Prime Ministers of France, Paul Ramadier (Political Affairs Committee) and Belgium, Paul Van Zeeland (Economic and Social Committee) and the former Spanish Ambassador to the League of Nations, Salvador de Madariaga (Cultural Affairs Committee).

Attending these first 'Estates-General of Europe' on an individual basis were 750 public figures from the most diverse backgrounds: distinguished statesmen, ministers and former ministers, and MPs from a range of parties (Christian Democrats, Socialists and Liberals predominated); religious figures; lawyers, professors, trade unionists and business people; leaders of social, women's and youth movements; scholars, intellectuals, writers and artists. It can therefore hardly be claimed that the Congress was a small-scale extremist conspiracy. Two hundred journalists covered the event. For four days, the participants debated Europe's future, seeking to reconcile approaches ranging from the most ardent federalism to the most lukewarm unionism.

Winston Churchill described the Congress's aims in terms which speak to us with undiminished force today:

The movement for European unity must be a positive force, deriving its strength from our sense of common spiritual values. It is a dynamic expression of democratic faith based upon moral conceptions and inspired by a sense of mission. At the centre of our movement stands a charter of human rights, guarded by freedom and sustained by law. It is impossible to separate economics and defence from general political structure. Mutual aid in the economic field and a joint military defence must inevitably be accompanied, step by step, with a parallel policy of closer political unity.

It is said with truth that this involves some sacrifice or merger of national sovereignty. I prefer to regard it as the gradual assumption by all the nations concerned of that larger sovereignty, which alone can protect their diverse and distinctive customs and characteristics and their national traditions, all of which under totalitarian systems, whether Nazi, fascist or communist, would certainly be blotted out for ever.

Churchill's declaration retains all its force today. The usual criticisms of pronouncements such as these in the mouth of a British speaker is that they are, by implication, being proposed for the Continent only. We must grant Sir Winston the benefit of the doubt. When it was necessary both he and his people demonstrated with deeds, and not mere words, that they were prepared to defend these values on the mainland, and to support the boldest of proposals, such as that for a joint Franco-British citizenship submitted by Monnet in 1940. Churchill's successor, the Labour Prime Minister Clement Attlee, went even further when, some months later, he stated in Strasbourg that 'Europe must federate or perish'. Churchill himself concluded his remarks with a proposal that a European Assembly should be set up 'in one form or another'. The debate as to *what* form immediately took the floor.

The following speaker, Paul Ramadier, said that European union was a necessity, and concluded that Europe could not be created by means of a kind of federalist revolution which would debilitate national governments without strengthening the community. It would be the sum of our efforts which, in successive waves, would lead to a solid structure.

The radical alternative was put by another prophet of European Union, the pan-Europeanist Count Coudenhove-Kalergi, who called for a 'continental constituent assembly' and pointed out that the September meeting of the European Parliamentary Union would be an appropriate moment. He was supported by Count Carandini, who proposed a genuine, disciplined political federation. Striking displays of aristocratic commitment to federalism!

However, the most direct response came from another former French Prime Minister, Paul Reynaud, who claimed that an Assembly was the 'only institution capable of saving Europe' and said that it should be directly elected because, in Spaak's words, 'in order to triumph it is necessary for the people to push their governments' and a second-tier Assembly would be 'a club for national MPs'. His proposal was given concrete form in an amendment submitted by the Gaullist Edouard Bonnefous, chairman of the French National Assembly's Committee on Foreign Affairs, and signed by all his colleagues except the Communists, advocating 'a European Constituent Assembly which will submit a Constitution for a single Europe to the different Parliaments'. Harold Macmillan spoke against this, raising a large number of political and technical objections (censuses, constituencies, electoral system) concluding that these needed to be resolved first, so as '. . . to avoid writing constitutions in the air. It is very easy to write constitutions; the difficulty is to make them effective and make them last.' Henri Brugmans, a long-time functional federalist, was also opposed to the amendment for doctrinal and tactical reasons.

Particularly worthy of notice was the speech by Dr Kramer on behalf of the German delegation, which included Adenauer, Hallstein and Heinemann. In it, he said that for the first time since the war and even before the Peace Treaty had been signed, a German delegation had been allowed to attend the Congress of Europe on an equal footing with the other nations, which implied a very great moral victory. This fact had made an enormous impression on German people. Many of his compatriots had understood for the first time that federalism was not an invention of victors intent on tying up the losers, nor a means of creating divisions, the better to control and to repress, but that it signified the right to organize freely – free union founded on the law in a spirit of good neighbourliness. There was, he said, no more efficient means of overcoming the German population's current great mistrust than to apply the selfsame principles to Europe. 'Let us federalize Germany, but let us federalize Europe at the same time, and thus we will demonstrate that it is the general principle derived from the best European traditions and that with it, Europe can build a better future'.

In the final session, chaired by Sir Anthony Eden, the rapporteur, Paul Ramadier, made a speech whose starting point was that the time had come to set up a European community, 'and the very foundation of this European Federation which we are seeking is European civilization, which can be defined in a single word, namely democracy. It is political freedom, popular sovereignty, with the recognition of the rights of the individual – in sum, respect for the human person, who is the object of social activity and whom it is society's mandate to safeguard'.

With regard to its scope, Ramadier said that it was a question of the countries' will to participate and used the traditional geographical definition of 'the region between the Atlantic and the Urals', (a formula which he cited as being classical, which means that De Gaulle cannot have had great difficulties in inventing it). At the Congress there were delegations from virtually all the central European countries which are currently seeking to join the Community. There was even a Turkish observer.

With regard to its legal form, he said that the Community had already been given a preliminary shape in the Treaty of Paris, and more notably in the 'Brussels Pact', the regional mutual assistance pact that had created the WEU, but the stage which had to be reached now was one in which the 'pact' phase (which left the integrity of each State's sovereignty untouched) would be left behind; and the conflict concerning the term was, he said, rather abstruse and confused, since words which expressed absolutes actually expressed nothing whatever and were prone to give rise to misunderstandings. He continued by saying that no common authority had been foreseen, and that the key lay in the constitution of this authority and in abandoning the unanimity rule, replacing them with the appointment of a legal person who would act in the name of all and who would be accountable, or, at least, to replace the unanimity rule with a majority rule. The idea of the High Authority, the Commission's predecessor, was already here in embryo.

The major points of the final resolution of the Congress were:

1 on *sovereign rights*, 'declares that the time has come when the European nations must transfer and merge some portion of their sovereign rights to secure common political and economic action for the integration and proper development of their common resources';
2 'considers that any union or federation of Europe should be designed to protect the security of its constituent peoples, should be free from outside control, and should not be directed against any other nation';
3 'declares its conviction that the sole solution of the economic and political problems of Germany is its integration in a federated Europe';
4 'demands the convening, as a matter of urgency, of a European Assembly chosen by the Parliaments of participating nations, designed: (a) to stimulate and give expression to European public opinion; (b) to advise upon measures to bring about the necessary economic and political union of Europe; (c) to examine the juridical and constitutional implications arising out of the creation of such a union and their economic and social consequences';
5 a *charter of human rights*, considering 'that the resultant union should be open to all European nations democratically governed and undertaking to respect a charter of human rights'. The Cultural Resolution developed this subject at greater length, affirming that the defence of human rights constituted the cornerstone of a united Europe but would not be adequately protected by a charter and needed to be made legally binding; it would therefore be necessary to back up the charter with a Convention between the Union's member states;
6 guaranteeing such rights implied the setting-up of a supranational body, a Supreme Court, a judicial monitoring body superior to the member states, to which individuals and groups could appeal and which would be capable of applying the requisite sanctions.

In this resolution there already appears, in embryo, institutions which share identical goals in an identical spirit: the Council of Europe and the European Parliament, the Court of Human Rights and the Court of Justice of the European Community. The resolution also identified personalities, discourses and arguments which have lost none of their actuality: from cautious advocates of a European alliance to revolutionary federalists, passing through the whole spectrum of gradualists or functionalists.

Moreover, we should note the curious fact that to date, this Congress represents the sole public constituent debate concerning the Community. Ever since, all the Community's constituent debates have taken the form of intergovernmental conferences held behind closed doors and for which no public minutes have been published.

Europe and Freedom

The Community's history has always maintained a curious ambivalence with regard to democracy. It does not begin with the drafting of the Constitution, or even of a Charter of Human Rights. Certainly, democracy is part of Europe's heritage, and basically the best part. Pericles' definition of democracy, made 2500 years ago in his funeral oration to the people of Athens, remains fresh and alive, while the institutions of the *ancien régime* of Europe can only strike us as mildewed with desuetude. Although in most of the current member states some form of medieval parliamentary life can be discerned, there is no disputing that democracy is a flower which throughout European history has been choked by the weeds of oppression, absolutism and intolerance for the best part of the 25 centuries which lie between Pericles and the present date. The consolidation of democracy as we know it begins with the 17th-century victory of the British and Dutch parliaments over absolute monarchs, and the parallel explosions of the French and American revolutions in the 18th century. The latter gave birth to the tradition of drawing up a Constitution as the supreme legal instrument, beginning with the dogmatic proclamation of the Declaration of Human Rights, which places the citizen firmly in the centre of political life, and establishing the structures of an organic system of division of powers. Two different democratic traditions have been born out of two different types of experience.

Of interest in this connection is R. Schuman's tale of his experience in London on 10 May 1950, i.e. the day after his famous Declaration, when he was made aware of the fact that his British allies disagreed with him: 'The fundamental reason was and is that "Englishmen cherish the principle of what they call the Unwritten Constitution." A Charter or Constitution must be adaptable to all circumstances, for which reason it must not be formulated with a rigid text. In France, the country of Descartes, on the other hand, everything must be given textual form; what is not in the texts is not of this world'[4]. Doubtless, Schuman's observations should be generalized, extending the formalist mentality to the whole continental tradition, both Latin and Germanic. We should not forget that Descartes had to go to Holland in order to be able to write in freedom. It was undeniable that both Schuman and Monnet knew that their proposal implied a rampant subversion of the vertical constitutional order characteristic of the nation-state, with its classical, structured legislative hierarchy.

Nonetheless, the foundations of a democratic Europe had already been laid with the participation of those who would be the member states of the Community, namely the Council of Europe and the European Convention of Human Rights, whose corollary was the setting up of the Strasbourg Court.

This framework has, since then, become the symbol and the forum of a free Europe, as Spaniards well know. The first European decision taken by the newly democratic Spanish *Cortes* in 1977 was to seek Spain's membership of the Council of Europe. Today, the Council continues to fulfil an essential role in educating and testing the democracies now being consolidated in Central and Eastern Europe, and it is to be hoped that it will provide the solid foundation of a democratic Europe.

Democracy: Deficit or Surplus?

Significantly, while democracy has been the Community's cornerstone, it had as a value merely been implicit in the Treaties. Only in the 1970s, when it was decided to hold direct elections

by universal suffrage to the European Parliament, were demo-
cracic values given explicit expression, while explicit recognition
of the Community's adherence to the European Convention
for the Protection of Human Rights has had to wait until the
TEU. The founding fathers undoubtedly took as their starting
point the need to make progress – to make sure that the jelly
set, creating a climate and a tradition of working together.

Progress has been made, little by little, with the setting-up of
structures which have been subject to criticisms summed up
in the expression 'democratic deficit'. Even cynical veterans of
European politics have been heard to say that if the Community were to seek membership of the Community, it would be
rejected because it was not democratic.

The most cutting, and as he himself said, 'dry and outra-
geous' riposte to his criticism was given by a judge of the
European Court of Justice, Federico Mancini: 'the Community
was not set up to be a democratic body'[5].

When we are assessing this deficit, we must nonetheless bear
in mind the sensible comment made by Laurent Cohen-Tanugi:
'as far as the deficit is concerned, the balance of 40 years of
European integration clearly reveals that this collective adven-
ture has put far more democracy into the participant states
than it can have deprived them of'[6]. In fact, the Community
has made a major contribution to stabilizing democracy and
helping it put down roots in countries like Germany and Italy,
and amongst members who joined later, such as Greece, Portugal and Spain – not merely by the fact of its being a *sine qua
non* for accession, but above all because it implies a genuine
collective psychological anchoring device. It even plays the role
of a safety net when there is a change of regime, as in France
in 1958 and in Italy at the present time.

Nonetheless, criticism concerning a democratic deficit is not
limited to the criticisms which can always be levelled within a
system which is by definition not transcendental and therefore
perfectible. The only infallible systems are those whose Heads
of State enter cathedrals underneath a canopy, or where the
Caliph is at the same time the Imam of the Believers. Where
there is liberty of expression and the possibility of taking turns
in power, change forms part of the essence of things. For that
reason, countries with democratic traditions are apparently

undisciplined and ungovernable and, at the same time, the most peaceful and efficient.

The expression 'democratic deficit', which was coined as part of the Community debate, refers essentially to the decision-taking mechanisms and to their control and accountability. In order to explain the principle features of this deficit and to avoid the usual pitfall posed by the labyrinthine complexity of the Community's structure, we need a brief description of the way in which the Community's institutions function and how they have developed. This will allow us, at least partially, to avoid one of the major errors committed during the TEU's gestation and ratification process, when certain well-meaning governments – firstly the Danes and then the French – sought to resolve the problem by publishing the text of the Treaty *en masse*. The result may be compared to publishing only the odd-numbered pages of a thriller, thus making any attempt to understand it a challenge even for readers addicted to hiero-glyphics, since essentially, the Treaty consists of amendments. It contains 57 new articles, 76 amended articles, plus 17 additional protocols and 33 declarations.

Furthermore, since we are discussing an ongoing constitutional process, we should look at the way in which the institutions have been given shape, how they operate and how they have been put together. In this sense, the Community has succeeded in tempering the presumptuous mainland European ambition to define everything once and for all in a Constitution (which has had the result of nine constitutions in France, seven in Belgium, four in Germany, seven in Spain, etc.) adopting a somewhat British evolutionary approach. Despite the fact that the expression 'ongoing process' is criticized by certain English Conservatives as being tainted with a certain pseudo-Maoism – when, in fact, the United Kingdom is the best example of this type of constitutional system – there can be no question that the Community's structure has been taking shape as a result of the successive reforms, with the contributions resulting from the interinstitutional agreements (whose significance is that of constitutional agreements) along-side the extremely important role of the Court of Justice.

The Court's jurisprudence has firmly established the Community as one focused on the rule of law by formulating three

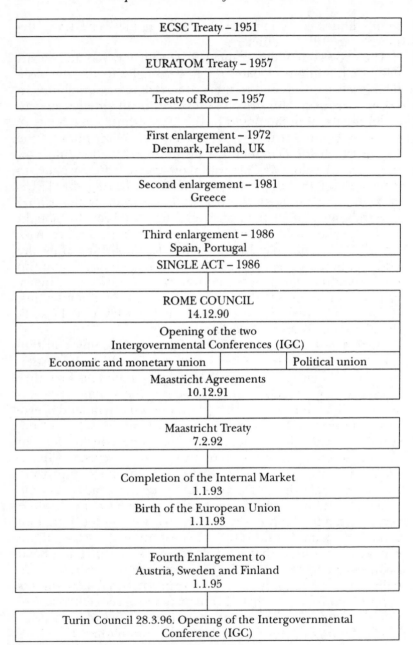

Figure 2.1 Steps in the ongoing constitutional process of the Community

fundamental principles: *direct effect* (i.e. Community laws directly create legal situations appropriate to citizens or legal persons, and do not need to be complemented by the national legislation of each country); *the primacy of Community law* over internal legislation of any kind; and *autonomy*, insofar as it is created and applied by the Community institutions[7].

Figure 1 shows, in historical order, the basic steps already taken in this constitutional process and those to come. The gestation process of the TEU has been shown in greater detail in order to help the reader acquire a better grasp of the steps involved and to indicate a way in which those scheduled for the immediate future will be taken – namely, calling a further Intergovernmental Conference in 1996 which, according to Article 2 of the TEU, must examine these provisions of the Treaty for which revision is provided, in accordance with the objectives set out in Articles A and B.

A final characteristic of this constitutional process is that, thus far, it has been carried out between states which by virtue of Article N of the Treaty are empowered to amend the Treaties through the offices of their representatives in the Intergovernmental Conferences by common accord and, following the signing of the Treaties, by means of the process of parliamentary ratification, complemented by referenda where appropriate.

3 The Community Labyrinth

> While it is true that both the market and democracy are characterized, to some extent, by competition, it is nonetheless the case that while liberalism is constituted by a single competitive-type market, democracy is a two-market system – i.e. a 'competitive monopoly' system – in which a monopolistic market of achievements is superimposed on a competitive market of advances.
>
> Ricardo La Conca

In order to understand the changes and modifications brought about by the TEU in the Community's structure, we should first of all examine its fundamental elements and the mechanisms which link these elements. This must be done with some care, since although the names of the institutions frequently coincide with those of Montesquieu's classical terminology of the division of power, important nuances and differences are also involved.

The fundamental institutional structure was set up in the 1951 Treaty of Paris establishing the European Coal and Steel Community (ECSC), which created a sectoral common market for coal and steel, the two fundamental industrial raw materials of the period, and also for the production of weapons. The structure rested on a triangle (see Figure 3.1), which featured the institution that allowed it to supersede the classical model of an alliance between states – namely the High Authority, the immediate predecessor of the Commission. The High Authority had one essential characteristic: a monopoly of the right to initiate legislation and to apply and implement what had been decided, in accordance with Jean Monnet's maxim 'decide first and explain later'. The Council was formed of representatives of the member states, and the Assembly by MPs elected within their respective national parliaments. The Assembly initially had an advisory function, while power of legislation was assigned to the Council of Ministers. The legitimacy of the members of the Council derived from their forming part of

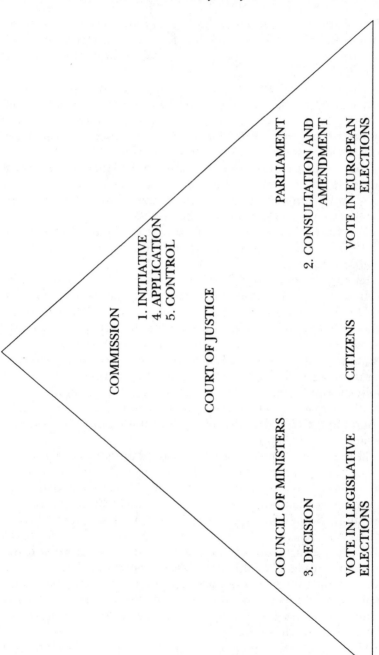

Figure 3.1 The Community triangle (basic scheme of institutional operations)

their respective national executives, and they represented their own country in the most classical terms of international law, i.e. voicing its wishes and undertaking obligations on its behalf.

The Court of Justice was also set up, to ensure that Community legislation was respected and to interpret that legislation.

Since then, the Community has acquired the Economic and Social Committee (ESC), an advisory assembly in which the full range of social-economic interest groups are represented, in three groups: entrepreneurs, employees and other interests (farmers, consumers and small businesses). It delivers opinions on Commision legislative proposals and on its own initiative draws up reports on specific issues.

The Court of Auditors was set up at Parliament's insistence in 1977 for the purpose of checking the management of the Community budget.

Finally, the purpose of the European Investment Bank (EIB) is the long-term funding of balanced Community development.

The Treaty of Rome extended the Common Market to the whole of economic life, establishing the four freedoms of movement, namely of persons, goods, capital and services. It also established a customs union with a joint external tariff and common agriculture, trade, competition, energy and transport policies, quite apart from the approximation of national laws. Finally, it laid down a twelve-year deadline for achieving a Common Market. The deadline was not met and the issue was taken up again later.

This is a very typical feature of Community history. It is not a question of systematically introducing brilliant innovations, but often of taking up and reconsidering old ideas which have not come to fruition and relaunching them at an opportune moment. Sometimes it is as though they have been thrown into a kaleidoscope which, after being given a few turns, comes up with the most unexpected combinations. Underneath the apparent modesty of the step-by-step approach, there lay hidden a tenacious revolutionary aspiration, to which we could well apply the words of Machado's poem: '*Caminante, no hay camino, se hace camino al andar...*' (Traveller, there is no road, the road is made by walking ...).

There are, however, many projects or proposals which are approved but not carried out, which are discarded or partially unsuccessful. A reference to the Fouchet plan in Community circles means the scheme submitted by the Gaullist minister Fouchet at the beginning of the 1960s, seeking to reinforce the intergovernmental nature of the Community; the Werner plan means the Luxembourgish Prime Minister's scheme for monetary union in 1970 (!); the 'empty chair' policy is a reference to the fact that the then Minister of Foreign Affairs of Gaullist France, Maurice Couve de Murville, did not occupy his seat in the Council for almost the whole of 1965, a situation which was resolved by the so-called Luxembourg Compromise – which sometimes puts in a spectral appearance at difficult moments – and which, despite lacking any legal basis, as Emile Noël[1] pointed out, extended the life of the unanimity rule in the Community by 20 years: unanimity in the Council, tantamount to a right of veto and to the Community's operating as an alliance of states. The result was the virtual paralysis of the Community, because, when it came to defending vital national interests, these were to be found in the calibration of screw-threads and the sizing of tomatoes. With some humour and a good deal of accuracy, one of the founders of the Community, the Belgian Albert Coppé, observed that 'even my family couldn't function if unanimity was the rule'.

In the 1970s, despite the worldwide crisis, Giscard and Schmidt working together were able to bring in important innovations: the setting-up of the European Council and the European Monetary System (EMS), to which we may add the introduction of direct elections by universal suffrage to the European Parliament.

European Council and Council of the Union

The European Council was initially conceived as a discussion forum for the heads of state and government, meeting twice a year. Inclusion of the heads of state is basically due to the Presidential nature of the French Constitution (which resulted in a French delegation at loggerheads with itself during the 1986–88 Mitterrand/Chirac 'cohabitation'; the Mitterrand/Balladur arrangement displayed a greater degree of harmony). The other members are heads of government coming from parliamentary-system backgrounds. A curious feature of the

Community is its division into eight republics and seven monarchies; an exact balance was broken by the Norwegian 'no'. This fact demonstrates two things: firstly, that the Community has been set up to carry out those things upon which it has reached agreement, and its purpose is not to rewrite history or create a superstate; secondly, the issue of whether states should be republics or monarchies – which, in historical terms, has been a source of bitter dispute in many Community countries, causing numerous armed conflicts and civil wars – now belongs firmly in the past. As President of the European Parliament, I have had audiences with all the Community heads of state. Without betraying state secrets, I can confirm that all the crowned heads are enthusiastic Europeans with a consummate knowledge of the Community.

With regard to the European Council, some terminological explanation is required. It is frequently confused with the Council of Europe, even in the media, and the conclusion has to be that criticism should be directed not so much at the ignorance of the man in the street or the mistakes made by journalists as at the Community's ingrained habit of choosing names and acronyms which lead to confusion or constitute the direct antithesis of transparency. For we also have to distinguish between the European Council, hitherto a forum for impulsion and orientation, and the Council of the Union, as the Council of Ministers now calls itself. Nonetheless the change of name has been approved by the British government on condition that it is specifically recognized that the Council of the Union 'is not recognized as a legal person in international law'. Therefore, the Council will be a Council of Ministers when it comes to signing. Although de jure, there is only one national Council of Ministers, there are de facto twenty[2].

There also exists a 'jumbo' Council, which on the odd occasion brings together the Foreign Ministers and ministers for whatever sector the subject under discussion affects.

The Central Council of Ministers is the General Affairs Council, composed of the foreign ministers of countries which were opponents for centuries and who today work together as Ministers of the Presidency, dealing with the Community's current affairs and with foreign and security policy. Next in order of importance is the Council of Agricultural Ministers, which for many years has managed the lion's share of the budget – even today, almost half of it – dealing with a subject vital to any democracy as a political system with a territorial basis. The Ministers of these two Councils meet one another almost as often as they meet with their own national cabinets. A third major Council is the Budgets Council, which, understandably, coexists on uneasy terms with the Agriculture Council.

Other Councils have their own peculiarities, such as the Transport Council, which was condemned by the Court of Justice in 1985 on a European Parliament initiative for having failed to set up and develop a transport policy.

However, the rising star is the Council of Economic and Finance Ministers, 'Ecofin'[3]. It brings together at Community level ministers who already meet in the context of the IMF Assembly (some of whom also meet within the G7). This Council of Ministers received its letters patent at the Maastricht European Council, the first which its members attended, and as Economic and Monetary Union goes ahead it will take on an increasingly central role.

The Presidency of the Council of Ministers, now called the Council of the Union, changes every six months, the order of precedence following the alphabetical order of the names of the member states in their own languages. So as to avoid an endlessly repeating pattern, the presidencies have at present been shuffled, and a new sequence has been negotiated until the year 2000 to take account of the enlargement process. The system has its moments; although six months is a very short space of time, the succession of presidencies has at certain periods created a highly respectable climate of competitive emulation, as with the approval of the 300 directives on the internal market, for example[4]. As far as Parliament is concerned, the process involves, first of all, an address by the new President of the Council (i.e. the foreign minister) at the beginning of the six-month presidency period, in which he or she gives a global view of what is planned, and, at the end of the presidency, an address by the Prime Minister of the country concerned to announce the success of the latest summit. Within the Council, both legislative and executive work is done, and there are informal brainstorming meetings and seminars which, in the case of the foreign affairs ministers, are called 'Gymnich'. Voting takes place on those subjects which fall under the aegis of the Community, i.e. where a majority decision is taken in Council and concerning which Parliament may submit amendments and appeal can be made to the Court of Justice. Votes are allocated as follows: France, Germany, Italy and the UK, ten votes; Spain, eight votes; Belgium, Greece, Holland and Portugal, five votes; Austria and Sweden, four votes; Denmark, Ireland and Finland, three votes; Luxembourg, two votes.

In certain areas, approval is by a qualified majority (two-thirds of the votes, since the Single Act, in the internal market, research and technology; its counterpart is the blocking minority). The Council meets behind closed doors, which does not mean that the meetings are secret. Traditionally, there has always been a listening room in the Charlemagne Building, where civil servants, often in a state of considerable anger, witness their respective ministers reaching agreements which they considered to be prejudicial to their country. Certain journalists – after Washington, Brussels has the highest concentration of journalists in the world – even go as far as to state a clear preference for meetings held *in camera*, because they believe that leaks are more valuable and more interesting. Gossip shops abound in Brussels, as befits its well-deserved fame as a city to eat out in.

We should also refer to the results of Council meetings. In principle, since there is no legal legislative hierarchy, the legislation can only take the form of directives or regulations, submitted in draft by the Commission on its own initiative (often encouraged by the member state or urged on by Parliament, or even at the suggestion of pressure groups). In reality, however, the terminological panoply is considerably more splendid, involving acts, decisions, agreements and recommendations. Within the Council, the power of the Secretary-General is equalled only by its discreetness: it commands over 2000 officials and, thanks to the six-monthly rotation of the politicians at the top, it constitutes a permanent authority lurking in the shadows.

No description of the Council would be complete if it did not include an institution which represents a genuine 'real power' in the Community, namely the Committee of Permanent Representatives or Coreper[5], made up of the ambassadors who function as plenipotentiaries at the head of the embassies of the member states. They deal with the day-to-day business and, in fact enjoy the enormous and concentrated power possessed by those who receive information before anyone else and who have the time to discuss the small print. For anyone who remembers the television series 'Yes, Minister', an appropriate comparison would be a 'collective Sir Humphrey' – according to a connoisseur of the more recondite areas of the Community world, forming a select, discreet and closed club in which they all 'live, eat and sleep together'[6]. Ministers, in fact, over and above living with one foot in the stirrup, as is normal for anyone involved in Community affairs, fly in from their capital cities where they are answerable to their national parliaments, and are obliged to reap triumphs as soon as they have arrived for the benefit of the Community journalists (whose sheer professionalism makes them a dangerous species), trying to convince them that these victories were won in a fight to the death. In fact, ministers often learn the final details of a meeting in the car from the airport or even before going into the meeting, from their PermRep. But it is not only a question of decisions; there is also the issue of implementation, and in this field there has blossomed a process, amenable to study only by initiates, which goes by the name of 'comitology', whereby national civil servants recover implementation and control of what has been decided. It is hardly necessary to add that this is a perfect example of the topicality of the Count of Romanones's famous aphorism: 'You lot make the laws and leave the regulations to me'.

Schuman gave a very exact definition of the sheer weight of the circle which surrounds ministers: 'The coalition of technicians is a fearful thing'. The Council's current status and its future calling raise many questions. Will the European Council become a Directorate? In what fields? What will its accountability be and to whom will it be accountable? How can the multiplicity of sectoral Councils best be managed? Will the Council continue to combine legislative and executive roles? Will it continue to legislate behind closed doors? Would it not be more appropriate and democratic to make the Council a Community Senate, putting faces to the current anonymous votes?

At home in each of the member states, there are questions to be answered. How is consistency to be achieved within each member state government? How do we go about debating and considering Community law in our respective national parliaments? How do ministers render accounts for their acts and decisions within the Council? How does the Council affect the balance and constitutional sharing of powers within regions and local authorities? The Treaty has given answers to some of these questions, as will be seen in Chapter 5, but many, nonetheless, remain unanswered.

The European Commission[7]

The Community's strongest claim to being an original political construct is the institution known as the Commission. It comprises a President, appointed by the European Council in agreement with the EP, and a College of Commissioners. In the Santer Commission, there are 20 of them, two for each of the five major member states (France, Germany, Italy, Spain and the UK) and one each for the others (Belgium, Denmark, Greece, Holland, Ireland, Luxembourg, Portugal, Austria, Finland and Sweden). There are differences in the way that they are appointed, with some countries proposing Commissioners and others appointing them without more ado. The British Prime Minister Margaret Thatcher dismissed Lord Cockfield, the author of the White Paper on the Internal Market, because he was too 'pro-Community'.

In accordance with the Treaties, a Commissioner is independent and may not take instructions from his government – and he gives a formal, sworn undertaking to this effect. Nonetheless, this independence is somewhat tempered by the discretionary aspect of the appointment and dismissal of Commissioners by their governments, over which there are no controls and for which there is no political accountability. The collegial responsibility, plus the cabinet organisation, sometimes makes the functioning of the Commission look like a Super Coreper. In fact, there are various options with regard to appointing Commissioners – and these are clearer in countries which possess two. They range from sharing the appointments either between the government and the opposition (as is the case in Spain at present) or between the members of the government coalition (Germany and Italy) to having a politically 'monochrome' team.

Since the outset, the personality of the President and his conception of his office have been crucial to his role. The first Commission President, the German Walter Hallstein, made a powerful contribution to shaping the office thanks to his protocolary pretensions, 'believing that the pressure of events would bring what he had in mind' according to De Gaulle[8]. In the case of Jacques Delors, his personal qualities – political courage, drive and tenaciousness, submitting proposals and ideas with no fear of controversy – have pushed both the office and the role of the President much more into the limelight.

The President takes part in the European Council and the G7 summits. But the Commission is not a strictly presidential organization, although the distribution of portfolios does have a significant role in defining the power enjoyed by the individual Commissioners.

Moreover, there is a certain degree of informal party-political grouping amongst the Commissioners which basically reflects the major European political family groupings: Socialists, Christian Democrats and Liberals.

With the passing of time, the Commission's relations with Parliament have been steadily consolidated, with the *de facto* creation of an embryonic system of answerability to Parliament thanks to 'Question Time', Commission statements, the submission of the legislative programme and of the annual programme, and even a semblance of a Speech of Investiture.

The Commission's fundamental weapons are that it holds the monopoly of initiative and of representing the Community as a legal person. This monopoly is not discretionary, and can only be exercised in those fields which the Treaties agree on as falling under the aegis of the Community.

Its principal functions are:

1 to submit legislative proposals to the Council of Ministers in Community policy areas in the form of directives, regulations, reports, recommendations and communications;
2 to manage the common policies and their budgets. Of outstanding importance are the EAGGF (Guidance Section) for modernizing agriculture, the ERDF for regional development, the ESF for social policy, the research programmes, aid to development through the European Development Fund, and humanitarian aid;

3   to negotiate, on a mandate from the Council, agreements
    with third countries and to represent the Community in
    numerous international organizations;
4   to monitor the correct application of rules, principles and
    decisions. It can investigate the incorrect application of
    legislation and impose fines for infringing the rules on
    competition. It may bring charges against national Govern-
    ments in the Court of Justice when Community law has
    been broken. To carry out its tasks, the Commission has
    14 500 officials, approximately two-thirds and one-third of
    the numbers employed in the Madrid and Paris City Coun-
    cils respectively.

In recent years, the power of the Commissioners and the vo-
racious appetite of the Brussels bureaucracy for regulations and
powers have become a source of enormous political controversy.

Certainly, neither the Commissioners nor the Community
officials are immune to the *vis expansiva* inherent in power of
any kind, and they tend to concern themselves with anything
and everything which they believe could help improve the
order of the fabric of the universe or, in this case, Europe.
Sometimes, the Commission looks like an orphaned government in search of a territory to govern. Since its very beginnings, the Eurocracy has been drawing up detailed regulations
and, as one of the bravest of Community politicians, Sicco
Mansholt, used to say, overburdening a thousand little regulations with technical details which serve only to obscure the
major issues[9]. This is not only the fruit of the mania of civil
servants for regulating every last detail which German *Beamte*
carry to such a peak of perfection. For although there is much
talk of the French universalist and rationalist mentality which
tends to treat and shape Europe and the world in its own
image and likeness, we tend to be unaware of the influence of
Teutonic civil servants and lawyers trained in the Great School
of 'Kameralwissenschaft'. One of the clearest indications of
the strength of the Eurocracy is that one normally speaks about
the 'DG' (Directorate General) rather than the Commissioner's portfolio.

The uncertain relations between member states and the lack
of elective legitimacy have made their contribution to this

meticulous 'regulationism', since the representatives of the national governments, seeking to ensure that all the hatches are fully battened down, have made sure that everything is covered in the small print. And it is not only they; the increasingly well-organized and active pressure groups keep an eagle eye on microscopic details when legislation is being drawn up.

The Commission's traditional philosophy has been to seek maximum harmonization in all fields, very much along the Napoleonic lines of a Europe with a single metric system, *code civil*, etc. At times, this is sensible. At others, it is not.

It has led to farcical situations which nonetheless have their importance – from regulations such as the 'noise threshold of tower cranes' to 'colorants or stabilizers which may be added to products or jam'. These matters are not trivial: behind them, businesses, jobs, markets – and, in some cases, even governments – are always at stake. The regulation on the fermentation of French cream cheese unleashed a wave of popular rebellion against Brussels's attack on an indestructible symbol of French identity. In fact, as was explained 'a posteriori' and hence, too late, the regulation had been drawn up in response to a request initiated by the French manufacturers with a view to guaranteeing the quality and character of their product. Nearer home, we have the case of the regulations on typewriter keyboards including the letter 'Ñ', which turned into a full-scale battle to safeguard Spanish national identity, with the *Real Academia de la Lengua* very much to the fore.

In this field, the case-law of the Court of Justice has achieved a Copernican revolution in the mentality that everything has to be standardized at all costs. The most outstanding cases, curiously enough, have involved food and drink, e.g. the historic 'Cassis de Dijon' judgement, which ruled against the German ban on importing this redcurrant liquor on the pretext that its alcoholic content was lower than that of the home brew, which paradoxically enough confused German purchasers. The Court took as its basis the approach that a product which was legally registered in one country should enjoy the same status in other countries, thus encouraging the principle of mutual recognition.

Other cases which have helped to make the question of recognition more flexible and have greatly speeded up the completion of the internal market were those of German beer and Italian pasta. In the first case, the Court ruled against the German ban on importing beer from other Community countries on the grounds that German production processes were natural and met the requirements of a recipe from a Bavarian monastery, dated circa 1500. The ruling also went against the monastic regulation. The third case was that of Italian pasta, in which German soft grain pasta producers were seeking the right to export freely to Italy, where the manufacture of pasta with hard grain is taken as an article of faith. Clearly, the difference in price is greatly to the advantage of a soft-grain pasta. The Court's ruling was in this instance in favour of the German case, providing the type of grain used was clearly labelled.

These rulings, amongst others, have made a far more decisive contribution to the internal market than hundreds of meetings debating preliminary draft directives or regulations *ad nauseam.*

After enjoying a period of exceptional privilege, with the Delors Presidency playing the leading role in the completion of the internal market, and the Commission defining by steps and stages what was good for Europeans, both the Commission and the Eurocracy have been subjected to the crossfire of accusations hurled by certain political leaders and to the reactions of public opinion. Claims that a monstrous socialist Moloch has been created in Brussels and that it is setting up a hyper-centralized, tyrannical state are mindless exaggerations. But there is no doubt that having played a leading part during the Community's creative stage – a part characterized by a certain 'gentle despotism', as Delors himself has said – today's Commission is faced with the problem of redefining its institutional role.

Will it become the Community government so longed for by the out-and-out federalists? Will it become a Technical General Secretariat or a Sub-Secretariat of a European Council converted into a Directorate? Will its role depend on matters being dealt with? What, in hard and fast terms, are its legitimacy and political answerability?

In Chapter 5 the answers provided by the TEU to some of these questions will be considered.

The European Parliament

The third fundamental pillar is the European Parliament, whose history falls into two stages. Between 1952 and 1979, it was a Consultative Assembly, and since then it has been a Parliament elected by universal suffrage.

Its initial role was that of a Consultative Assembly comprising members elected by their respective national parliaments. Its career, broadly speaking, follows that of all parliaments, in their struggle to play their own role throughout European history.

Like the Council and the Commission, Parliament has problems with defining its own identity and establishing its own space, although, funnily enough, Parliament has been the only institution whose name has not had to be changed as a result of the TEU; it designated itself as a Parliament in 1962, and obtained formal recognition of this name in the Single Act. For all that, it has the problem of not being surrounded by the aura of respectability and mystery generated by power, above all when power is exercised behind closed doors. Parliament has had a bad press for years. Media, particularly in the English-speaking world, have created a stereotype of a chamber located somewhere between a gravy train and 'Congress on holiday' – for its detractors – and, for its defenders, located between the UN and a student talking shop.

It is undeniable that the *vis expansiva* of a Parliament which lacked a solid institutional profile did not help to clarify matters, since in dealing with subjects of all kinds, Parliament felt increasingly free to express itself the greater the distance between the problem in question and the Community. However, it is not fair to draw up a merely negative balance sheet. At world level, Parliament's resolutions on the political situation and human rights in many countries have been applauded by democrats and provoked unfavourable reactions from dictatorial governments.

In the field of domestic affairs, Parliament has battled to place the Community on a democratic basis. The Tindemans Report of 1975 represented a first demand for a revision of the institutional system so as to improve the Community's democratic equilibrium. It proposed two things: the election of the

EP by universal suffrage and a reform which would give it an active role. The first demand was achieved in 1979; the second had to wait for the Single Act and the introduction of the so-called cooperation procedure. Even the obligatory nature of consultation had to be affirmed, on pain of declaring the measures in question null and void, by the Court in its ruling 'SA Roquette Frères' against the Council of 29 November 1980.

In this field, we should highlight the consolidation of Parliament's rights which the Court of Justice obtained when it recognized Parliament's passive legitimation in its ruling on the case of the French Greens versus the EP for discrimination in the funding of the information campaign of 24 April 1986 – and, more importantly, active legitimation in the Chernobyl case, with the annulling of measures decided by the Council without respecting Parliamentary prerogative. Then to think that this very right had been denied Parliament two years earlier in the ruling on 'Comitology'. The Chernobyl ruling was described as the 'most blatantly political ruling ever given' by the Thatcherite Bruges Group[10].

The EP's longest battle to establish its own identity and position has unquestionably been in the budgetary field, in which it was for many years at loggerheads with the Council, with Parliament rejecting the 1979 and 1984 budget because it did not agree with the spending priorities. In this protracted battle, Parliament was fighting for the sharing of budgetary authority between the Council and Parliament. Ruling 34/86 of the Court of Justice defines this sharing of power on the basis of a need to arrive at agreement between two branches of the budgetary authority. Since then, the EP's preferred model for legislative co-decision takes as its basis the shared budgetary authority and the way in that is balanced.

Following its election by universal suffrage in the early 1980s, Parliament launched the project of drawing up a draft constitution, better known as the Spinelli Treaty, which, although it failed to achieve its objective, made a decisive contribution to reawakening optimism in a Community which had fallen into 'Euro-pessimism' – thanks to its inspired and innovative text which went hand in hand with the Adonino Report on a 'People's Europe'.

The response was the Single Act, greeted by Parliament with a 'yes but' to the legislative cooperation procedure, which by means of a complex system of two readings allowed Council decisions to be amended or rejected by an absolute Parliamentary majority; if these are approved, the Council can only reject them by a unanimous vote. Even though this is a 'negative power of consent', it allowed the package of 300 internal market directives to be dispatched on time and in due form, at the rate of one a week, and with a significant proportion of Parliament's amendments being accepted (60% at first reading and 40% at second reading).

The experience was enormously enriching for the Community's institutional triangle, giving rise to and establishing political, Parliamentary, negotiating and interinstitutional agreement practices which constitute authentic constitutional agreements. Over and above the Declaration on Racism, Fascism and Xenophobia which concluded the Evrigenis Report (16 January 1986) by the Committee of Inquiry set up for that purpose, which became a Solemn Declaration by all three institutions, there have been other agreements of importance. The most decisive was undoubtedly the Agreement on Financial Perspective and Budgetary Discipline (1987–1992) which I myself proposed in my Report on Future Funding, allowing the Community to pull itself out of what was, technically speaking, bankruptcy, and to replace the endless interinstitutional jockeying for position with constructive collaboration. This agreement was renegotiated and successfully extended for the 1993–1998 period, on the basis of the Colom Report by the EP.

In the Parliament elected in 1994, the number of MEPs increased first from 518 to 567 as a result of the agreement reached at the Edinburgh Summit, which took up the European Parliament's proposal in order to reflect German unification. In January 1995, the total number has risen to 626, following the entry of representatives of three new partners. The following tables show the breakdown by countries and 'political groups'[11]:

There are ten 'political groups' to which members belong, according to the rules that discourage as much as possible the creation of national groups. From one side, there are the big traditional ideological European families – Socialists, Christian Democrats and Liberals. The two main groups – PES and EPP – keep the majority of the chamber and have strengthened

Table 3.1 Breakdown of MEPs by countries, January 1995

	Tot	B	DK	D	GR	E	F	IRL	I	L	NL	A	P	FIN	S	UK
PES	221	6	3	40	10	22	15	1	18	2	8	8	10	4	11	63
EPP	173	7	3	47	9	30	13	4	12	2	10	6	1	4	6	19
ELDR	52	6	5	–	–	2	1	1	6	1	10	1	8	6	3	2
GUE	31	–	1	–	4	9	7	–	5	–	–	–	3	1	1	–
FE	29	–	–	–	–	–	–	–	29	–	–	–	–	–	–	–
RDE	26	–	–	–	2	–	14	7	–	–	–	–	3	–	–	–
V	25	2	–	12	–	1	–	2	4	1	1	1	–	–	1	–
ARE	19	1	–	–	–	–	13	–	2	–	–	–	–	1	–	2
EDN	19	–	4	–	–	–	13	–	–	–	2	–	–	–	–	–
NI	31	3	–	–	–	–	11	–	11	–	–	5	–	–	–	1
Tot	626	25	16	99	25	64	87	15	87	6	31	21	25	16	22	87

Table 3.2 Breakdown of MEPs by political groups, January 1995

PES	Group of the Party of European Socialists
EPP	Group of the European People's Party
ELDR	Group of the European Liberal, Democratic and Reformist Party
GUE	Confederal Group of the European United Left
FE	Forza Europa Group
RDE	Group of the European Democratic Alliance
V	The Green Group in the European Parliament
ARE	Group of the European Radical Alliance
EDN	Europe of Nations Group
NI	Non-attached Members

their representativity thanks to the incorporation of the British Conservatives into the Christian Democratic group and the former Italian Communists into the Socialist group[12].

From the other side, there are the smaller groups that defend other visions of Europe than the mainstream: Greens, Communists, the new green-communists and the nationalists or populist groups (Forza Europa, Europe des Nations, Rassemblement des Démocrates Européens or Alliance Radicale).

There is a presence of the extreme right too, with the French *Front National*. If we look at the relative weight of the national delegations, it is directly proportional to their presence in the big families. This is true for the German, Dutch, Belgian, British, Spanish and Luxembourg members, while it is a traditional handicap for the French.

The Parliament brings together men and women from every corner of the Community. These individuals do not participate in the European institutions on the basis of special qualifications or acknowledged technical aptitudes, but because they have been elected by their fellow citizens, sometimes on the basis of pro-Community or anti-market lists (in the latter case, above all in Denmark and the UK). It is no exaggeration to claim that the Community experience, in this institution as in others, is a return to school insofar as one learns something new and at the same time revises one's outdated ideas of history, discovering affinities and things in common with one's traditional rivals. It is a process of cross-fertilization which foments tolerance, cooperation and solidarity. For this alone, the Community venture would have been worth undertaking. A complex aspect of Community life such as the use of eleven working languages is all the more apparent in Parliament, which could be described as a 'Tower of Babel that works'. In fact, almost a third of its budget is spent on translation and simultaneous interpretation, which allows debates to be held in eleven languages. Over against the experience of not being understood by one's own language speakers, the daily life of the EU demonstrates that where there is a will, the opposite way is possible. It is certainly complicated; but this is a fact which remains intractable, despite crackpot attempts to discover magic formulae. I think, with Umberto Eco, that 'Europe should be multilingual'.

There is also a school of thought which believes that the election of the EP by universal suffrage came too early and thinks that it would have been more appropriate to consolidate the Community framework first of all. This thinking, to all appearances, is based on a certain degree of prudence, although it appears to be unaware that history is not written in advance. The history of democracy, like the history of life, is made up of sudden breaks with the past which, with the passing of time, turn into causes for celebration, such as the night of 4 August in France, the Boston Tea Party or the rebellion of the US Constituent Assembly, not to mention the complex and picturesque ritual world of Westminster.

Certainly, its functions cannot be assimilated to those of national parliaments consolidated in struggles which have gone on for centuries. Its freedom to tackle certain subjects (e.g. the Gulf War and the conflict in the former Yugoslavia) has been greater, since it does not suffer from the discipline of a governmental majority – a fact conducive to far more open and dynamic debating. But it is significant that, insofar as it has been able to generate its own customs and practices, or has been assigned functions, Parliament's capacity to digest and exploit has been instantaneous. The experience of the Single Act and the cooperation procedure is conclusive in this respect.

Undoubtedly, Parliament's image is limited insofar as there is no consolidated body of Community public opinion, but every time interesting, topical subjects have been dealt with, the response has been positive (drugs; racism, fascism, xenophobia; anti-pollution or health measures and quality of foodstuffs).

The questions which arise with regard to Parliament stem on the one hand from its role in legitimizing the system and on the other from the popular vote. Should it 'invest' the Commission? What is the Commission's accountability to Parliament? What it its relationship with the Council? How should the EP exercise democratic control over issues jointly decided on? How should it exercise the right of initiative? What should its relationship with national parliaments be? The Treaty, despite its shortcomings, offers possible ways of answering these questions.

The Power of the Court of Justice

In sum, the Community's ongoing constitutional process has not only created an institutional framework but has also engendered a legal 'corpus', the *acquis communautaire*, which means all the legislation which has to be accepted *en bloc* in order to be a member of the Community. Those who are interested could have a look at the Spanish *Boletín Oficial del Estado* of 1 January 1986, which has over 50 000 pages. The countries that have just entered have taken an almost double amount of legislation on board. The result is a system in which the weight of the Law, which is typical of the Anglo-Saxon tradition, takes centre stage, as against absolute concepts of parliamentary constitutional sovereignty reflected in a single law.

The decisive role of the Court of Justice, which since 1964 has enshrined the principle of the primacy of Community law over national law, is a key element in this process. Jean Foyer has called it a 'juridical *coup d'état*'. Certainly, we are speaking about justice which is not being administered in the name of the king, people or a sovereignty, but which rests on the Treaties.

More recently, anti-Court of Justice criticism in Germany has been stepped up, saying that the Court has placed itself at the top of the Community pyramid, through to the critical remarks made by Chancellor Kohl himself in the Bundestag debate of 4 December 1992 and the reply of the *Frankfurter*

Rundschau, 'Im Zweifel für Europa' ('if in doubt, for Europe'), which gives positive expression to the preoccupations of the leading German politicians, and not only them, on the Court's role. If there has been a coup in the Community, it was not in Maastricht. It happened many years ago with the full consent of those concerned and their acceptance of it.

The authentic interpretation is always an authorized source. It is therefore apposite to remember Schuman giving the inaugural lecture of the College of Europe in Bruges: 'We are dealing with an unprecedented upheaval in our political conceptions. The community idea has to lie at the base of all future relations between the belligerent countries, and this community is the prelude to a full-scale community, a political community, a military community, an economic community, beyond coal and steel. This is the fatal chain, because the essential thing was to achieve a change of attitude'.

Today we have, according to the definition of the Court of Justice (the ruling cited above, on the Greens versus the European Parliament), a 'constitutional charter of a Community law', comprising the Treaty of Paris establishing the ECSC (1951), the Treaties of Rome setting up the EEC and the EAEC (1957), the Treaties amending certain budgetary and financial provisions (1970–1975), the Treaties of Accession of new members (1972, 1979 and 1985) and a Single European Act (1986). To these we now have to add the Treaty on European Union (1993).

To these texts, we must add the fact that general principles are enshrined in the jurisprudence of the Court of Justice, and the constitutional agreements between the Council, the Commission and Parliament.

All these elements have gone into the building of a constitutional system whose characteristics, according to the current President of the Court of Justice, Gil Carlos Rodríguez Iglesias[13] are:

1   The supreme position of the Treaties, even where no legislative hierarchy exists, expresses a clear definition of Community laws from a legislative point of view (there are directives, regulations and various kinds of measures). The Treaties assign the power of control of Community legality to the Court, which at the same time fulfils a constitutional

function, the procedural validity of measures requested by national courts. In this connection, the 'Greens' ruling already referred to defines the EEC as a community of law, in so far as neither its member states nor its institutions may abstract themselves from control of the conformity of their acts with the fundamental 'constitutional charter' constituted by the Treaty.

2   Moreover, there are the general principles which are common to the member states' legal systems, which are not explicitly included. The most characteristic case here is that of fundamental rights, which was enshrined in case law in principle (ruling of 17 December 1970) to become the subject of a joint interinstitutional declaration in 1977 and finally, the expressly included Article F2 of the TEU which recognises the Rome Convention. For its part, the EP has drawn up a declaration of fundamental rights.

3   A third element is the constitutional outlook of the Treaties as the basis of Community powers and their allocation to the various Community institutions.

It should be recalled in this connection that 'the Community, unlike sovereign states, possesses no general powers, but only those assigned to it by the Treaties', although it has to be equally borne in mind that the Communities 'assume broad powers of a legislative, executive and judicial nature in areas traditionally reserved for the sovereignty of the state'.

In short, 40 years of experience, of progress and setbacks, agreements and splits have gone into creating a regional international organization which is very much *sui generis*, constantly evolving towards a more advanced type of integration, whose name is the European Union, and some of whose final outlines we can discern, but which is not yet politically or juridically defined. The reality of this situation reminds me, if my memory of Roman law serves me right, of the way in which law arose as an agreed norm, following a period of gestation in the shape of contracts and customs. In the case of the Community, since the member states are the subjects of the constitutional process and are alone legitimately empowered to reform it, we rely on them for the initial impetus and their voluntary acceptance of the Community yoke. The Community as such does not possess coercive instruments: the member states' decisions to accept the Commission's monopoly of initiative on Community subjects, to obey Community laws and to respect the rulings of the Court of Justice are all voluntary decisions. Of particular interest is the ruling of the German Federal Constitutional Court of 12 October 1993, which removed the last obstacle to the definitive ratification of the Treaty. Although all the institutional courts and similar bodies of the member states have pronounced on aspects of the TEU, the Federal Constitutional Court, a key institution in the Federal Republic, had to rule on a fundamental appeal submitted by Mr Brunner, the former head of Commissioner Bangemann's private office, alleging that the Treaty ran contrary to German parliamentary democracy. The ruling took as its starting point the principle of democracy, which lays down that the authority of the State (the Bundestag) is legitimated by the popular vote, but that 'this principle' does not prevent the Federal Republic from becoming a member of a supra-nationally organized Community of States. On this basis, the Court was of the opinion that the TEU is bringing about an ever closer organization of the peoples of Europe, without creating a European people, for which reason the national parliaments continue to be sovereign 'with tasks and powers of particular significance'. Moreover, the Court said, in the present stage of development, the European Parliament enjoys a decisive legitimating function which would be strengthened if its electoral system were to be rendered uniform in all the Member States and its influence in the policies and legislation of the European Communities were to grow. What was decisive, the Court said, was that the democratic basis of the Union should advance on a par with the integration process, and that a full democratic life should be upheld in the member states. The challenge of constructing a 'compound' democracy resting on a double legitimacy lies, therefore, at the heart of European integration.

4 The Gestation of the TEU

There has never been a political system which promoted democratic civil liberties and at the same time abolished Parliament. Similarly, there has never been a political regime which maintained Parliament whilst at the same time abolishing civil liberties. And, until now, there has never been a political system where a post-capitalist civil society combined profound political liberties and an active and vigilant parliament. The building of just such a system could be considered one of the greatest historical challenges facing contemporary socialist tradition.

J. Keane
Democracy and Civil Society

The description in broad terms of the institutional triangle allows us to go back to the original issue, i.e. democracy, and to ask the key question as to the legitimacy of the gestation of the TEU, examining the changes it entails and the questions which remain as yet unanswered. Introducing innovations is the most difficult thing in life, particularly in an area as complex, versatile and perilous as politics. Nevertheless, this is a more useful way of discussing Maastricht and its repercussions than making grandiloquent speeches, somewhat out of fashion on the video age, in defence of immutable historical destinies or all-or-nothing stances. There are areas of discourse concerning certain analytical approaches to the future of the Community that ignore the existence of a Community governed by the rule of law, with its own institutions and dynamics.

Nevertheless, the phase which culminated in the TEU did not begin with such an ambitious goal in view. Once the Single European Act was ratified, which in most cases was merely a formality in the respective parliaments, the most worrying problem was that of finding a solution to the Community's technical bankruptcy. The matter was resolved at the extraordinary summit in Brussels in February 1988, which saw the adoption of the basic decisions concerning the CAP reform and of the financial perspective until the completion of the Internal Market. At the Council of Hannover in June of that same year, it was decided to begin preparations for the EMU, with the setting-up of a Committee of Experts chaired by Delors, consisting of the Governors of the Central Banks and certain other specially designated experts. At the Madrid Council of 1989, it was decided to establish the EMU. The strategy of the Commission and of the European Council was to continue the gradual process to enable Political Union to take place in the mid 90s.

The Hand of History

However, history constrained and altered the patient plans of the planners and guiding brains. 1989 saw a deviation from the plan, thanks to the events behind an Iron Curtain which was corroded at its very foundations. Indomitable Polish rebeliousness and Hungary's patient dissociation of itself from the Eastern bloc were joined by Gorbachev's policies of *perestroika* and *glasnost*. The thaw provided an opportunity for the citizens of the then German Democratic Republic to rush to the then Western paradise via Hungary, and in early November it breached the Berlin Wall. The subsequent domino effect led to calls for parliamentary democracy from all the peoples of Central and Eastern Europe, resulting in the bridging of the ideological division of the continent: for the first time in history, all the countries of Europe were subscribing to a single set of values, to be enshrined in the Charter of Paris only one year later.

The recently-elected European Parliament had to deal with this situation and with its most decisive aspect, namely German unification – an event which, in addition to changing the make-up of the Community itself, filled many of its citizens with hope and many others with unhappy memories of the past. Above all, it came unexpectedly. I remember that I was first told about it whilst on an official visit to Italy, by a journalist on the telephone. I reacted by asking whether the fall was symbolic or real. He was unable to answer at the time. Events were to do so later. In that same month of November 1989, the debate in the EP showed that a large majority supported it and that the solidarity shown would be able to overcome the spectre of the past. The joint appearance at my invitation before Parliament of the President of the Council, François Mitterrand, with Chancellor Kohl was a powerful political signal. In the debate that followed, the main problem raised was how to translate the term *Selbstbestimmung* (self-determination), whilst attempting to bring together such divergent traditions in this respect as that of Germany and of older states. The term itself has the most highly charged political and emotive connotations, ranging from the romantic conception of Germany, which brought about its 19th-century unification and its reaffirmation after the Treaty of Versailles, to Third-World emancipation from the colonial yoke following the Second World War. This term created a concept which for the pantheists of nationalism begins with the existence of a people, an eternal entity, which exercises this self-determination without consideration for the individual's wishes, and with the inescapable consequence of its constitution as a discrete State. The German case is an example of the opposite, in that unification came about as a result of elections following the reclaiming of political freedoms, a process which was closely followed and monitored by its neighbours and partners.

Certainly, the unity achieved was fundamentally that of Germany, but it had a Community dimension which, in terms of protocol (the golden rule in politics) were reflected in the privileged places reserved for Mr Delors as President of the Commission and for myself as President of the European Parliament on the right hand of President von Weizsäcker of the Federal Republic of Germany at the ceremonies of 3 and 4 October 1990 at the first session of the united Bundestag. On that same day, 3 October, I had the honour of speaking at the Paulskirche in Frankfurt on the invitation of the city's mayor and at the initiative of my old friend and comrade Rudi Arndt, former Chairman of the Socialist Group in the European Parliament. In this setting – pregnant with symbolism for the Germans, since it was there that the 1848 revolution was proclaimed and the first Constitution was created – I was able to answer the question 'What does Europe expect from a united Germany? We expect, because we know it to be true, that the German people are now in an even better position than before to play their proper role in the common endeavour for democracy, liberty and peace, contributing to making a united Europe a reality and benefitting from this process'.

Finally, the Community adopted an exceptional procedure to adopt the legislative package for the integration of the five new federal states with all their provisional and transitional regulations. This procedure was made possible by an inter-institutional agreement which resulted from the shared aspirations of all concerned.

A final important aspect, because of their repercussions on the life of the Community, were the economic terms under which unification took place. Even though there was an immediate show of solidarity on the part of the Community, including the less developed members – namely, the granting of structural funds equivalent to those received by Spain – the fact remains that the terms governing the monetary exchange rates and the union were set by the German Government. For my part, I advocated from the very beginning that the process, then called '2 + 4' (the two Germanies plus the four occupying powers, i.e. the United States, the United Kingdom, France and the Soviet Union), should be supplemented with a '2 + 12' process, i.e. the two Germanies plus the Community as a whole, and that the Community as such (and this was the position of President Delors) should assume the direct co-responsibility of the reconstruction process of Eastern Germany. This was not the route chosen and this has been one of the causes of our subsequent problems in the economic field.

Be that as it may, there are two noteworthy aspects of the unification process: firstly, for the first time in history such a unification has taken place by peaceful means and with the acceptance of the partners and the neighbours of those involved, including the countries of Central and Eastern Europe and Russia in particular; and secondly, this has not only been done with explicit reference to the process of European unification but has acted as a powerful catalyst to accelerate the process towards political union within the Community. This is not merely an expression of blind faith in Europe, but rather an observation based on a fundamental principle of European politics: Germany has always caused problems, both when it has been very strong and when it has been very weak, due to its central position in the continent, its human, economic and cultural importance and its lack of well-defined borders. The latter concept is difficult for Englishmen, Swedes or Spaniards to understand but easy for somebody in neighbouring Maastricht, for example, as I showed in Chapter 1. It is for this reason that the 'incardination' or embedding of Germany in the process leading towards European unity is so important, and it is for this reason also that the idea of keeping this country free but under close observation, eternally under suspected designs to leave 'the common home', is so fruitless. A quick look at history shows that all the European nations which have had aspirations to establish a hegemony have taken their turn at committing atrocities; the fundamental problem with Germany is that it has made the most recent attempt at hegemony. Still, the most notable element is this incardination-in-principle with European unity, since, as Habermas remarked, 'the fact that Germans belong to western Europe has only become evident in the decades following the Second World War' – and not because of a fear of fleeing eastward, but rather because of the idea of the *Zentrum*, the ideology of the centre, deeply rooted from romanticism till Heidegger, described by Adorno as the 'fundamental anti-civilizing and anti-western current of the German tradition'[1].

These days, the institutional structure of Germany seems to be conceived for the Community. Federalism – with the systematic application of the principle of subsidiarity as well as cooperation, the integration of the social partners, the independence of the Central Bank, in other words, the basic elements of a 'culture of stability' – means that Germans can view the Community as yet another tier, as the attic story of their political edifice.

From Walking Speed to Gallop

This vertiginous acceleration of history resulted in a leap in the strategy of progress which envisaged at first the completion of the internal market, to be followed by economic and monetary union and culminating in political union. As President of the European Parliament, I was able to play a privileged role in, and be a close eyewitness of, the gestation of the TEU, since the beginning of my term in office coincided with the beginning of the thaw in the summer of 1989 and ended with the adoption of the Treaty. During this period I had the opportunity of explaining the European Parliament's position on the situation and on the integration of Europe to the European Council following the tradition initiated by my predecessor, Lord Plumb, of giving ten-minute talks ('time is money') summarizing Parliament's debates and resolutions on current issues.

This task of summarizing and prioritizing issues before a High Council (a cross between a panel of examiners and a synod) is not an easy one, for one has to set out one's position in a clear manner, avoiding both acrimony and servility, in a speech which may not, and as a rule should not, always be to the liking of the audience.

Some of the old hands had told me that some heads of government did not even bother to use the headphones (an absolute necessity for most of them) but I was able to see from the very beginning that this was not so. It is an attentive and quiet audience, their gestures and nods of approval when quoted betraying both their human nature and their courteous attention. A convention has grown up between the Presidency of the Council and that of the European Parliament, namely of suggesting the inclusion of a given subject, particularly where it concerns last-minute developments, as in the case of the eruption of the Yugoslavia question at the Luxembourg Council.

Another achievement has been that the declarations of the Presidency, such as the conclusions of the Council, should include Parliament's position. These documents make for interesting reading, showing how one's position conditions one's perspective: while the Council routinely congratulates itself and assigns tasks to the Commission, Parliament merits the occasional mention or ticking-off.

The Strasbourg Council provided the first opportunity for positing the theses which had been maturing in the recently constituted Parliament as a result of a combination of the internal impetus and the bewildering political changes in Europe, which demonstrated the need to proceed with European union, not merely as an economic and monetary grouping but also as a political union. On the basis of this fundamental premise, I drew up a decalogue, this being the most effective method of presenting a programme known since the time of Moses: to ensure active involvement in the process of constitutional reform, proposing the 'Interinstitutional Preparatory Conference' (IPC) and the meeting of the national parliaments: a call for an inter-governmental conference to be held in the autumn of 1990; a shortlist of the key issues for Parliament (legislative, co-decision, the investiture of the Commission and the making public of legislative debates within the Council) involved in establishing the federal foundations; the granting to the European Parliament of the power to ratify the reform; the association agreements with the emergent democracies, and the setting of the year 2000 as the deadline for European union.

Parliament's new approach was noticeably different, for the situation had changed significantly. In the previous reform around, the EP had drawn up a draft Treaty on Political Union envisaging a Constituent Estates-General. When Jacques Delors, then an MEP, was appointed President of the Commission, he decided to go back to the traditional Community approach and seek a motivating factor in the economic field. He chose the Internal Market, espousing and adding to the unfulfilled historical commitment, and introducing majority voting and legislative cooperation as additional political elements.

The Single European Act was the fruit of negotiations between the Governments with only token involvement of the European Parliament. Nevertheless, good ideas eventually succeed, and the proof is that the Treaty on European Union drawn up by the European Parliament, also called 'Spinelli' after the determined Italian federalist who was its greatest champion, was to be found in the briefcases of many participants in the IGCs.

At the Dublin summit of March 1990, the first urgent issue I raised was Community incardination of the unification of Germany and the challenge it posed for the future of the EC, NATO and the Warsaw Pact: at the same time I announced the establishment of a temporary committee to deal with the necessary legislative adjustments required by the transformation undergone by a member state, i.e. Germany. Taking as my basis the Kohl-Mitterrand initiative, which reaffirmed the need for a political union focusing on three fundamental issues (institutional legitimacy, efficiency and foreign and security policy) I announced the dates of two fundamental initiatives:

the first IPC on 17 May in Strasbourg and the announcement of the conference with the national parliaments called by the European Parliament, to be held in Rome that autumn. The invitation was rather bold, but it was a question of ensuring that the European Parliament would not merely be left watching from the sidelines, and it worked. Moreover, it was in keeping with the finest Community tradition of fixing times and places, in a pragmatic anticipation of the reality to come.

A few days later I was invited, by the amiable Irish Minister for Foreign Affairs, Mr Collins, in his capacity as President-in-Office of the Council, to come for after-lunch coffee with the Council of Ministers in the gigantic, drab Charlemagne Building (the architecture of the Community institutions is unlikely to outshine the Athens of Cleisthenes in terms of aesthetic appeal).

Following numerous consultations between Ministers by means of the COREUR, I was finally invited to have my coffee and to set out Parliament's position. In the narrow, cramped dining room where the Ministers, Secretaries of State and Ambassadors were seated with the interpreters' cabins hanging over the table, the President asked me to take the seat on his right. Following the obligatory small-talk, whilst coffee was being served and cigars were going round, I put forward a proposal that for the first time in the history of the Community there should be a dialogue on the constitutional reform that lay ahead. Once I had finished, the President courteously thanked me for my positive contribution, thus letting me know that my time was up; I had to point out that I had not yet had my coffee. I did manage to get it drunk; there was not time to enjoy the cigar, though . . . But seriously, I have gone into such detail in describing these events to show the apparent lack of communication and reticence which characterized inter-institutional relations as recently as 1990. On leaving, I remembered how much strategic importance Jean Monnet had attached to the dining room of the Commissariat du Plan in the Rue de Martignac.

The IPC, the Beginning of the Dialogue

The opening meeting of the IPC in the Council of Ministers chamber of the Council of Europe Building in Strasbourg was a success. For the first time ever, the twelve Ministers for Foreign Affairs of the member states sat face to face with a delegation of twelve Members of Parliament to initiate a forum for discussion and dialogue based on mutual respect and trust. Previously, there had only been conciliation meetings on specific issues of legislation, particularly on budgetary matters.

On this occasion, opinions were expressed more freely, since it was not just the Presidency that spoke, but all the participants, and each Government set out its views on the reform of the Communities. The ever discreet and efficient activity of Paco Fernández Ordoñez played an important role in ensuring the success of the initiative.

Encouraged by that success, we suggested broadening the discussion to include the issue of economic and monetary union; a delicate subject, since it entailed strengthening the role of the rival ECOFIN council. However, with the active cooperation of the Italian Presidency, we managed it.

The 'Rome I' Council posed the greatest problems. The very fact of this being called at all was criticized as 'useless and superfluous' by Mrs Thatcher when I greeted her in the baroque atmosphere of the Palazzo Madama. At the time she was fighting her last battle to survive as Prime Minister, and she was deposed only a few days later by the Praetorian Guard of the Conservative Party, precisely because of her stance vis-à-vis Europe.

The atmosphere was tense. My own speech, particularly as regards 'double democratic legitimacy' and the eternal question of the seat of the European Parliament[2], gave rise to some lively and critical reactions in the discussion that followed and which later appeared in the Press. In the lobby I had a private word with Chancellor Kohl about the situation of the eighteen German observers in the EP, on which occasion I was able to explain the complex problems posed by German unification and the cooperation being developed with the Bundestag which was in order to try and find a solution. Later, my speech was the object of a certain amount of criticism in the Council which was quickly leaked to the press. There were two central issues: firstly, 'double democratic legitimacy' which, it seems, triggered a debate between the political leaders. The second controversial issue was the perennial one of the location of Parliament's seat, which, according to many of those directly involved, has aroused more passions and cropped up more frequently than any other problem since the ECSC itself was set up.

The European Parliament has, without doubt, been the institution which has suffered the most as a result of the vicissitudes of the negotiating process. The status quo, defined by the Council in 1965, was that Parliament's Secretariat and officials were located in Luxembourg, while the committees and political groups normally worked three weeks a month in Brussels with one week in Strasbourg. This migratory system was just about bearable in 1965, when the Assembly basically played a merely consultative role. By 1990, with the workload involving a new directive every week and an average of 45 different issues (legislation, political declarations, debates on current issues) on the agenda for each of the week-long plenary part-sessions, the situation was practically unsustainable. Each month all the issues had to be grouped together in order to adopt decisions on them during one week of marathon sessions; a mass migration exacerbated by the fact that 90% of the officials based in Luxembourg had to be coped with; and even a simple one-page document or amendment needs to be made available immediately in the nine working languages. For the EP the situation meant torture on a daily basis. It gave rise to endless conflict between the member states of the Council, and for two member states in particular, Luxembourg and France, it was the cause of repeated disagreements and appeals to the Court of Justice.

Under the presidency of my predecessor, Lord Plumb, it was decided to rent the Congress Building which a private consortium was building behind the EP complex in Brussels. Under my Presidency, in March 1990, Parliament's Bureau was able to reach an agreement which, for the first time ever, enjoyed the approval of the French Vice-Presidents and offered a balanced solution to the question of Parliament's three places of work (Brussels, Luxembourg and Strasbourg). The essential elements of this agreement were later upheld at the European summit in Edinburgh.

These factors, together with that speech to the 'Rome I' conference, resulted in a significant increase in my popularity as President of the European Parliament. As far as the issues to be dealt with were concerned, Mrs Thatcher's negative attitude was hardly justifiable: they included the culmination of the German unification process, the annexation of Kuwait by Iraq, and the establishment of economic and financial assistance to the crumbling Soviet Union. As regards the reform of the Community, in addition to the first IPC on EMU, I put forward three proposals, namely that the documents prepared by the European Parliament should be considered as working documents, that the Presidency should be able to attend ministerial meetings, and that the European Parliament should be the first to give its approval.

The Inter-Parliamentary Dialogue

I also announced the first conference between the national parliaments and the European Parliament which was to be held the following month in Rome. The origin of this initiative was twofold: firstly, there was the proposal originally put forward by Felipe González as President-in-Office of the Council, and later expanded upon by President Mitterrand in a similar capacity, that parliamentary *Assises* be held to discuss the prospects for achieving a union. Secondly, there were the increasingly closed contacts which had followed the entry into force of the Single Act.

Admittedly, relations had existed since the very beginning of the Community, and had been put on an institutionalized basis in 1962; but generally speaking they had been dominated by the consideration of the European issues as 'foreign policy' questions; a speciality of parlamentarians with an enthusiasm for travel and foreign languages and, from 1979 onwards, by the undeniable jealous desire of a directly elected assembly to deal with matters where the dividing line with internal affairs was not – and is not – all clear. The feeling of mutual distrust was accentuated by the leap forward produced by the Single Act and the avalanche of legislation which followed: in which connection, the statement by Commission President Jacques Delors that 80% of decisions adopted in the field of economics and social affairs were of Community origin came as an eye-opener to many members of national parliaments at a time when plain sailing was a thing of the past and the Community found itself facing the rough seas of increasingly problematic internal situation.

External and internal difficulties notwithstanding, my position from the very beginning was that this represented an absolutely vital step. It formed part of the whole challenge of Community democracy, whose hour had struck with the end of 'enlightened despotism'. Moreover, it was, and continues to be, a matter of extending everyday experience to all the institutions, as the best form of re-education, allowing everyone to learn to discuss, work and reach joint decisions with people who belong to the same political families and who share many aspects of their basic philosophy and experience. In fact, the overwhelming majority of Members of the European Parliament are former members of national parliaments, and some continue to have a double mandate. Moreover, the European Parliament has had amongst its members a former President of the French Republic, many former Prime Ministers and a substantial number of former Commissioners and Ministers. This growing institutional osmosis is thus a fruitful source of knowledge and experience.

That the *Assises* were possible at all was due to the patient collaboration and to the pro-European convictions and enthusiasm of a significant group of presidents ('speakers'), of national Parliaments, notably the President of the Belgian Chamber of representatives, M. Nothomb, who tabled the Conference's motion for a Resolution; the President of the Bundestag, Rita Süssmuth, and the then Presidents of the French National Assembly (Laurent Fabius) and of the two Italian Chambers (Nilde Iotti and Giovanni Spadolini). Following patient, laborious persuasion and the timely revival of the practice of 'self-convening' (a formula used during the beginning of the Spanish transition to democracy in order to avoid causing offence), we worked together to reach unanimous agreement on all the essential issues. This meant that members of one's own political group had to be persuaded of the merit of the initiative. At the same time, the problem of linguistic *faux amis* had to be overcome. The meaning of the French word 'assise' is quite different from that of the Spanish 'sentada' which means a 'sit-in'. But, as usual, the most difficult problem was with English, since 'to go to Assizes' means to be tried in a criminal court (from the name of the Court of Appeal). Experience has taught me that the most complicated, treacherous and controversial relationship between two

languages is that between French and English, at least since
the Battle of Hastings[3].

The goal was not to establish an alliance between parliaments, far less to create a 'joint congress' – a French initiative
which would have brought about a sort of Diet within each
Presidency, consisting of the European Parliament and the
national parliaments of the member states. Such an assembly
would have been akin to the institutionalization of the
European Council as a 'Directorate'. The intention was, on
the contrary, to hold an exceptional meeting for the purpose
of defining the broad objectives of the European Union, which
were to be considered by MPs from throughout the Community.
The preparatory work allowed an initial assessment of the situation to be made and experiences in dealing with Community
issues were exchanged.

The most elaborate traditions of examination and scrutiny
are those of the Danish Folketing and of the Palace of Westminster. The Danish system, with its Committee on the Market
and a tradition of minority coalition governments, is the most
advanced, since it gives a great deal of weight to the mandate
conferred on Danish ministers before and during negotiations
within the Council. However closely it monitors the preparation of Community regulations, it has to be acknowledged that
this Committee works in camera and no minutes are taken of
meetings. In the British case, a 'select committee' of the House
of Commons holds prior debates on the regulations, whilst the
House of Lords has in the past drawn up excellent reports
on Community policies. The report prepared by the House of
Commons for the Conference gave a detailed description of
the process, confirming the conclusion reached by the Foster
Report, to the effect that the United Kingdom had given an
undertaking, as a condition for membership of the Community, to accept the collective authority of a legislative body (the
Council of Ministers) in which only one of the twelve members was accountable to the House of Commons. In fact, the
principal historical consequence of Community integration has
been the transfer of power from the legislature to the executive of each country rather than from the national capital to
Brussels, with the Council of Ministers exercising the legislative power behind closed doors and without bearing collective
responsibility as a body.

Another system is that used in Belgium, where the *Comité d'Avis* brings together national and European Members of Parliament on equal terms. Its opinions and resolutions are distinguished by their quality and insight.

In other cases, bodies have been created such as the *Commisión Mixta para las Comunidades* in Spain, the *Europa-Ausschuss* of the Bundestag or the *Délégation pour les CE* established in the French National Assembly. In general, however, the Community process has been regarded as an aspect of foreign policy, and an awareness of its immediacy and scope has developed only recently.

This careful, diplomatic preparatory work bore fruit. From the very moment of its constitution in the majestic assembly hall of Montecitorio, and following the adoption of a point of order raised by Laurent Fabius to the effect that members should be seated by groups instead of by country, the three days of discussion and the resultant resolution, adopted by a wide majority and clearly worded in favour of a European Union, constituted a clear message to the Council to proceed, thus breaking a psychological barrier and paving the way to ratification, subject to the agreement that the European Parliament should first give its assent.

The Conference has not remained an isolated incident. In fact, in recent years there have been numerous working meetings at committee or delegation level on an almost weekly basis. Moreover, a body called the Conference of European Community Affairs Committee has been established to coordinate the work of the national parliaments and of the European Parliament. Throughout the negotiations on the Treaty, however, I defended the European Parliament's opposition to any form of institutionalization of this relationship in the Treaties which might result in the creation of a body akin to a Congress or Diet. The end result was a declaration on the role of the national parliaments in the European Union, which proposed that the supply of information to and consideration of Community affairs by the national parliaments should be improved, and their relations with the European Parliament should be upgraded. Other than that, each parliament should be free to organize its work as it saw fit. What we are seeking to create is not an 'anti-executive' alliance, but rather a climate of interest and cooperation. As far as the holding of plenary

Conferences is concerned, I believe them to be of use only at times of constitutional reform.

The eventful Italian Presidency culminated in the Rome summit, where the important issues of the day included the signing of the Charter of Paris, the need to define the framework of relations in Europe, the Gulf crisis, aid to the Soviet Union and the difficult situation reached in the GATT negotiations (which led me to declare that what might have seemed Utopian at the beginning of the year was now a matter of necessity, not to say utter urgency), and after reporting on the Conference of Parliaments, stressed the need to place 'the citizen' at the very heart of European integration, with a view to consolidating the Community dimension.

Finally, at the Rome summit it was decided to convene the intergovernmental conferences to consider political union and economic and monetary union.

Intergovernmental Conferences

The Intergovernmental Conferences (IGCs) were at work throughout 1991. The Conference of Economic and Monetary Union advanced over terrain which had been being cleared and prepared since 1988 by the Committee of Governors and the Delors Report; it was also facilitated by the fact that it only had to deal with the single issue of currency. On the political front, the issues were, understandably, vastly more complex and wide-ranging: the Luxembourgish Presidency, which was responsible for the strategically important task of drawing up the first draft of the Treaty, did so on the basis of proposals, memoranda and reports totalling not fewer than 1500 pages on 35 different subjects. The Presidency, whose period in office was dominated by the Gulf Crisis and the situation in Eastern Europe, rose to the challenge, and was able to prepare a draft on the basis of this extraordinarily rich and variegated material. Curiously, roles had been reversed; Parliament insisted on a short list of subjects, whilst the select group of personal representatives discussed all manner of subjects under the sun. At the second Luxembourg Summit, I was able to explain Parliament's criticisms of the first draft. These concerned above all its very layout, following the debate at the informal Council meeting in Dresden on whether to adopt an 'architectural' or a 'botanical' approach.

In Dresden, the model of the Greek temple with several pillars (Community, intergovernmental and intermediate) had been chosen in preference to the idea of a Community 'tree' (which had been the basis of the Treaties). I remarked that the result bore a closer resemblance to the Labyrinth of Crete than to the Parthenon, and that in any event, if we were going to talk about pillars, these should be those of double legitimacy. As for specific criticisms, these concerned the regulations on European citizenship, the principle of legality and the hierarchy of legislative acts, legislative co-decision, the need for a double investiture of the Commission, a serious definition of what cohesion actually meant, and the fact that there was a risk of insufficient accountability in the management of EMU (which provided for the consultation of Parliament in only 4 out of 28 types of decision).

At the same time, I announced the EP's final offensive, which consisted in holding bilateral meetings between the IPC delegation and all the members of the European Council. This allowed our position to be strengthened. At any rate, the Luxembourgish Presidency took on the important, and advantageous, task of putting down in writing what had been debated.

The final straight was run by the Dutch Presidency, which unsuccessfully attempted to force the pace of things with a more federative preliminary draft. During this stage, we used every available means to influence the final wording. There were a total of fifteen preparatory conference (IPC) meetings with all the Heads of Government and with the French President, and I was able to launch my last two philippics during the meetings of the Council of Foreign Affairs Ministers on the eve of Maastricht. My oratory must have been particularly harsh at the meeting in Noordwijk, near the Hague, where I was forced to pull out all the stops in my repertory, in keeping with a wise remark of Paco Fernández Ordoñez: 'If you really want to draw attention at a meeting with simultaneous interpretation, you have to raise your voice and bang your fist on the table'. On that occasion, I resorted to provocation: in the draft treaty the term 'High Ranking Official' was capitalized, whilst the term 'minister' was written without an initial capital, a 'lapsus' the mention of which somewhat disconcerted the members of Council. I even warned them that the European Parliament could recommend to the national parliaments that they should not ratify the Treaty. In view of the situation, the German Minister, Hans Dietrich Genscher, strongly recommended to his colleagues 'to take what President Barón says seriously'. In addition to my speech, the fact that the journalists had been left back at the Ministry in the Hague, some twenty kilometres from this foggy North Sea Benidorm, created a certain electricity and expectancy which proved to be of major help in publicizing Parliament's view.

Some important issues such as the recognition of the European political parties were resolved at the last minute in a telephone conversation with the President of the Council, Prime Minister Lubbers; at the same time I offered him a better wording of Article 189B, concerning co-decision, on the basis of experience gained in the budgetary procedure. This proposal was not accepted by those who advocated a third reading as a safeguard.

Thus we arrived at the Council of Maastricht on a cold, sunny morning when it fell upon me to take my leave as President with an appeal to the Council to pave the way for a European Union of a federal nature, with a unitary, coherent treaty, based on double democratic legitimacy, with a philosophy shared by all, a legal personality and appropriate decision-making procedures, a clear definition of legislative co-decision, the legitimization of the Community executive, the espousal by the Community of a common foreign and security policy, and an EMU coupled to political union, in which cohesion and the social dimension should be taken into account.

For almost two days, the political leaders negotiated the terms of the Treaty in a last round of give and take before finally deciding to take the historic step.

It has been my privilege to have been involved in two constituent processes. The first was in my own country, as a member of the Cortes which became a constituent assembly by virtue of the people's decision at the ballot box. It had not been a constituent assembly when it had been convened, but it became one on 16 June 1977. In the debates on and the drafting of the Constitution, based on a reconciliation of the Spanish people and the recognition and respect of human rights, we were collectively able to set our own history to rights and to reconsider the very nature of our society, seeking answers from our own history, even though entombed as they had been by an alien Jacobinism and a dictatorial and intransigent regime. In this way, we were able to recognize the multinational reality of Spain, through negotiated constituent processes which culminated in the 'Statutes of Autonomy'. We were also able to lay the groundwork for a constitutional monarchy with a parliamentary government, reconsidering certain essential aspects of sovereignty and providing for Spain's incorporation into the European Communities. This experience shows that in an old and complex nation state, with a distant imperial past, it is possible to re-think the form of the State and its very nature adapting it to new forms of organization which, undoubtedly, to imply a certain relativization of 'sovereignty and its traditional attributes'.

Above all, however, there was an important democratic element, namely that the debates were public and minuted, and were not subject to 'guillotine' deadlines: this allowed the public progressively to absorb ideas and suggestions and gain an accurate idea of the proceedings from the minutes of the sittings.

The Community process is a more complex issue. Certainly, the fact that a climate of dialogue has been established (after a patient strategy of courting, which bordered on besieging) has in this case helped to establish a form of communication which is equivalent to what in information technology is referred to as 'interfaces'. However, it is clear that one cannot continue with this method of negotiation, not only because the European Parliament, for whom the community process is its own very *raison d'être*, failed to obtain the right of ratification, but also because the national parliaments are only given a one-off opportunity to 'take it or leave it' on decisions which may involve the modification of a significant number of the articles of the Constitution and a historic change of role.

This criticism is not the voice of frustration: the step taken has, after all, been quite significant. It is meant as a warning to the *next* intergovernmental conference, wisely provided for by the Treaty and scheduled for 1996, with the purpose of adopting specific steps and reviewing the progress made with regard to political and economic commitments. In view of the experience gained in the debate on the Treaty on European Union, the days of carrying out a constituent process 'behind closed doors' should be regarded as over. To continue with this approach, trying to mitigate and minimize the effects of the agreement, would be to run the danger of provoking negative public reactions like those seen in connection with the ratification process, and, at the same time, it would provide those most assiduous of political analysts, financial speculators and operators, with opportunities to take advantage of any loopholes – particularly in this case, where the decision on the how and when of economic and monetary union is already marked on the calendar.

5 The Treaty on European Union

> We use the word 'Greek' to describe not so much those of
> the same ethnic origin as ourselves as those who share our
> way of life.
>
> Isocrates

At Maastricht, the governments of the Twelve decided, at the
European Council, to turn the Community into the European
Union, comprising 'political union', based on common citizenship, and 'economic and monetary union', to be crowned by
a single currency. Before examining the changes and progress
achieved in this area, we need to pass political judgment.

From the very beginning, I deemed the decision courageous
and opportune. And I said so, the day after the Maastricht
Council, to that 'holy of holies' of Europeanism, the EP's
Committee on Institutional Affairs. Subsequent events have
only strengthened my opinion. In April 1992, the EP voted by
a large majority for the Martin Report, which approved the
Treaty and recommended its immediate ratification, although
it pointed out no fewer than twenty omissions and major issues,
alongside an equal number of hits. This opened the process of
parliamentary ratification by the member states – happily concluded, despite the fact that the 1 January 1993 deadline was
overrun. In any case, the national parliaments were ahead of
public opinion in Denmark (with an 80% majority) and in
France (with 70%) while in the United Kingdom, the reticent
attitude of the Labour Party was due to the exclusion of the
Social Charter, and not to the Treaty itself – an attitude which
also presupposes an historic change.

More complex was the debate at public opinion level. At the
outset, it was thought that it would be a question of rubber-
stamping, but reality took over and demonstrated that the hour
of democracy had struck. The Danish 'No' came as a resound-
ing knock on the door that dramatized the debate, which
became a political paroxysm with the French referendum,
aggravated by a profound political, cultural, psychological and

above all economic crisis that called Europe's very *raison d'être* into question. This time, not because the leaders had fallen short of their responsibilities, but to the contrary, because they had gone too far.

In the public debate which arose, all kind of arguments were raised, particularly in the UK and France. Criticism was particularly acerbic in certain intellectual circles, demonstrating that while the etymology of the words 'intelligence' and 'intellectual' may be the same, their meaning is not. Full-scale rejection frequently came in the name of 'The Other Europe', which, like Dulcinea, is both unattainable and faceless.

Another frequent criticism was the claim that the Treaty was conceived during a period of prosperity and was rendered obsolete by the crisis. It's a poor knot that comes undone when pressure is applied! But the European Union's very beginnings were born not of abundance but of misfortune and devastation.

The Union's Objectives

Undoubtedly, it is more useful, rather than expressing unqualified support for the Treaty or rejecting it outright, to examine its contents. In the political field, the introduction of Title I is of fundamental importance, containing as it does the façade of the temple. 'The High Contracting Parties establish among themselves a European Union' . . . 'this Treaty marks a new stage in the process of creating an ever closer Union between the peoples of Europe, in which decisions are taken as closely as possible to the citizen' (Art. A). Here, the mention of the Union's 'federal vocation' was finally dropped due to implacable UK opposition, and the Treaty of Rome's formulation of 'an ever close Union among the peoples of Europe' was retained.

Title I goes on in Article B to state that 'the Union shall set itself the following objectives:

1 to promote economic and social progress which is balanced and sustainable, in particular through the creation of an area without internal frontiers, through the strengthening

of economic and social cohesion and through the single currency in accordance with the provisions of this Treaty;

2   to assert its identity on the international scene, in particular through the implementation of a common foreign and security policy, including the eventual framing of a common defence policy, which might in time lead to a common defence;

3   to strengthen the protection of the rights and interests of the nationals of its Member States through the introduction of citizenship of the union;

4   to develop close cooperation on justice and home affairs;

5   to maintain in full the *acquis communautaire* and build on it with a view to considering, through the procedure referred to in Article N(2), to what extent the policies and forms of cooperation introduced by this Treaty may need to be revised with the aim of ensuring the effectiveness of the mechanisms and the institutions of the Community.

Article B further states that 'The objectives of the Union shall be achieved as provided in this Treaty and in accordance with the conditions and the timetable set out therein while respecting the principle of subsidiarity as defined in Article 3(b) of the Treaty establishing the European Community.'

Other Articles provide that 'The Union shall be served by a single institutional framework' (Art. C), in which 'the European Council shall provide the Union with the necessary impetus for its development and shall define the general political guidelines thereof' (Art. D).

1   The Union shall respect the national identity of its Member States, whose systems of government are founded on the principles of democracy.

2   The Union shall respect fundamental rights, as guaranteed by the European Convention for the Protection of Human Rights and Fundamental Freedoms signed in Rome on 4 November 1950 and as a result from the constitutional provisions common to the Member States, as general principles of Community law' (Art. F)

In essence, these articles take the decisive step of turning the Community of States into a Union based on states and citizenship. The Union rests on three pillars: in addition to the

Community pillar, CFSP is introduced as a policy with an intergovernmental basis and a potential for common development, and intergovernmental cooperation on justice and home affairs is proposed under a single institutional framework.

In this connection, the most relevant fact is the inclusion of the European Council as the supreme Community body, a collective Directorate which dominates the whole. Moreover, the Declaration of Rights is included, even if it is only by means of subscribing to the Rome Convention, and not of a new formulation such as that proposed by the EP.

Citizenship and Double Legitimacy

The most democratically relevant fact is the recognition of European citizenship over and above that of each state, not only as a declaration, but conferring new rights and duties.

This long-standing goal of the EP was opportunely emphasized by Felipe González in a missive to his colleagues on the Council when they were negotiating to fix the agenda. Initially, it was welcomed, and no major reservations were expressed, but with the passage of time, Danish second thoughts emerged (even occasioning an *a posteriori* interpretative statement), as did British and even French reservations when it came to ceding certain civic rights, such as the right of passive suffrage, to Community citizens.

In essence, citizens are to enjoy the right of active and passive suffrage in European and municipal elections; freedom of movement and of establishment throughout Community territory; and diplomatic protection in third countries in the embassies and consulates of the Member States. They also 'shall have the rights to address . . . a petition to the European Parliament on a matter which comes within the Community's spheres of activity and which affects him directly' (138 D), and Parliament enjoys the right to 'set up a temporary Committee of Inquiry to investigate . . . alleged contraventions or maladministration in the implementation of Community law'. In fact, the EP was already making full use of both of these facilities, with the UK MEPs proving quite outstanding in submitting reams of signatures to petitions from their constituencies. The Ombudsman's office was also set up, 'empowered to receive complaints . . . concerning instances of maladministration in the activities of the Community institutions or bodies'.

Moreover, we should highlight the fact that in the TEU, there appears for the first time the characters and protagonists who are to make use of the institutions so that these will be more than a stage-set or an architect's drawing: 'political parties at European level are important as a factor for integration within the Union. They contribute to forming a European awareness and to expressing the political will of the citizens of the Union'.

This article was included in the Treaty at the last minute – thanks to my efforts in collaboration with the Belgian leadership of the three families (Wilfried Martens for the EPP, Guy Spitaels for the PES and Willy DeClercq for the Liberals) and the decisive support of President Lubbers.

In reality, the nucleus of Community citizenship was established many years ago, in 1962, when the jurisprudence of the Court of Justice established the direct effect[1] of Community legislation when creating subjective legal situations, since individuals may avail themselves of the provisions of the Treaty insofar as the provisions of the Treaty itself explicitly confer rights on them and impose on the member states such clear, precise and unconditional obligations as mean that they can do without the measures of application (Van Gend & Loos v the Dutch Fiscal Administration).

In 1979, an essential attribute of citizenship was recognized when the right of Community citizens to stand for election and to vote for the EP was recognized. This is now enshrined in the Treaty, creating a fundamental basis of legitimacy which is different from that of the popular will conceived a whole which creates a nation, along the lines of 'we, the people . . .'. Here we are dealing with a citizenship which takes as its starting point the fact of belonging originally to a state as an organic whole, but which defines itself on the basis of participation in a public sphere comprising values, rules and decisions which constitute an institutional system. It is a concept of citizenship similar to that 'constitutional patriotism' which Habermas defends in the German and European instances, which rests more on rationalized affection than on blazing, exclusive, impassioned nationalism. Habermas says that examples of multicultural societies, such as Switzerland and the USA, demonstrate that a political culture in which fundamental constitutional principles may take deep root in no way needs to be based on ethnic, linguistic and cultural origins shared by all citizens. A liberal political culture merely constitutes the common denominator of constitutional patriotism, which concerns itself equally with the multiplicity and integrity of the various ways of life coexisting in a multicultural society. In a future European federal state, too, the very principles of law will have to be interpreted from the standpoint of the different liberal traditions, of the different national histories. One's own tradition has to be engaged with from a standpoint relativized by the standpoints of others, so that it can be included in a shared, supranational Europeo-western constitutional culture. Democratic citizenship, according to Habermas, does not need to be rooted in the national identity of one people, and the multiplicity of the different cultural ways of life apart, it demands the socialization of all citizens within a common political culture[2].

There is no need to indulge in long historical descriptions or windy theorizing to demonstrate the difference between this concept of citizenship and the out-and-out nationalist concept: a heart-rending example is given by what is happening in the former Yugoslavia. In fact, the forging of this culture has been taking place as the Community slowly matures. Which helps to explain the favourable reception extended to external signs such as the European 12-star flag, passports and driving licence. Today, with the recognition of European citizenship, the principle of double legitimacy now rests on a solid foundation.

Such was the simple point of departure for the EP's thinking – to look at the world through the eyes of the citizen, who participates in the Community in two ways: firstly, by electing a national parliament, which produces a majority government occupying one of the seats in the Council of Ministers, with its weighted votes, where the fifteen Member States take their decisions; and secondly by voting in the elections to the European Parliament. There is, hence, a double democratic legitimacy such as is characteristic of federal systems. Hence, the solution to the problem of democratic deficit consists in centring the system on the citizen as the basis, with a harmonious, viable and effective balance between the various powers (Hamilton's 'checks and balances'). The goal is not so much to ask always for more powers for the EP as to achieve a genuinely democratic, answerable and balanced system. In this perspective, the Union is endowed with the proper basis for all democratic systems, namely the legitimacy of the ballot box.

The Façade of the Union

On the basis of this foundation, we can make a drawing of the façade of the temple (see Figure 5.1). Until the TEU, there were, essentially, two fundamental pillars: on the one side, there was the Community pillar, in which the Commission enjoyed a monopoly on initiating legislation, the Council voted by a majority, sharing legislative power with the Parliament (since the latter could amend and modify), and controls on legality and constitutionality were exercised by the Court of Justice.

On the other side there stood the intergovernmental pillar, ruled by unanimity within the Council, with the Commission enjoying associative status and Parliament, at the very most, being consulted, with no legal appeal against decisions being possible.

Since the Treaty now includes common foreign and security policy (CSFP) and policy on justice and home affairs (PJH), we talk about three pillars, with the intergovernmental one subdivided in two. Nonetheless, I have preferred to include four pillars, since the major innovation of the Treaty, economic and monetary union (EMU), cannot be assimilated to the Community structure as such because the Community pillar is, in its turn, subdivided into two.

With regard to the ambit of the strictly Community pillar, there is, first of all, the raising of economic and social cohesion to the category of a Community objective, with the setting up of the Cohesion Fund and the redefinition of the Structural Funds: the European Regional and Development Fund (ERDF); the European Agricultural Guideline and Guarantee Fund (EAGGF) and the European Social Fund (ESF), which has led to an extension of the areas covered, both at regional and state level.

New fields of action are also included, such as industrial policy, the development of major trans-European transport and telecommunications networks, energy, consumer protection, vocational training, health and culture.

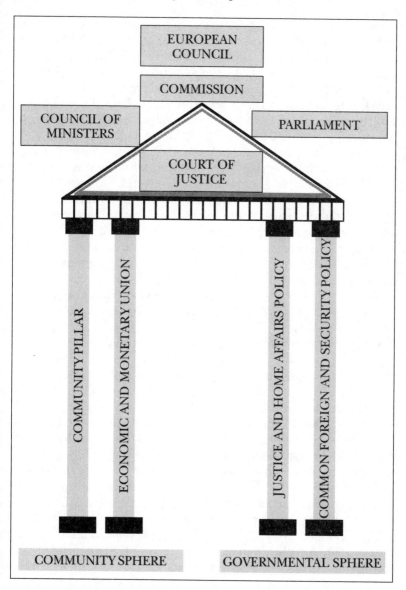

Figure 5.1   The façade of the temple

Community affairs subject to co-decision are, essentially, those which involve the internal market, extended to include the right of establishment and the freedom of movement of citizens, consumer protection, special arrangements for foreigners (non-legislative measures), vocational training, research and technology framework programmes, environmental action programmes, guidelines for the trans-European network and measures to stimulate public health and culture.

Outside the sphere of co-decision remain, however, transport, social affairs, agriculture, development, the environment and the regional and social funds, where the Council decides by a qualified majority. Unanimity is upheld with regard to taxation, energy, exploitation of environmental lands, research and development plans, provision of the structural funds, etc. There are also procedures in which Council unanimity is upheld as far as legislative intervention is concerned, such as the research framework programme and culture.

The mere listing of powers in terms of decision-making formulae is of a labyrinthine complexity bordering on confusion in some cases. The fundamental reason is that we are dealing with last-minute compromises in which one or more member states believe they have a special interest, and every effort has been made to reach agreement between spokesmen whose situations and sets of problems are very different.

A subject as sensitive as social affairs also receives special treatment. The Treaty of Rome had already stated the need to promote improvements in living and working conditions, and the Single Act provided for issues concerning safety and hygiene in the workplace to be regulated by majority decisions. In December 1989, eleven member states had adopted the Social Charter, a fact which brought about scarcely any progress, since unanimity remained in force.

The TEU laid down that, henceforward, decisions should be adopted on an eleven-man basis, as the UK negotiated an opting-out clause. For improvements in the working environment, working conditions, informing and consulting workers, sexual equality and the reintegration of those excluded from the labour market, decisions are now to be taken by a qualified majority. Unanimity is required for social policy, social protection of workers, protection in cases of dismissal, collective representation and defence of workers and employers and the conditions of employment enjoyed by immigrants from third countries. Issues such as wages, trade union rights, the right to strike and management shut down are excluded from Community legislation.

As a whole, the division is a model of casuistry and clearly lends itself to large-scale 'shadow-boxing' in which complexity can achieve undreamt-of levels of refinement in the hands of officials whose virtuosity is undeniable.

To smooth the rough edges, fill the holes and untie the Gordian knots of this system will require a very large dose of technical mastery and cooperative goodwill indeed. The major Gordian knot is in the co-decision procedure, since Article 189b(6) confers the right of approving a text on the Council, even if conciliation with Parliament should fail. The text becomes law unless the EP, within six weeks of the date of confirmation by the Council, rejects the text by an absolute majority.

Within the Community colonnade, the EMU pillar has its own logic and involves the setting-up of ad hoc institutions such as the European Monetary Institute (EMI), set up on 1 January 1994 with its own independent legal personality as successor to the Committee of Governors and the precursor, in its turn, of the European Central Bank (ECB) and the European System of Central Banks (ESCB). (The process and its phases will be examined in the appropriate chapter.) In this field, the key element is the Council of Economic and Finance Ministers (ECOFIN), with the Commission now taking on the role of draftsman of reports and recommendations, appropriate to a technical general secretariat, and Parliament being reported to on action taken and consulted with regard to appointments.

On the intergovernmental side of the colonnade, the Council enacts its decisions unanimously. The Commission is 'fully associated with its work' and may submit proposals to the Council, with the EP having the right to be informed and consulted and, in certain cases, to give its assent (authorization by an absolute majority vote in the Chamber). On these issues, no appeal can be made to the Court of Justice.

Cooperation in the fields of justice and home affairs is the very prototype of intergovernmentality, covering policies such as border crossing, immigration and residence of nationals of third countries, legal cooperation in civil and penal matters, customs, and policing against terrorism, drug trafficking and crime, involving the setting up of the European Police Office (Europol).

With regard to the last pillar, Common Foreign and Security Policy (CFSP), this too is based on the criterion of unanimity within the European Council, which lays down its general guidelines. On this basis, the Council of Ministers decides 'that a matter should be the subject of joint action', also unanimously. The details, procedure, deadlines and limits of the joint action are decided on by a qualified majority. This change in the nature of political action leads to the formulating of transversal *passerelles*, 'walkways from one pillar to another'.

Security falls fully within the competence of the European Union, and the definition of a common security policy is established as one of the Union's tasks (including, according to Article J of the Treaty, 'the eventual framing of a common defence policy, which might in time lead to a common defence'). The very wording reflects the laborious gestation of the idea.

To this end, the Union requests the WEU 'which forms an integral part of the development of the Union' to 'elaborate and implement decisions which have defence implication'. At the same time, this means that an organization whose life has been largely latent for a long time is being adopted and delegated to; the TEU mandates it to become the Union's defence dimension.

Systematically, there are the four major pillars. As you can see, we are not dealing with unadorned, rectilinear Doric columns, but with a baroque structure of Salomonic columns with complex embellishments.

On the façade, we may place the institutions which channel the double legitimacy at the corners, and the Commission, as the body which receives the confluence of both, at the top of the triangle. The apex is occupied by the European Council, the collective directorate enshrined in the Treaties.

The Court of Justice, which is often placed on the fringes, should of right appear in the centre of the pediment, given its powers of initiative and constitutional amendment.

All schemes are a simplification of reality, and so is this. The most difficult problem, undoubtedly, arises from the sharing of attributes which have belonged to the central nucleus of the 'nation-state' since its appearance at the time of the Renaissance, namely property, defence and foreign policy. Although in any case there is a clearly discernible will to establish a common policy, what has been set up is organized cooperation and mutual aid, which imply not a transfer but joint management. For this reason we should not lose our sense of perspective and think that the member states will entirely lose these powers, which will become the exclusive and direct responsibility of the Community. What they are doing is managing them jointly. The question is wide open as to whether this Community can be symmetrical with the current one. With regard to defence, the problem of the two member states on the UN Security Council (France and the UK), which moreover possess nuclear weapons, accepting a rotational system with partners whose armies are virtually non-existent does not strike me as admitting of an easy solution – no more than does the problem of a country like Germany accepting, in the monetary sphere, the need to manage its currency on a virtual equal footing with a clearly divergent partner.

A further decisive element is the question of inter-institutional relationships, i.e. just how the precision mechanism of checks and balances interlocks, and how these checks and balances actually channel democratic legitimacy. In this field, the Treaty has produced the most important step forward in regard to the strengthening of the Community pillars.

The Investiture of the Commission

The new Article 158 lays down the system for appointing and electing the Commission. 'The governments of the Member States shall nominate by common accord, after consulting the European Parliament, the person they intend to appoint as President of the Commission' and 'shall, in consultation with the nominee for President, nominate the other persons whom they intend to appoint as members of the Commission'. These persons, thus nominated 'shall be subject as a body to the vote of approval', tantamount to an investiture, and they will be appointed by the Governments. Moreover, after much struggle, we in the EP succeeded in ensuring that the mandate of the Commissioners coincided with the five-year parliamentary legislature. Initially, there were government ministers who expressed astonishment at the insistency displayed by the Parliamentary delegation. Nonetheless, the reason is perfectly clear, since it achieves the structuring of a parliamentary system in the election of the Commission and the expiry of its term of office, whereby the patient labour of creating and developing usages and practices carried out by the EP with a view to defining the responsibility of the Community executive requires real meaning. Hence the 'investiture speech' is the programme of the Commission, whose workings are given concrete expression in the annual legislative programme, declarations, interpellations (oral questions), question time and regular appearances by the Commissioners.

The investiture of the new Commission after the European elections of 1994 has allowed us, with lightning speed, to put the theory into practice. As a matter of fact, the selection process was full of vicissitudes, manoeuvres and rejections that drove to exceptional votes at midnight after the dinner in Corfú, followed by the British veto to the Belgian candidate and the final appointment of a senior although little known member of the Council, the Prime Minister of Luxembourg, Mr Jacques Santer. In fact, the behaviour of the Council responded to an unwritten pact that was seemingly reached in Maastricht: namely, the successor should come out of the ranks of the Council. Mr Santer had to face a hard and unexpected electoral campaign in the EP to get a favourable vote. The consultation of the new Article 158 became a confidence vote hardly won. I had the opportunity to comment with him in Strasbourg that, in an irony of history, he was running a real risk to be hanged with the rope he had offered to the Parliament, remembering our negotiations when he was preparing the first draft of the Treaty as President of the Council that led to the incorporation of the investiture.

Democratic Complexity

The criticism of the labyrinthine and baroque nature of the system is justified, but it should be examined with a certain care if we wish to avoid merely repeating what we have heard second hand. In fact, the only systems whose operations are perfectly straightforward are dictatorships or absolute monarchies, the world of '*Yo, el Supremo*' – Roa Bastos' superb novel – where everything which is not obligatory is prohibited. We have been privileged to contemplate how, as the Treaty was in gestation, how right before our very eyes a monolithic world of absolute certainties was disintegrating, a world which rested not only on an absolute faith, but also on one of the most powerful armies in the history of mankind. Not because it was defeated, but because the weight of absolutism and the popular passivity which was its counterpart meant that the first breath of fresh air reduced the entire worm-eaten structure to dust.

Democratic regimes which appear, on the contrary, at first sight to present a picture of insecurity, division and complicatedness, are, in the long run, the only ones which achieve lasting consensus. The Venetian Republic, an oligarchic system of more than 100 000 citizens which lasted over 1000 years, possessed an institutional mechanism which was complicated in the extreme, involving the election of the Doge by a mixed system of voting and random chance, in twelve successive steps, in which the *ballota* (little ball) – a modern political key word – served as an electoral mechanism, with the Grand Council, the Little Council and the Council of ten. In the case of the Helvetic Confederation, the power-sharing system upholds a rotating government with a broad coalition base, with frequent recourse being had to direct democracy, and limitations which strike a Community citizen as unthinkable – such as teaching qualifications being valid only in a given canton.

The majority of European parliaments have second or third reading mechanisms for bills, which allows them to ripen and to be revised. In this, the most peculiar case is that of the UK, where the existence of a consuetudinary tradition in a perpetual and continuous process of adaptation meant, for example, that no British politician was prepared to go beyond what the bookmakers were offering (bets on political forecasts) as far as the date of ratification of the Treaty of Maastricht was concerned.

A simple reading of the declarations annexed to the Treaty exemplifies the very complexity of life itself. The first protocol limits the acquisition of second homes in Denmark to foreigners, a country which has no Mediterranean coast and, therefore, runs little risk of being invaded by investors. For enthusiasts of comparative federalism, an examination of the operation of the United States' political system in the light of its Constitution constitutes a useful demonstration of the inextricable complexity of a mechanism which in general is considered choked and inefficient, but which achieves the undeniable result that the USA is the world's leading power.

This raises the question of the pace and the objective of European integration which, since its outset, has been a parallel task of creating both society and institutions. As one of its leading figures, Jean Monnet, said in his memoirs, 'the germ of Europe was a political vision, but even more, a moral vision'. Europeans had little by little lost the ability to live together and to pool their creative forces; their contribution to progress, their role in the civilization which they themselves had created appeared to be in decline. Undoubtedly, they no longer possessed institutions capable of guiding them in a changing world. The national model had proved its unsuitability.

> I saw in the new, common institution, the sole appropriate means of giving Europeans back their mastery of the exceptional qualities which had characterized their history, and I was prepared to make an effort because the men listening to me in the ECSC Assembly shared that feeling.
>
> For many years now I have been impressed by a thought voiced by the Swiss philosopher Amiel, to the effect that experience begins anew in each person, and only institutions become wiser, accumulating collective experience, and thanks to this experience and wisdom, human beings subject to the same rules will see not so much a transformation of their nature as, gradually, of their behaviour.[3]

This would be, if it were necessary, a sufficient justification for the Community institutions. The bottom line is that they have produced and are continuing to produce a change in individual and collective behaviour – a process which is patent in all those people who are involved, for whatever reason, in the Community institutions, and which extends to whole nations that for centuries engaged in confrontation and hatred and today practise good neighbourliness, accepting that any Community citizen can become a village mayor, or find everything from a common passport or driving licence to common groceries perfectly normal and appropriate.

Community history is a continuous linking-up of society and institutions, with progress in social integration taking place on the basis of the dialectic of the specific and the commonplace. In this way, it has proved possible painlessly to set in motion and to forge the basis of the most important social revolution in our entrepreneurial, manual or vocational activities – which now have a greater area available to them, with fewer barriers and greater liberty to achieve self-fulfilment in a society that can only live if it is supported by active citizens, in a synthesis between competition and cooperation and also between the market, the role of the public institutions and social concertation, as Jacques Delors[4] has affirmed. In short, it is a clear-cut triumph of the open society as conceived by Popper.

Of course, we are not talking about simple deregulation. Curiously, Eurosceptics who are critical of the Maastricht Treaty are normally ardent defenders of the internal market, without realizing that it is responsible for most of the things they do not like.

There has been a veritable competition to find the most farcical way of describing the Brussels bureaucrats' mania for standardization. From the attempt to describe English sausages as 'tubes full of emulsion' in 'Yes, Minister' to the colour of flamingos or the size of eggs, there are stories for all tastes. The UK Government's Foreign Office has published a leaflet called 'Euromyths', in which it refutes, *inter alia*, claims that curved cucumbers are to be banned or that Ecus are to be minted bearing the effigy of Delors. These caricatures are often linked to bitter complaints on the lack of protection of consumers or the dismantling of industries as a result of the lucubrations of some petty bureaucrats in a windowless office. Nonetheless, it has been the very spread of the principle of mutual recognition, in preference to that of complete harmonization, since the mid-1980s, that has allowed us to complete the internal market.

The judgements mentioned above on the Cassis de Dijon liqueur, German beer or soft-grain pasta have allowed the removal of barriers which were invisible, hidden or based on tricks. Barriers which were *peccata minuta* alongside those which existed in so ardent a defender of free trade as Japan, where the carrier of a handful of rice at the customs was running the risk of a prison sentence, as would someone taking peanuts to the USA. The Community is a far more integrated market than the US in the banking and financial sphere.

Many matters are perforce resolved in the Community context. The extension of anti-pollution laws for motor vehicles under 1400 cc is due to an EP amendment, since the combined pressure of various European industries had prevented its introduction. Or the laws protecting European productions in the *télévision sans frontières* directive challenging the monopolistic sway of the USA. In fact, the first decision which I took as President was to grant the Council an additional month in which to accept the parliamentary amendment including protection of European productions.

This activity is both the object and the result of constant demands from interest groups, associations and sectorial organizations (employers, professionals, consumers, etc.), the lobbies, devoted to the task of convincing politicians of the merits of their cause and ensuring that it is reflected in an amendment or in a law. An activity which in itself is not ignoble, but intrinsically democratic; although clear rules are needed to distinguish between the interests and passions involved, and to eliminate behaviour which stretches from supplying information to trading influences or even criminal conduct.

This concern led me as President to propose the regulation of lobbies in the European Parliament. Following a first census, which registered over 3 000 lobbies, the Galle report was drawn up to define and regulate a code of conduct for a supervision of their activities. On this basis, the Commission has brought about an analogous regulation, a job all the more necessary insofar as conventional thinking has it that Brussels is where you have to lobby if you want a result.

The Regulation – Deregulation Dilemma

We are thus dealing with a regulation-deregulation process within a new framework, since, despite what certain apologists for neo-Conservatism claim, the pure and simple suppression of laws is not a miraculous panacea; normally, what it does is to leave the field open for the strongest to dictate their laws.

Certainly, an excess of regulationism and compartmentalization leads to social initiatives being suffocated, although the existence of laws is absolutely essential to the life of a society, no less the organization of its economic relationships. In brief, we are dealing with a debate on the sharing of power and how the rules of the game are established.

In the case of the Community, the underlying issue in the debate before Maastricht and, more intensely, in the ensuing debate is how Community authority is structured, how codes of conduct are fixed and the establishment of priorities, as well as balancing centralization and decentralization. A simplistic answer is to leave it all to the would-be miraculous 'invisible hand', but it seems more reasonable to think, as does an experienced European like Etienne Davignon, that 'happiness will not arrive because we cease to concern ourselves with problems[5]', and that therefore it is necessary to establish the principle of an authority, certain rules of behaviour and a guarantor of conduct, because if not, he who cheats wins. This demands explicit legislation, since we cannot leave everything to the hazards of negotiation: as Davignon himself rightly points out, 'if everything is negotiable, what are we negotiating?'.

The question is decisive, insofar as a general process of opening-up has taken place, with greater freedom within the Community, a development which demands legislation that will allow the capitalist system to operate with an adequate level of respect for social equilibrium, and within a context in which the rules of competition are evolving at a dramatic rate. This raises questions which have become issues of the greatest moment, such as, at the political level, the debate covered by the word 'subsidiarity' or, at the economic level, the word 'competition'. It is no coincidence whatever that both debates should have become central throughout the ratification process.

The Discovery of Subsidiarity

The appearance of the principle of subsidiarity as a central political issue is suggestive of the change brought about. A principle whose very name has been subject to endless criticism above all in the Saxon world, when everybody immediately understands the word 'subsidy', derived from the same

Latin root (*subsidium*), which describes aid or help of an economic nature, and corresponds to the legal principle relating
to action or responsibility which supplements or strengthens
the main action or answerability. It is a concept to be found
in political life from Aristotle to Tocqueville, although its modern formulation stems from Christian thinking and federative
thought, in so far as citizens believe that the closest possible
level of government is the desirable level.

The principle was taken up by Catholic thought in 'Rerum
Novarum' and developed in 'Quadragesimo Anno', published
in 1931, which theorized the concept in the face of the progress
of totalitarism, saying that tasks which individuals were capable
of realizing on their own initiative and in their own way should
not be transferred to the community, and that it would also be
unjust and highly damaging to the social order if functions
were withdrawn from smaller entities which were perfectly
capable of carrying them out on their own and transferred to
a larger and greater collective unit.

But, independently of its theoretical basis, subsidiarity had
already taken flesh as a nuclear element in federative political
systems, whereof it is an intrinsic component, forming part
of their basic culture, as happens in Switzerland and Federal
Germany, as an element to counter-balance the congenital temptations of power. In the case of the USA, whose starting point
consisted merely of territorial communities, the experiment
rests on the fact that every governmental body, whether federal,
state or local, is a government; political authority and power
reside in the people. Theories of the state commonly accepted
in Europe, however, claim that sovereignty is indivisible and
that the state is the source of political authority and of power[6].

The inclusion of the principle of subsidiarity in the Treaties
was advocated in the European Parliament's draft of 1984. In
the preparation of the TEU, it was the subject of a report of
the then MEP Giscard D'Estaing, the former President of the
French Republic, who displayed, in his brilliant defence of this
principle, an openness of spirit comparable to that of an ex-
Pope putting up a convincing defence of the principle of free
investigation – affirming that the Community intervenes only
in a subsidiary capacity by virtue of a principle of exact suit-
ability, which states that each level should be assigned only
those powers whose nature and scale means that they can be

effectively and conveniently exercised at that level. This principle was enshrined in Article 3b of the Treaty: 'In areas which do not fall within its exclusive competence, the Community shall take action, in accordance with the principle of subsidiarity, only if and insofar as the objectives of the proposed action cannot be sufficiently achieved by the Member States and can therefore, by reason of the scale or effects of the proposed action, be better achieved by the Community.'

We must here list some specific aspects of the Community's application of the principle of subsidiarity. In the first place, its formulation does not take the citizen as its starting point – the issue is one that arises between Member States and the Community; secondly, the wording mixes up the principle of subsidiarity and proportionality. The latter claims that the means used by the Community and the objectives laid in the Treaty need to be properly adapted from one to the other. The nuance is important, because this principle has repeatedly been defined in case-law, which considers that when there is a choice of various appropriate measures available for achieving a given objective, the least restrictive must be chosen. While proportionality makes reference to the need to make the means fit the ends, subsidiarity implies that specific action should be taken at appropriate level in order to produce the most desirable effects.

The principle of subsidiarity is neither yet enshrined in the case-law of the Community, nor kitted out with established lists of the ways in which powers are to be shared out. However, the Treaty clearly lays down the scope of the Community's powers: it can take action only in a given sector or policy when explicit powers exist in the Treaties or when, via Article 235 of the Treaty of Rome, the Council achieves unanimous agreement that the Community should adopt secondary legislation in the sector in question.

All this is no doubt very long-winded and complicated for the non-specialist reader, but is has important consequences: on the one hand, the Council can extend its sphere of competence, and on the other, the Court of Justice may correct certain aspects of the current lack of definition by drawing attention to criteria which differ from those established by the Council. In any case, public interest in this subject demonstrates that it is not a merely academic or legal issue.

The debate on subsidiarity dominated the year 1992 in political terms, at a time when, having taken the step of Maastricht full of bright hopes, it appeared that the world was falling about the Community's ears. Moreover, the alphabetic roulette of the rule governing the rotation of the Council produced the coincidence of Denmark following the UK in the Presidency, openly raising fears – and in politics, fears like hopes, are tangible; they are not mere impressions – that a gargantuan superstate had been born, a veritable Saturn devouring its parents.

In the case of the UK, where the debate on federalism was causing havoc even before the Treaty was signed, the government used the principle of subsidiarity as a missile. This was curious in a legislative union such as the United Kingdom, based on England, which has been the most centralized state in Europe since the Middle Ages; Scotland, with its own official church, central bank and legislation; Wales, which enjoyed a certain degree of administrative and cultural autonomy and Ulster, with its own parliament – a state in which the Thatcher government cut back the autonomy of local authorities to a minimum with its proposal to return to the medieval poll tax. This crusade had its own nuances, because, when it came to the details of applying the principle of subsidiarity, what was being called for was basically the renationalization of Community policies, with a return to the inter-state alliance set up and apparently effective attack on Brussels centralism, which consisted in scrapping a whole series of directives, not approving others and submitting all decisions to prior examination (i.e. veto). Latin words, as in this case, frequently change meaning when they cross the Channel; for example, when you see a sign announcing *diversion* on an English road, it does not mean that it ends in a fun park.

In the Danish case, with its tradition of open government and thoroughly decentralized political life, concern was focused on 'nearness', a principle closer to the traditional meaning of subsidiarity.

However, it is undeniable that the problem exists, and all the more acutely at a time when substantial additional powers have been granted and there has simultaneously been a massive rise in public awareness of what is happening. For that reason it is necessary to find a political solution to the question, before the 'government of judges' is forced to lay down the criteria.

The Interinstitutional Agreement of October 1993 on 'democracy, transparency, subsidiarity' as its global philosophy, which consists essentially of a statement of democratic will with regard to a working method as far as subsidiarity is concerned, and of an intention to improve the Council's transparency, specifically in the form of certain proposals concerning publicity and information, has been a first joint answer. This Interinstitutional Agreement is complemented by agreements concerning the application of co-decision and the statute establishing the Ombudsman, both central issues in the process of bringing citizens closer to the European Union.

The Treaty also gave constitutional status to a consultative committee of regional and local authorities. This decision recognizes the existence and importance in Europe both of regional and local identity, which in some states, has constitutional status (Germany and Belgium as federal states, Spain as an autonomist state, Italy as a regional state). In the latter the Treaties have heightened sensitivity with regard to the Community take-over of powers which are not the explicit prerogative of a central government, but which are shared, or occasionally appertain exclusively to the regions. This is an issue that needs to be resolved above all in each state, in accordance with its own legislative arrangements and its own 'federal or autonomous loyalty', and to be reflected in the way in which it is represented on the Council.

The state which has the greater experience in this field is Germany, where the Bundesrat (a chamber comprising the ministers of the *Länder* with a weighted vote) is equipped with a European Committee which, when the Treaty was being ratified, put its conditions to the Federal State (Bund) on Germany's participation in the Council.

Municipalities have also played a major role in Europe since its beginnings. In the Community, there are over 150 cities with more than 100 000 inhabitants, and some Community countries are, historically, constellations of city states, such as Italy, Belgium or the Netherlands. Moreover, it is at local level that many of the policies of basic concern to citizens, such as environment, education, employment, housing etc. are raised and dealt with.

In any case, it seems difficult to limit the debate on subsidiarity to the relationship between the member states and
the Community, when we are dealing with a principle which
produces a chain reaction from the citizen's point of view. To
seek to limit it to relations between states is another matter. In
this sense, one can understand the concern expressed by a
resolute defencer of inter-governmentalism like Miguel Herrero
de Miñón about both the ambiguity of how it is to be regulated and its 'explosive character'[7]. If we respect the different
traditions and organization of each state, regional bodies will
play a major role in certain Community policies (management
of regional aid, agricultural guidelines, environment . . .), which
means that they should participate. Certainly, there are more
radical attitudes, which call for a progressive replacement of
the twelve member states by some 140 regions, a proposal
which is not destined to gain credibility in the foreseeable
future and does not fit the very structure of the Community.

To conclude these reflections on the Community institutional system, I would return to my initial questions. Is it preferable to draw up a constitutional text or to continue with an
open-ended constitutional process? Is federalism a model to
be followed?

Federalism

The debate on the federal nature of the Community is one of
the most impassioned and longstanding of its history, comparable in intensity only with that of the seat of the Institutions.
We saw how at the 1948 Congress there was a radical federalist
block of opinion which called for the immediate establishment of the United States of Europe. Since the very beginning, the idea of federation has been present. The Schuman
Declaration itself mentioned it as a final objective.

At the Intergovernmental Conference, both the word and
the concept were the subject of heated discussion. The term
'federal vocation' appeared in the draft Treaty in Article A's
definition of the European Union.

However, the word disappeared from the text and was replaced by the classical 'ever closer union' as a result of implacable British opposition and more discreet reservations on the

part of other members. A curious animadversion, when 21 of the 42 countries throughout the world which apply federal principles actually belong to the British sphere, as against seven from those whose political traditions derive from the Iberian peninsula and six from that of the Holy Roman Empire[8]. At the Nordwijk conclave, I had occasion to remind those present, in the presence of Douglas Hurd, the British Foreign Secretary, of the letter of Queen Anne of England in 1706 to the Scottish Parliament, when she called for 'entire and perfect union' as 'the solid foundation of lasting peace' between England and Scotland'. If a union is ever closer it will perforce eventually end up complete and perfect; it cannot be an endless process of drawing 'ever closer'.

Curiously enough, the term 'federalism' has always been supported in another old-established nation-state, France, where, despite presidentialist rule over a historically centralized and Jacobin state – the very antithesis of what is normally conceived of as federalism – there exists support for the idea, compensated by the Gaullist conception of *L'Europe des Patries*. The Federation of Nations proposed by Delors is an interesting definition. In Germany, clearly, the concept arouses no opposition, as it is a natural component of German sort. In any case, the question is why so many doubts exist at all. In fact, Germany history presents us with the best and the worst examples of European union, namely the Federal Republic and the Third Reich. Italy has always supported maximum European unity, and in this, she coincides with her fellow 'new nation'.

In the case of Spain, the proposal poses no particular problem; this is undoubtedly a result of the rethinking of the State enshrined in the 1978 Constitution which completely revised out-of-date centralist concepts.

Belgium has just become a federal state, and the idea is popular in Holland, while other countries, such as Portugal, Greece, Denmark or Ireland, have reservations. A curious state of affairs, since smaller bodies are always over-valued in federative systems, doubtless reflecting their concern to retain their own national identities.

Without seeking to engage a complex theoretical disquisition, I should like to specify some characteristics of federalism, an undoubtedly more complex exercise than that of describing an absolute monarchy. The concept signifies, originally, alliance (*foedera*) by means of treaties. Its most genuine creation is the Helvetic Confederation, now 700 years old, which, at the heart of Europe, unites people of four different cultures within a long-established democracy. In its modern version, it arose from the North American constitutional debate between those who sought a stronger central government and the anti-federalists who supported the old confederal system.

Its principal features are, according to Madison's description at the end of the 18th century (which remains valid today), the following:

1   *Non-centralization.* Power resides in an alliance of sovereign states and is deliberately shared so as to safeguard the liberty and vitality of the latter. The system is contractual, and the power cannot be rescinded unilaterally or arbitrarily by the central government.

2   *Negotiationism.* Decisions are adopted in an ongoing process of negotiation between the federated states and the federal power and, often, between the associates themselves, which constitutes a shared process of decision-making, in which the parties have a guaranteed voice in defining the administrative, financial and other obligations of the central power.

3   *Constitutionalism.* In federations, there is normally a Constitution which binds the alliance of the parties to the basic purpose, mission and principles of the overarching institution. It also covers the powers, rights and responsibilities of the parties, who have their own constitutions, in so far as these do not violate the basic principles of the federation.

4   *Territoriality.* Precise frontiers exist between the constituent units, with 'dual citizenship', of the federated state itself and the federation, which leads to a bicameral system.

5   *Balance of powers,* between both the central power and the federated powers and between the latter, guaranteed by a Constitutional Court.

6   *Autonomy.* The federated states are free to exercise self-government, in so far as they do not violate the fundamental principles necessary for the maintenance of the Union[9].

Over and above these features, federalism implies the existence of consensus and active cooperation between individuals and institutions which, in their turn, pride themselves on the preservation of their respective integrities[10].

Federalism takes as its basic starting point an attitude and a state of mind of federal loyalty, in the sense of accepting conflictive cooperation and the sharing of power. It is not so much a method for resolving problems of diversity as a process for channelling the positive potential of forces which could become destructive if they were in confrontation with one another. It actually allows and upholds diversity, because it is founded on the implicit recognition of the fact that diversity generates strength. It is not without significance that federative principles are those which underpin the major form of productive organization in this century: the large multinational corporation.

If a political system establishes itself as a whole comprising two or more fora, planes, spheres, layers or levels of government, each of them enjoying legitimacy and having a place in the constitution of the system at large, which possesses its own institutions, powers and responsibilities, that system is heading towards being a federal one[11].

The European Union already matches this description almost completely. If it fulfils its own forecasts and undertakings, establishes a single currency and a common foreign and security policy and democratically resolves its finances (on the principle of 'no taxation without representation'), it will be a federal system in its own way. Each and every one is. The ever closer Union of the Treaty cannot eternally remain at the level of a platonic engagement or an occasional encounter; it must move on to being a shared destiny. The best-balanced and most democratic in history are federal destinies.

The Constitutional Debate in Waiting

After forty years of history and laborious institutional construction, and the 'constitutionalization' of the Treaty of Rome by the Luxembourg Court, in the words of Judge Federico Mancini, there does not seem to be a great deal of sense in calling for a revolutionary 'Estates-General'. The debate between federalists and unionists at the 1948 Congress has proceeded down a path which at that time no-one was capable of foreseeing. History is never written in advance. For that reason we cannot convincingly imagine a scenario like the oath of the

'Jeu de Paume' and the night of 4 August 1789 in France, or like the 'Constitutional Convention' of Philadelphia rebelling against its mandate and drawing up a new US constitution.

With the ratification of the Treaty of Maastricht and its coming into force on 1 November 1993, a difficult stage has been traversed, although it is undeniable that the proposal to endow European integration with an effective democratic constitution, comprehensible to citizens and capable of allowing the extension of the Union, as the European Parliament proposes, could appear to be an invitation to put oneself in the lion's mouth. Of course it is absolutely necessary to undertake the work of recasting, rewriting and redefining the concepts. The text drawn up by Emilio Colombo, Marcelino Oreja and Fernand Herman successively for the EP Committee on Institutional Affairs is a useful tool.

But it is not merely a question of stylistics. If we set the Treaty alongside the calendar of work which it contains, very specific in the economic and monetary fields and less so in the political one, we realize that if this work is to be carried out by the year 2000 there is no time to lose. It is not a question of internal pressures merely; there are candidates knocking at the door who have been assured of accession. Developments in economics, industry, trade and security in Europe and the world at large will not wait for us to make up our minds.

Moreover, a new date, 1996, has been set for a fresh Intergovernmental Conference, with the extremely wide mandate of examining the provisions of the Treaty, in accordance with the objectives laid down in Articles A and B of the common provisions (those defining European Union and its objectives).

In June 1995, the celebrations of the 40th anniversary of the opening of the conference that laid the groundwork for the Treaty of Rome took place in Messina. An event with a 'touch of middle-aged angst' as rightly described by Lionel Barber, that concluded with the inauguration of the reflection group charged with preparing the Inter-Governmental Conference to review the Maastricht Treaty. The main question that the select group of representatives, appointed by the national governments, chaired by Carlos Westendorp – a Spaniard of European breed – and with the participation for the first time of two Members of the European Parliament, Elisabeth Guigou and Elmar Brok, set itself, was a daunting one: what is the common cause and vision of the fifteen member states, and how do they propose to respond to the external challenges confronting the Union?

The answer was presented to the European Summit at Madrid in December 1995 as a report of the majority, with a clear reservation of the UK government. In the index, for the first time, appear the Citizen and an Efficient and Democratic Union. In the meantime, the fifteen leaders had an appointment on the inspiring island of Mallorca for reflection. On this occasion, there was a general consensus that the debate must be democratic, clear and transparent. The problem is how to implement these good principles. There is another advantage; the fact that the process has already been launched, with the publication of the reports of the EU institutions and other bodies.

Certainly, the mood is not so good as it was in the last round that led to Maastricht. In 1989, the tidal wave of the fall of the Berlin Wall gave a new push to the self-accelerating process of building the single market, and we were ready for new challenges and horizons. Although we have recovered from the deepest economic crisis since the World War, accompanied by an existential anguish, the prospects are not so bright nowadays. We are not depicting new worlds or frontiers, nor a castle in fairyland. To build a common house is a difficult task that requires accuracy and perseverance. And the main challenge is getting and maintaining the support of the people for the embodiment of the project of the Union, whose realization will clearly be in the next millennium.

A common feature of the British and Spanish peoples, shared with many fellow Europeans, is that we are more willing to fight and make sacrifices for epic or heroic causes than for everyday matters.

And the issues that more concern the everyday life of European citizens are how to create jobs and how to provide stability and security in their lives. We are undergoing a period of historical transition and reassessment, in which the old certainties do not provide a safety net. For these reasons, the Maastricht Treaty and the Union itself have become a kind of scapegoat for everyday miseries.

Nevertheless, if we look to the ongoing debate in each one of the countries of the Union, we shall see that its objectives and substance are on the stage, either in an explicit way or as an underlying factor. The most striking example of an open and dramatic debate is the United Kingdom; the best example of a non-open debate is, perhaps, France.

In fact, the debate on the IGC was launched by the so-called 'Schäuble-Lammers' paper, issued by the CDU-CSU parliamentary group in the Bundestag in September 1994, imbued with a clear federalist faith, with the underlying German anguish of a 'Sonderweg', a way of exception and loneliness, and proposing clearly to create a common European defence. The document broke the ice, and was widely criticized for two of its features: one, the definition of the 'Kern' or 'hard core' of states able to take the definitive step towards economic and monetary union as early as in 1997–1999; and the other, mentioning by name the states that were in a winning position in the race towards achieving the objectives of convergence.

This undiplomatic behaviour is not new in itself; every day, the newspapers publish such rankings. The problem was that the author represented the main ruling force in the strongest partner of the Union, in which the main question was how to get a balanced structure between political and economic and monetary union.

The presidential electoral campaign in France has shown the complex situation in this founding and key member of the Community. The majority RPR-UDF is deeply divided on Europe, between the Gaullist 'Europe des Patries' and the openly federalist vision of Giscard d'Estaing. Chirac tried an impossible synthesis, with contradictory proposals in the campaign, even proposing a referendum on the single currency. The succesive economic programs of the Juppé Government reflects the complexity of the situation, and the revolt of December the mixed feeling of anguish an despair in most of the people.

In the case of Great Britain, the position of Prime Minister Major, as expressed in his speech at the University of Leiden in September 1994, showed a British outlook on Europe very reluctant to make any move forward, although he recognized that 'the IGC of 1996 is likely to bring many issues into sharp focus'. How, for example, can we fashion a fairer voting system? Can we develop simpler and more transparent legislative procedures? Should the Council exercise more control on the Commission? Is the number of Commissioners becoming unwieldy as the Union enlarges? Should the Commission have new powers in some areas, for example to pursue budget fraud into the member states themselves?

In spite of the bold, almost revolutionary aspects of proposals like the creation of a kind of Euro-FBI squad to pursue fraud, the British approach was 'flexible and workable'. The more recent developments demonstrate this position as too advanced. In the field that matters the most for the UK, security and defence, the proposal of placing the WEU as a parallel structure to the Union is a clear step backwards. But the most decisive fact is that already everybody agrees that there will not be a decisive British engagement before the UK's next general election.

From their side, two of the European institutions – the Commission and the Parliament – have prepared reports that show very similar views on the current situation and the main issues that are at stake. In order to face them, we must not forget that the IGC of 1996 is an appointment made in Maastricht, in the same Treaty. There are several reasons for this, such as the end of the Treaty of Brussels of 1948 that created the WEU, but perhaps the most important was awareness of the necessity of testing the changes and the new instruments with the possibility of adjustment in 1996 – a wise precaution, similar in principle to that was adopted in the Spanish Constitution, in the area of implementation of the political and financial devolution to the regions. It is true that the forecast was the entry into force of the Treaty on 1 January 1993, in a smooth process. Facts turned out differently, not only because of postponement for almost a year, but also because of sudden enlargement and a wave of new candidates.

What will be the terms of the conference? In principle, the implementation of the EMU and the introduction of the single currency are not on the agenda, nor are the budgetary aspects related to enlargement. These are two key issues that cannot be ignored and will have a clear influence on public opinion. European construction needs prosperity as the oil that lubricates the change. And we must not forget that the big question is how to find a balance between political and economic union.

Looking at the institutional aspects of the IGC, there are four main issues: the rule of majority as the general one; the merger of the three pillars in a single institutional framework;

the implementation of the common defence policy with the absorption of the WEU and a balanced codecision legislative procedure.

In order to explain the aims and priorities to the ordinary citizen, I have drafted a ten-point programme that represents the most important conclusions of this chapter:

1   *Consolidate the European Union:*
    The aim of the IGC is to reform in order to build a democratic and jointly binding Union among states and peoples, based on common citizenship and a single currency.

2   *Reform in order to enlarge:*
    It is necessary to strengthen the double democratic legitimacy, decision-making capacity and clear accountability, in order to enlarge the Union to accommodate those states and peoples that want to share our destiny.

3   *Do together what we can jointly better achieve:*
    The Union must pursue only the objectives agreed in common, respecting the national identity of each one of its Member States. Decisions must be taken at the closest possible level to the citizens.

4   *Contribute jointly and with enough means,* enabling us:
    –   to promote a balanced and sustainable progress, strengthening economic and social cohesion, and establishing economic and monetary union;
    –   to affirm a common identity on the international stage, organising a common foreign, security and defence policy that works;
    –   to ensure that the Union's citizens can exercise their rights and freedoms.

5   *Ensure the unity and workings of the institutional system* through
    –   a simplified Treaty, with a charter written in clear and inspiring language;
    –   a merging of the three pillars in the common institutional framework, with flexibility within unity.

6   *Reinforce and democratize Union institutions:*
    –   with the priority of clarifying and achieving an appropriate balance between the two pillars of democratic legitimacy, not transferring new powers;
    –   ensuring that the Council will work with qualified majority voting as the rule, on a fair basis;

- ensuring that when the Council is acting in its legislative capacity, its proceedings should be public and its agenda binding;
- ensuring that the European Parliament should have equal status in all fields of EU legislative and budgetary competence, with simplified and balanced procedures.

7 *Reassert and reinforce the role of the Commission,* whose President should be elected from among a list of names put forward by the European Council. The members of the Commission will be selected according to the tasks of the Union. The Commission will be appointed through a vote of confidence by the European Parliament and will be accountable to it.

8 *Give full means to the Court of Justice* to ensure the respect of EU laws and the EU institutional balance, extending its authority to include foreign affairs and justice and internal affairs.

9 *Recognise the right of the majority* of the States to advance to go ahead toward the accomplishment of objectives of the Union. States unwilling or unable to join this 'avant-garde' should not be able to veto it.

10 *Provide that the revised Treaties* will come into force with the approval of the Council and the European Parliament, and the ratification of two-thirds of the Member States.

In any case, it must be an open constitutional debate. Within it, it is desirable that the EP should maintain and fine-tune the mechanism of the PIC, as well as its right of initiative, but it would also be reasonable to demand that the sittings of the IGC be public, in broad daylight and with stenographers in attendance, so that MPs, economic and social leaders and – why not? – the ordinary citizen, the people, can follow, become involved in, criticize and grasp issues as vital to how we are going to achieve a definitive union of our destinies and a single currency. This time round, there will be no possibility of presenting a *fait accompli*.

6 From The ECU, Illegitimate Child, To The Euro, Sole Heir

'Más valen en cualquier tierra
(¡mirad si es harto sagaz!)
sus escudos en la paz
que rodelas en la guerra.
Y pues al pobre le entierra
y hace propio al forastero,
poderoso caballero
es don Dinero.'

[Of greater worth in any land
(On his dumbfounding prowess gaze!)
Are his ecus in time of peace,
Than round shields in war.
No poor man can against him stand,
He soothes all foreign hostility –
A puissant knight at arms is he,
Sir Currency!]

                                        Quevedo

'The second major aim of the Treaty on European Union is to promote balanced, sustainable social and economic progress, principally through the establishment of an area without internal frontiers, the strengthening of social and economic cohesion and the setting-up of an economic and monetary union which in due course will require a single currency. The ultimate objective is, therefore, to achieve a single currency which will henceforth be known as the ECU' (Article 3A).

This is all that the Treaty has to say on the objective to be achieved: a gradual monetary reform to be completed by a date which has yet to be firmly established, although 1 January 1999 has been mentioned as a deadline. Such an undertaking would, in terms of timescale, be unprecedented.

The case of the USA demonstrates the difficulties involved

in consolidating a common currency and creating a central bank. Washington created the National Bank on the basis of the plan drawn up by Alexander Hamilton, whose reasoning was based on the doctrine of implicit powers, as opposed to Jefferson, who based his reasoning on the Tenth Amendment, under which all powers that are not delegated to the United States by the Constitution, nor prohibited by the Constitution from being delegated to the States, are reserved for the States or the people. This constitutes an early American form of subsidiarity. The US First Central Bank collapsed in 1811 because of pressure from the States. In response to currency depreciation, Congress set up a Second Central Bank in 1816, the reorganization of which was vetoed by President Jackson. Only during the Civil War were national banks set up with stable currency, in spite of which four instances of financial pandemonium occurred, by comparison with which the problems of the EMS are trivial. The Federal Reserve was set up in 1913, i.e. 124 years after adoption of the Constitution, in spite of which the central monetary authority continued to be openly distrusted, a state of affairs which led to the setting-up of Reserve Banks in each State. Even today, the American financial and banking market is much less integrated than its European counterpart.

In Europe, German monetary unification based on the Reichsbank came about in 1875, although the old names and face values of currencies which would henceforth be inextricably linked were maintained. Within the Community, other interesting cases of monetary union are to be found: the most trustworthy country in the economic and monetary field, Luxembourg, does not have its own currency but shares the Belgian Franc with Belgium, whilst the Scottish pound has its own notes within its union with the English pound.

As regards the case under consideration, it is interesting to remember that the currency has already been christened twice. The first name was the ECU. With reference to this the circumstances under which this name was bestowed are worth recalling. Former President Giscard d'Estaing tells the story[1] of how, at the 1978 Bremen European Council, he persuaded the then British Prime Minister, James Callaghan, that the new accounting unit should not be given a special name but should simply be designated by its function: European Currency Unit, abbreviated to ECU. According to his account the formula was approved, with Callaghan whispering his satisfaction into the ear of David Owen, Helmut Schmidt immediately understanding the pun, which he seemed to find amusing, and the Belgian Prime Minister Leo Tindemans giving a smile on seeing how neatly an English abbreviation and the name of a medieval French coin could be combined in one word. However, Community reality is, unfortunately, more complex; the name met a strong opposition in Germany, where the word sounds like the plural of the word for cow – 'Kühe' and more important, had lost more than 20% of its value since its creation – which led to a new christening as EURO in the Madrid Summit of December 1995. It must not be forgotten that the German Mark is not just a stable and well-managed currency; it is also a basic symbol of German identity and, as Michael Stürmer points out, the symbol of the only happy and successful phase in 20th-century German history[2].

Wallet or Purse

Money is the subject of varying conceptions which are reflected in everyday habits. In northern Europe, men normally keep coins in a purse which forms part of their wallet, whilst in southern Europe, loose change is a dead weight which has to be got rid of as quickly as possible. This is an area in which the Italians demonstrated their imagination years ago by introducing the use of sweets, postage stamps or matches as small change, the custom of giving 'change in matches' in the Andalusian towns of my childhood. This cultural difference gives rise to the fact that, in the northern countries of the Community, the basic unit of currency can be divided into hundredths, whilst in the south even the unit of currency itself already seems very small. The change of habits which came about in France following the introduction of the New Franc shows that change is possible. It is also curious to note that, when budgets are being discussed, a Dutchman, a Briton or a German will normally talk of cents, pence or pfennigs, combined with a fierce ritual criticism of extravagance, whilst amongst the countries of southern Europe it is more normal to talk in terms of billions.

The fact is that, in Germany, replacing the mark by something else (whether better or worse) is strongly resisted. This is something to be borne in mind since Germany is the country with the strongest currency within the Community, a currency which plays a central role in the system as a reference value and as anchorman. It is the currency of a society which experienced the tragedy of disastrous hyperinflation in the 1920s and which retains a fear thereof which is branded on its collective memory, a society which subsequently experienced the two most important post-war monetary reforms: that of 1948, which established the Deutschmark, and the one which occurred more recently at the time of unification. In Denmark and the Benelux countries the prime objective is to stick as close to the mark as possible. France achieved better results in 1993 recently as regards the basic economic indicators – the 'fundamentals' – and even toyed with the idea of becoming a second anchorman. However, it is symptomatic that, in opinion polls, the French Right, still heavily burdened by its hegemonic nostalgia in political matters, had no difficulty in declaring itself to be overwhelmingly in favour of monetary union. In the United Kingdom, sterling's exit from the EMS and its subsequent devaluation had the same effect that the sinking of an invincible British Armada would have had.

In the case of Spain, nobody has set out to defend the peseta. The days in which the '*real de a ocho*' or '*Peso duro*' (the sorcerer's *peso*, according to the Chinese) was the main currency in world trade and, in the words of Braudel, defined monetary circulation in the Mediterranean or the Far East thanks to the Nao of Manila, or in which the first dollars were made as IOUs in Spanish milled dollars, are now long gone. Only the stylised figure 8 on the Pillars of Hercules has survived as its symbol ($)[3]. It is now more than a hundred years since we agreed to give our currency the humble name of 'little coin' in Catalan. The comment on its value which has stuck longest in my mind is one I heard from a respected financial expert at the first post-Maastricht debate I attended; 'When I retire I want my pension to be paid in the currency which is most like the German mark'.

The purpose of the above comments is not so much to provide facile stereotypes of Europeans in their attitudes towards money as to raise the most serious political problem regarding economic and monetary union: its ability to move and inspire the citizens of the Community. The matter is certainly a delicate one and requires both substantial technical preparation, together with enormous sensitivity so as to ensure the success of a fully supported referendum and the introduction of a new currency. The cultural aspect must be taken fully into account in the process and not just the technical side.

When dealing with money we should never forget what the ancients used to say: 'Money has the heart of a hare and the feet of a rabbit'. The current neglect of the ECU does not help much, as Professor Peter Kenen, an American advocate of EMU, has rightly pointed out: 'If the peoples and parliaments of Europe say no to monetary union, the architects of EMU will have themselves to blame. Caught up in seeking to understand *how* monetary union could be made to work, they ceased to ask *why* one should want it to work'[4].

Indeed, achieving EMU is not an objective which is self-evident, nor is any explanation given as to why it should be desirable. In newspaper reports the disadvantages associated with the establishment of EMU are standard fare (instability of the national currency, attacks by speculators, etc.). When something more intellectual is attempted the pages are covered with graphs which are suspiciously reminiscent of the temperature, heart rate and blood pressure charts of hospital patients.

However, the question is neither trivial nor marginal, since it refers to an item which is of interest to everyone insofar as it serves as a reference point for social relations as a whole. As a matter of fact, money was not initially created by law; it was a social institution originated by trade and division of labour. The first coins were shells, cocoa grains, . . . Indeed, it is the only power acting on everyday life. It cannot be denied that many people will not worry excessively about the form which joint legislative decision-making and subsidiarity take in the Treaty but it would be difficult to find anybody who is unconcerned about what happens to his money, not out of pure greed but on account of its role as a benchmark, given its value as a unit of exchange in an open market economy. Thus a small child, an illiterate person, a bold speculator and a mendicant friar understand and attach importance to money and its value, although clearly for very different reasons which do not always correspond to the stereotypes; Mr. Soros, for example, is dedicating a substantial amount of the money he made by speculating on the pound sterling to financing foundations in Central and Eastern Europe, whilst certain religious orders which have taken the vow of poverty have amassed wealth and luxury in amounts which are unparalleled in history.

Recognition of the Son

The prime concern must therefore be to convince people that a single currency is both appropriate and necessary because it is better for everybody.

The Commission's first line of argument is that the establishment of a single currency would put the finishing touch to the internal market. Its arguments are summarized in a document entitled 'One market, one currency', supplemented by the report on the ECU by Michael Emerson and C. Huhne[5], and in the Cecchini report on the advantages of the internal market. The essential argument is based on a cost-benefit analysis detailing the efficiency gains and the growth to be brought about by a single currency, starting with the disappearance of exchange costs arising from bank commission charges and fluctuation margins. The example of 'doing the rounds' of the Community capitals with the sum of £1000 which is changed successively into the respective currency of each country and which, on one's return home, is found to have lost approximately half its value is a highly instructive one, even though most people are not regular travellers but merely tourists once a year. However, the argument is a sound one if we consider the benefits to economic activity (small and medium-sized businesses in particular), the reduced risks for investors, the improvement in economic prospects and, above all, the strength which comes from greater power.

In fact the ECU was born before the internal market was even thought of. Its creation in 1979 is associated with that of the European Monetary System, which was designed as a 'basket' containing a fixed amount of each of its component currencies and may thus be regarded as a 'cocktail of currencies'. At the same time it acted as a safety device since it reduces the fluctuations in each of those currencies. The ECU survived and lived on – or, rather, there were two ECUs, an official one and a private one, which lead parallel lives, the first as an illegitimate child and the second as an orphan.

The official ECU came into being as the 'contra' to the reserves deposited in the European Monetary Cooperation Fund (EMCF), a body set up in 1973 to administer the 'monetary snake' exchange mechanism and the transfer of funds between central banks. For this purpose it received 20% of the Member States' reserves as a deposit, created ECUs as a 'contra' and ran the central banks' ECU reserve accounts. The ECMF has been wound up and has become part of the European Monetary Institute (EMI), which has the job of setting up the Central Bank during the second stage of EMU. Progress in the recognition of the illegitimate child, has been made, changing even its name.

As regards the orphan, the private ECU, its survival was due to various concurrent factors: the weight and stability of the strong component currencies and support from the Community institutions. For this reason, more extensive use is being made of it in international financial markets for lending operations by banks, large companies, international organizations and national, regional and local governments, and in money markets for the development of loans, bank deposits and the clearing system. Furthermore, it is used as an accounting and settlements currency by many European companies and increasing use is being made of it in private transactions. Certain Community member states (Belgium, France and Spain) have even issued ECU coins, although at the moment these have only numismatic value. However, its acceptance in commercial deals and transactions is limited, with the Benelux countries in the lead thanks to their favourable attitude to its use, and Germany bringing up the rear.

However, we cannot leave everything to the efforts of this street urchin. Highly commendable work is being done by the Association for the Monetary Union of Europe that has drawn up a complete timetable and programme for the introduction of the single currency into everyday use, with the general public to be educated on the subject in stages.

The conclusions of the Maas Report on the preparation of the changeover to the single European currency commended by the Commission are of the utmost interest. It attaches vital importance to promoting awareness, minimising uncertainty and potential fears, while broadening support amongst the general public. It proposes as a leading criterion that the single currency must be based on the strict implementation of the Maastricht Treaty; there will not be a possibility of an instantaneous new EURO introduction comprising all aspects of a single currency on the first day of Stage III of EMU, but it is very convenient to introduce the currency in a smaller number of steps, taking into account the complexity of changing the accounting systems, producing and distributing notes and coins and adapting the thousands of slot machines everywhere. This is why an early ongoing dialogue between public authorities and the private sector is of the utmost importance.

From the start of Stage III, the EURO will become a new currency in its own right, managed by the independent European Central Bank, and the basket will disappear. This gives extraordinary importance to its institutional framework and its anti-inflationary credentials, and above all points to the need to be aware that 'the move to the single currency implies a definite change of habit of each citizen'.

The Economic and Monetary Pillar

Setting criteria and an objective is not enough; achieving EMU involves adding a new pillar to the basic structure of the Community, by means of which a system for decision-making and the assumption of responsibilities may be set up. The definition of such a system is the subject of the new Title VI of the the Treaty and three annexed Protocols (Nos. 4, 6 and 10) and includes the following:

1 Consolidation of the ECOFIN Council to coordinate the economic policies of the Member States and sustainable convergence of economic performance, with the possibility of making recommendations to the member states. The Commission acts as secretariat and has the job of drawing up reports and recommendations.
2 As regards monetary policy, the European System of Central Banks (ESCB) is to be set up, comprising the European Central Bank (ECB) and the central banks of the member states.

The EMI Leading the Way

What basically needs to be done is to create a focal point where decisions can be taken and responsibilities assumed. Jurgensen rightly points out that neither Monetary Committee members nor central bank governors – who appear to some extent to be in competition with government ministers, in view of the publicity given to their work – nor Eurocrats are elected, for which reason they cannot assume political responsibilities. There is no one leading the way[6]. Setting up the EMI and appointing a president to run it implies that a pilot has been placed at the controls of the system. The structure of the EMI is federative and is based on that of the Bundesbank (Bund means 'federation'), on whose board the governors of the *Länder* (German federated states) banks sit. In the case of the EMI the board members are the governors of the central banks. The EMI is the most fully federative body within the Community, since it has adopted the 'one man, one vote' principle in response to the proposals that votes should be weighted according to an individual currency's significance within the EURO, which would have produced a system based on relative financial strength. In other words, the chairman of the Bundesbank will have the same weight within the EMI Council as the chairman of the Institut Monétaire Luxembourgeois, a financial 'fortress' without its own currency.

The EMI has various things to do in order to carry out its task of preparing the transition to the third stage of EMU: securing greater coordination of monetary policies with a view to ensuring price stability, preparing for the establishment of the ESCB, implementing a single monetary policy, creating a single currency during the third stage of EMU and supervising the development of the EURO, including the design and production of banknotes. In all this the EMI must be able to operate independently and its members are to act in accordance with their own responsibilities. In carrying out its duties the EMI Council may not request or accept instructions from Community institutions or bodies or the governments of the member states.

In October 1993, the Brussels European Council appointed as President of the EMI the Belgian banker of Hungarian origin, Alexander Lamfalussy, who until then had been chairman of the Bank for International Settlements, based in Basle, an institution whose importance in the international financial world is matched only by its discretion. It was set up to oversee the payment of reparations by Germany after the First World War but in fact it has acted for many years as the seat of the Committee of EC Central Bank Governors.

It comes as no surprise, therefore, that Mr Lamfalussy, at the hearing held in the European Parliament at the time of his appointment as President of the EMI, said that the Institute's first task would be to promote cooperation amongst the central banks of the Community with a view to achieving the second stage of EMU, and to ensure a smooth transition period within a framework in which responsibility for monetary policy would remain in the hands of the national authorities until the start of the third transfer of monetary authority to the ESCB, an extremely complex and hazardous task which will only succeed if a common Community policy emerges before such a step is taken. An essential requirement for this is to ensure that the internal market continues to operate properly by means of effective cooperation, not just in monetary terms but also as regards 'policy mixes', i.e. an appropriate combination of policies. Accordingly, extending the EMS band to 15% has radically changed ways of formulating monetary policy and 'preventing exchange market operators from being able to continue gambling without risk at the expense of the monetary authorities'. But the president of the EMI warned that: 'If there is no exchange rate stability, it will not be possible to achieve the principal objective of the internal market, which is to secure productivity gains resulting from a better allocation of European resources.'

It has now been decided that the EMI will be based in Frankfurt, thus resolving the contradiction of an official Community body having its seat in Switzerland, outside Community territory. Their proximity to the Bundesbank is not just of symbolic value and will require parallel efforts to achieve a balanced and pragmatic economic decision-making system.

Thus we are now at the threshold of the decisive stage during which the demanding task must be accomplished of making the EURO the single currency. Convincing the people of the Community of the advantages thereof is one of the major challenges facing us as we enter the new millennium. It will require careful handling, and a curious example of role-reversal: whilst economists have taken to writing political pamphlets, our elected representatives must make careful co-ordination of their budgetary, fiscal and economic decisions their main task. Despite what the Treaty may say on this matter, it is difficult to imagine that a parliamentary debate at the time of moving to a single currency is to be held only in the two countries which have clearly expressed such an intention (Denmark and the United Kingdom). The German Constitutional Court has also expressed the necessity of a such kind of approval in a country in which it and the Bundesbank represent ideals which in Germany are perceived as being outside day-to-day politics[7]. According to the Ratification Act on the Maastricht Treaty, the vote of the Federal Chancellor in the European Council is subject to the approval of both chambers of the German Parliament (Bundestag and Bundesrat).

Legitimizing the EURO will have to be an official act, willed by everyone both individually and collectively. Otherwise, it will fail.

7 Sailing Towards Convergence

BOOK OF PROPHECIES
Two eclipses one after the other. The worst is the conjunction of Mars and Saturn. It always brings great storms and rought seas. We have gone 700 leagues since the Blessed Isles. We have only 50 or 70 to go before we reach the Archipelago of the Eleven Thousand Virgins which the Pilot marked on this deathbed map. I think it must be the archipelago that surrounds Cipango, as described by all the cosmographers and travellers from Pliny to Toscanelli and Pope Aeneas Silvius to Marco Polo. Please God that the route of the Florentine and that of the pilot will lead me to the same destination.
Please God that it may consist of pearl-bearing reefs, or better still, whole headlands of natural gold. The mutiny would evaporate on the instant, though the ensuing struggle to bite off pieces of those gold-bearing rocks would be a fierce one.

Augusto Roa Bastos
Vigilia del Almirante

Stages Towards Convergence

Now that the final objective of a single currency has been defined, it is worth studying the process leading up to it: convergence and its various stages.

This process follows the dictates of common sense: 'You don't put the cart before the horse'. This approach is based on the need for the various economies to come together gradually in a manner which can be sustained through lower inflation and a reduction in the budget deficit and overall debt, as well as lower interest rates, so that economic and monetary union will come about as the logical conclusion. The alternative would have been the creation of the EURO in one stage by means of radical monetary reform.

In order to achieve convergence and attain the objectives of EMU, 'the activities of the Member States and the Community shall include, as provided in this Treaty and in accordance with the timetable set out therein, the adoption of an economic policy which is based on the close coordination of Member States' economic policies on the internal market and on the definition of common objectives . . . these activities shall include the irrevocable fixing of exchange rates leading to the introduction of a single currency, the ECU, and the definition and conduct of a single monetary policy and exchange-rate policy the primary objective of which shall be to maintain price stability and, without prejudice to this objective, to support the general economic policies in the Community', which 'shall entail compliance with the following guiding principles: stable prices, sound public finances and monetary conditions and a sustainable balance of payments'. These criteria are in themselves unobjectionable: they are the principles dictated by any judiciously cautious approach. Nevertheless, there is a considerable difference between agreeing that these criteria are sound and successfully putting them into practice. Five convergence criteria have been defined, termed nominal criteria (nominal in economic jargon being used to refer to circumstances as they exist in the real world, while real refers to circumstances as they exist in the minds of economists)[1]. They are:

1 respect for the narrow bands of the EMS (±2.25%) for two years;
2 inflation rate that does not exceed by more than 1.5% the average rate of the three states with the lowest rate for one year;
3 budget deficit less than 3% of GDP;
4 public debt less than 60% of GDP;
5 long-term interest rate not exceeding by more than 2% that of the three countries with the lowest inflation for one year.

It appears from these criteria that the sole objective of EMU is monetary stability and that no specific binding provisions have been laid down to implement the principles enshrined in Article 2, chief among which are harmonious and balanced

Table 7.1   The timetable for EMU

01.01.93 • Completion of the internal market
         • Entry into force of the Maastricht Treaty
         • Freezing of the composition of the ECU

01.01.94 • Creation of the European Monetary Institute (EMI)

31.12.96 • Decision of the European Council
         – Following a report by the EMI
         – Following a report by the Commission

         If a majority of states fulfil the convergence criteria, transition to a single currency

         If not,

01.07.98 • Decision of the European Council
         – Following a report by the EMI
         – Following a report by the Commission on which members fulfil the convergance criteria (no majority required)

01.01.99 • Transition to a single currency by those states which fulfil the convergence criteria

---

development, sustainable and non-inflationary growth which respects the environment and a high level of employment and of social protection. The preponderance of monetary experts has doubtless influenced the institutional and political structure. Nevertheless, actual circumstances have made growth and employment fundamental priorities, and these have taken centre stage.

What is Convergence?

It is important to remember that the purpose of the convergence process is to bring about a single currency. According to the dictionary, 'to converge' means 'to tend towards a single point', which in this case lies between 31 December 1996 and 1 January 1999. Until then, each step will be assessed and the pace will be set by all fifteen partners.

The word 'convergence' has acquired new shades of meaning in Community Eurosperanto; it featured in the Treaty of Rome, which laid down that conjunctural policies, balance of payments and economic policies are matters of common interest, and acquired increased significance in the texts establishing the EMS and the Single Act, culminating in its current usage, which is both richer and more ambiguous. It can be understood both as the harmonization of policy and an approximation of economic situations. The extent of the demands which this entails varies from one interpretation to the other, since the former involves finding a common rhythm while the latter involves coinciding as regards the final outcome. This distinction can be compared to that drawn in law between an obligation as regards the means and and obligation as regards the results. The strictest interpretation is that upheld by the Germans and Dutch, while those encountering greater difficulties in passing the convergence tests are more flexible.

Convergence can also be understood as a process of bringing together the 'stragglers' and those 'at the top of the class', through a more intense effort or by tending towards a common meeting point, which would be the average. This is the position upheld by France with its systematic criticism of asymmetrical effort.

Once again, reality has provided more dialectic than plans, and in 1993 the roles of France and Germany were reversed. Even measured against the most demanding criteria, France obtained better results than Germany. In themselves, competition and emulation with a view to progress are no bad thing.

The famous convergence criteria are not written in stone, nor are they a yoke imposed from Brussels; they are principles of sound management which should be followed in any case. Their application nevertheless requires profound changes in company and social behaviour, for example in relation to inflation, since many industrial and service sectors will be forced to stop rounding up their results by means of a price hike. Social attitudes to inflation may change: the Germans see it in negative terms, while the French have traditionally had higher inflation despite strong interventionist policies: social behaviour in relation to inflation began to change when price controls were removed. Cheaper money in Spain is a desirable objective for everybody, particularly industrialists and consumers, but it will require a dramatic process of rationalization and improvement in our financial system. As regards the deficit and debt, the problem is the creation of a single currency: are we prepared to agree to help pay off the current debt of Italy or Belgium as our contribution to the Community patrimony?

Some people also hold the view, though without much basis in theory, that the key emphasis placed on inflation is a reflection of conservative principles. The argument is based on the importance of real variables in relation to nominal variables, for example in setting unemployment against inflation: it is held that it is more important to deal with unemployment than to combat inflation, or that it is preferable to accept a certain degree of inflation if this makes it possible to achieve greater growth.

While recognizing that the two subjects are very different, this is as if, in medicine, it were claimed that a slight fever could stimulate or improve the state of a sick patient. Inflation has effects equivalent to those of prolonged fever, leading to a perversion of values and favouring those with variable incomes over those with fixed incomes (wage earners and pensioners) who do not recover the value lost until later and suffer from fiscal drag when income tax rates rise without any improvement in purchasing power. Consequently this represents a negative mechanism of income distribution which leads to social disintegration. Moreover, the country becomes relatively more expensive, reducing its ability to compete on the world market.

A study of the industrialized world shows that countries with high inflation have more unemployment and lower per capita income than countries with low inflation[2].

This law also applies in the European Union: the most developed countries with the most regular growth and best income distribution are those with the lowest inflation over long periods, i.e. Germany, the Netherlands and Denmark – countries with an established welfare state – while the more lax countries experience the greatest difficulties. This is one of the basic lessons to be drawn from the financial hurricanes which hit Spain, Portugal and above all Great Britain and Italy in 1992–93, even though it was not the sole cause.

To Sail or to Float

Given that nautical imagery is often used to describe the state
and process of convergence – 'anchoring' a currency to a fixed
point, with 'flotation' as an alternative – it is worth recalling
the old image used by C. Tugenhadt, comparing the Community to a convoy of galleons[3]. Indeed, convergence is not a
simple process of approaching the destination via successive
stages of a level and obstacle-free route. It can be seen as a
journey to a destination which is desired but has not been
explored or surveyed in advance. The harmonious navigation
of the second half of the 1980s made it seem that it was mainly
a question of maintaining the course. Paradoxically, since the
Treaty was signed we have entered a stormy patch of tempes-
tuous seas, with inadequate navigational charts.

The hurricane of historical events by which we are being
battered, made more acute by the difficult situation arising
from economic recession, has made it tempting to wonder
whether it is worth continuing together or whether it would be
better to abandon the attempt to construct the European Union
and to manage on our own, leaving its objectives for better times
and, in the most extreme cases, criticizing them as idealistic.

This is the option which lies at the root of the dialectic
confrontation between convergence as a goal to be steered
towards and the alternative of flotation, which leads to the
formation of diverging policies. Staying with the nautical terminology and bearing in mind that to converge means to tend
towards a single point, we need to set a course in order to
reach the chosen destination. The safe harbour is the European Union – political, economic and monetary union –, which
is not merely an objective contained in the programme of a
party or government but a decision which has been ratified by
all the Community countries. Even though it is legitimate to
contest this final destination on a political level, this would
first entail denouncing the Treaty. Otherwise, we would have
to ask how convergence could be achieved in a better and less
costly way, i.e. how we can come together and ensure that we
move on at the same pace. To continue with the maritime
image, we must decide whether we want to weather the storm
on our own or form part of a convoy which offers us safety,
help and guidance in our journey. What we cannot do is fix a
destination and then sail in the opposite direction or lie to.

At the moment we are sailing through heavy seas. We are living in a context of free movement of capital and a world market which is growing constantly thanks to the development of information networks, with transactions amounting to $1 trillion taking place every day, of which only around 5% corresponds to actual trade in goods and services. The market tends to adjust and rationalize in the medium term, which does not mean that it is not on occasion foolish or hysterical in the short term. It is therefore surprising that some people should demand that we return to isolation or float . . . (with what kind of a life-jacket?). Even taking into account the painful problem of unemployment, it must be open to question whether we could make better progress by struggling on alone in a difficult overall world situation. The experience of those Community countries which have been forced, much to their regret, to drift alone on the high seas is not very promising.

In the European framework, moreover, we are living in a highly integrated economic area, which raises the question of what margins are available. The solution of leaving the system through 'competitive devaluation' means denying the essence of the internal market and coordination of economic and monetary policy, since it generates a chain reaction of disintegration, with the partners being forced to pick up the bill. In contrast to this option, it might be recalled that economic and monetary union is based on 'cooperative disinflation'.

The difficulties largely stem from the degree of rigidity built into the exchange-rate system at a time when the various national economies were showing very different results in terms of fundamental data (inflation, balance of payments, growth). We must start from the assumption that no country has devalued its currency on a whim of its own. Even those countries which have been forced to leave the EMS have experienced their departure as a humiliation linked to a feeling of being left on the sidelines.

The Bermuda Triangle

Experience shows that progress towards EMU is more a journey into the Bermuda Triangle than a pleasure trip. This situation has been aptly described by the Italian economist Tomasso

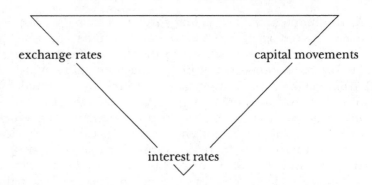

Figure 7.1 Padoa-Schioppa's EMS triangle

Padoa-Schioppa[4], who has compared it with the sacred and infernal figure of the triangle, the sides being the three basic requirements of the EMS, i.e. fixed exchange rates, freedom of movement of capital and interest rate harmonization:

The problem is how to make them compatible. If complete freedom of movement of capital is maintained and attempts are made to establish fixed exchange rates, interest rates are the only remaining lever with which the process can be regulated, leading to a excessive increase in the price of money. This is what happened with the EMS in the period from 1987 to 1991, when it attracted capital to the EEC where, as the IMF economist Morris Goldstein has pointed out, it found unparalleled stability and unreasonably high returns. Business confidence in the convergence plans changed in response to trends in the fundamentals and the upsets which occurred in connection with the ratification of the Treaty.

The decision taken by ECOFIN in the summer of 1993 to extend the flotation bands to 15% has enabled the convoy to continue its progress for the moment. Significantly, there have been no major changes, and no more participants have been separated in the storm. Short-term interest rates are highly important for currency speculators, while investment funding is determined by long-term rates.

In fact, as Padoa-Schioppa rightly remarks, trade freedom, full freedom of capital movement, fixed exchange trade and autonomy of national monetary policy constitute in the long run an 'unconciliable quartet'[5]. The way to conciliate them would be to follow the logic of complete financial integration and unrestricted mobility of capital to its conclusion –, a common world currency. It is not necessary to stress that this is not politically feasible.

One of the main lessons to be drawn from the experience of these last years is that, as Delors has rightly pointed out, the free movement of capital requires traffic regulations and we may need to consider imposing such rules, which Tobin and Dornbusch among others have shown to be technically feasible, even though they might pose political difficulties. It was in Germany that attempts to tax returns on capital at Community levels failed when the government retreated over a withholding tax. Dr Nölling, a former member of the Bundesbank Council, rightly observes that the complete mobility of capital is very far from being an indisputable virtue and concludes that 'it is no exaggeration to speak of an abdication of democracies vis-à-vis the anonymous, uncontrolled forces of the market. As Thomas Jefferson said, banks may be more powerful than armies in action[6]'.

Without wishing to reduce short-term currency speculation or the role played by financial institutions, investment and pension funds – which, according to Peter F. Drucker, already represent the greatest concentration of capital and will do so more and more in the future[7] – to shady manoeuvres, a tax on capital returns within the Community framework should be seriously considered, particularly with regard to windfall profits resulting from speculation which, in the case of the Spanish banks, accounted for half of all profits in the first half of 1993.

In any case, the policy option made in the TEU follows the theory of 'parallelism' between the monetary and economic integration process. In fact, it is a middle-of-the-way thesis between the two radical ones that oppose economists: from one side, the essentially German *Krönungstheorie*, which considers the monetary union as the culmination of a long period of perfect convergence reached with policies decided at national level; from the other, the monetarist one, which gives absolute priority to monetary integration, regardless of convergence conditions. The option reflected in the Treaty considers that monetary and economic integration must run parallel, as a process more than a perfect syntonic state.

The Culture of Stability

The defining features of the Community monetary system essentially follow the German approach: price stability to be guaranteed as an absolute priority, independence of the European Central Bank and establishment of a multilateral surveillance system. These are the conditions for setting up EMU which have been accepted in the Treaty, in conjunction with progress on a stage-by-stage basis in accordance with the essentially Germanic theory of culmination, the *Krönungstheorie*.

Given the prominent European role which the Bundesbank has acquired *de facto*, it is worth defining its role in relation to the objectives listed above. Firstly, it is a German and not a European institution whose absolute priority as established by law is to maintain price stability, since the only stable money is good money. As the German economist M. Matthes has pointed out, 'the FRG's dominant role in the EMS stems less from its economic size than from the importance which it attaches to price stability'[8]. Memories of the hyper-inflation of the 1920s, of postage stamps costing thousands of millions of marks and wheelbarrows full of notes just to buy bread, remained engraved on Germany's collective counsciousness. Defending currency stability is therefore laid down as the Bundesbank's essential and primary objective in the Law on its organization of 1957, complemented by the provisions of the 1969 Basic Law on stability and growth, which further entrusts the Federal Bank with the tasks of contributing to the maintenance of exchange-rate stability, growth and employment as complementary objectives.

The fundamental pillars of the culture of stability are thus as follows: at monetary level, the independence of the Central Bank vis-à-vis the executive power at the same time as it is deeply embedded in the country's federative structure; at political level, decentralization and the distribution of fiscal and budgetary powers between the Federation (*Bund*), the *Länder* (federal states) and municipalities, and in industrial relations, the *Partnerschaft* system of negotiation between employers' organizations and trade unions and co-partnership in large undertakings. Ironically enough, these three features were favoured by the Allies after the war in order to avoid the reconstruction of a strongly centralized Germany.

The option followed in the Treaty basically involves adopting selected key elements of this culture of stability, mainly in the monetary field. Is this a result of imposition or imperialism on the part of a unified Germany? The question is relevant, given that a significant number of intellectuals, ranging from free-market conservatives to the 'caviar Left', have turned the study of Germany's state of mind and possible unpredictability in relation to Europe into an inexhaustible source of speculation. The answer may be too simple: it is a complete and coherent system which considers the management of monetary policy to be a fundamental political issue. The German notion is quite different from the monetarist theory of Friedmann as followed by Thatcher and Reagan.

There is a marked difference between this notion and that of the Bank of England, which starts from the premise that currency is a good which operates in a self-regulating market, with the central bank being assigned the function of injecting into the economy the amount of money which it requires. In fact, banks also create money by granting loans, with the result that only the price is left to the central bank. In contrast, the Germanic notion of monetary policy is based on the view that the market is a forum for the decisions of free agents dealing with something which is more than a good. There is something Faustian in this concept. The Bundesbank treats the market as an adversary and therefore likes to act in an unpredictable manner. The money supply needs to be carefully regulated by an institution which is a democratic emanation of the community and is not subject to short-term ups and downs and political temptations or, worse, to financial innovations, which are highly unpopular in Germany. This is a characteristic illustration of the profound difference between Californian and Rhine-Main capitalism which has been so effectively defined by Michel Albert[9].

The culture of stability does not rest solely on the greater or lesser success or skill of the government in office but on the three pillars listed above. It embodies a balance encompassing various agents and spheres which act as counterweights and form the backbone of civil society. This culture is the fruit not so much of any infallible Teutonic rationality as of lessons drawn from bitter experience of crisis and suicidal adventures. Paradoxically, the main problem was first that, as a consequence of German unification, internal imbalances have arisen which are difficult to influence.

Moreover, the dominant role of the Bundesbank while the Union's monetary institutions are not yet shaped creates a growing *de facto* dependence on its role as the central bank of the Union, and that in a situation in which there is no counter-weighting political power as such.

The best way of outlining the issue is to ask whether the crowning theory is appropriate, regardless of whether or not it is seen as being essentially German. The most convincing aswer is doubtless that given by Philippe Jurgensen, the French expert and member of the Delors committe which drew up the report on EMU: 'The best law is always that of the most sensible'[10]. In other words: the German model is accepted because it is the model desired by the remaining countries.

Is a Single Currency Inevitable?

In principle, a single currency appears to be the natural complement or culmination of the single market. Nevertheless, this is not an economic dogma, nor is it inevitable. The most radical standpoint is that taken as long ago as the 1948 Congress of Europe by the Nobel-Prize-winning economist Maurice Allais, who postulated that politics took priority over economics and time would be lost by disregarding this fact. He has never wavered from this standpoint, taking a highly critical view of Community policies.

The neo-liberal economists of the Chicago School have re-iterated their opposition to the economic necessity of a single currency. One of the most detailed criticisms was made by Martin Feldstein, the former chairman of President Reagan's Council of Economic Advisers, in his article 'The case against EMU'[11] in which he maintains that monetary union is not necessary in order to enjoy the advantages of a free-trade zone and concludes: 'I can understand, however, that there are those who are willing to accept these adverse economic effects in order to achieve a federalist political union that they favour for other non-economic reasons. What I cannot understand are those who advocate monetary union but reject any movement towards a federalist political structure for Europe. That is a formula for economic costs without any of the supposed political benefits.'

Whether or not one shares Feldstein's views, his analysis is correct in highlighting the links between the political and economic dimension. This was also rightly stressed in the article replying to his criticism written by a group of economists favourable to EMU, who stated that 'there are a few things which monetary policy can do which cannot also be achieved through budgetary policy; the fundamental difference between them being that one is voted on and the other is not. EMU would impose an additional restraint on governments, but its substance is in fact democratic in nature'[12]. The single currency is a crucial element of a federal-style European Union, as is illustrated by the structure of the EMI, the forerunner of the future Central Bank.

These links between economics and politics have been demonstrated by the difficulties experienced by the Community in the last years. After a phase of cruising along, it appears that events have conspired to test not only the validity of what had been agreed upon but also its durability in the most severe crisis since the last war.

Even though ups and downs are a normal feature of society's development and a key element of what Schumpeter defined as the creative destruction of capitalism, not only the mechanisms for coordination but also our resolve have been put to the test. In order to arrive at a single currency, we have to find a common pace; not only as regards currency management but also in economic policy. It must also be borne in mind that the Community as such does not exist in a glass case and must face frequent 'competitive devaluations', both of the dollar and the yen.

The independence of the monetary authority has become a commitment which is forcing modifications to be made to the structure of central banks in the Member States and their relations with the executive power. Clearly, the proposal is not purely technical in nature but involves sweeping changes in the practice of government management and, above all, in the budget management of the state and other public authorities. This is aptly demonstrated by the fact that, in order to progress to the second stage, they have had to forego the possibility of automatic appeals to the Central Bank or privileged access to financial institutions.

Nevertheless, independence should be seen as decision-making autonomy within the body's own sphere of competence which, in the case of the EMI, encompasses coordination and cooperation between the central banks, monitoring the EMS, managing the EURO and promoting its use. In the third stage, the ESCB is to carry out the functions of defining and implementing the Community's monetary policy and managing the official reserves and payment system. In parallel, the governments will be obliged to coordinate their budget policy as closely as possible and endeavour to reduce any negative effects to the minimum.

The plan poses a significant problem of democratic control, since it requires a body which can provide a counterweight to the governing monetary authority in drawing up economic policy. More specifically, two decisions give particular cause for concern: the Council is to decide on economic policy by a qualified majority, while the European Parliament is to be informed only after the decision has been adopted; and recommendations addressed to the member states are not to be made public, not even to the parliament of the state concerned. The topics covered include budget guidelines, inter-state financial assistance, sanctions imposed on a state which fails to comply, decisions on reducing excessive deficits, measures for states experiencing difficulties as regards their balance of payments, derogation made for one Member State regarding the introduction of the EURO as a single currency, and assessment of convergence problems. The democratic deficit emerges once again as the recurring theme.

Curiously, this criticism, contained in the Martin report by which the European Parliament approved the Treaty on European Union in April 1992, largely tallies with the criticism made from a variety of widely differing points of view, not only traditional federalist circles but also the Bundesbank, which can surely not be suspected of harbouring revolutionary tendencies and which has stressed the need for the Union to make parallel progress on both fronts, the economic and the political. The prospect of so much power being accumulated without any counterweight appears to have caused some dizziness.

Dr Otmar Issing[13], an influential member of the Bundesbank's Council and considered a monetary hawk, bases his criticism on the fact that the sanctions envisaged for governments who fail to comply with budget discipline are inadequate, arguing that, with a single currency, public debts will be 'communitarized', i.e. they will be distributed among all members without any need for a specific commitment making them jointly responsible.

In the absence of real convergence, the system risks punishing the thrifty and rewarding the extravagant, even though there are mechanisms designed to cushion the additional efforts which some countries will have to make in order to align themselves with the average.

From the internal point of view, the monetary crisis has demonstrated the inevitability of monetary realignment in order to respond to external shocks or divergences. In fact, policy was being conducted in the first stage as if we had already entered the third stage, with parity considered fixed due to obstinacy or reasons of prestige. In a regatta, it is important to know how to make the best possible use of the prevailing wind rather than being forced to change course. The problem is that, when the third stage begins, parity will be fixed and devaluation will no longer be possible. A country experiencing economic problems due to higher inflation or lower competitiveness will have to adjust by means of a relative cut in wages and living standards, particularly if there is also a lack of flexibility and geographical mobility. Currency alone cannot be seen as a mechanism for levelling out income and wages.

If divergences are to be narrowed, the only real solution is to increase transfers from the richest countries and areas to the poorest. Significantly, during the negotiations on the Cohesion Fund and Structural Funds, all the member states in the Council and all Members of the European Parliament showed a clear interest in receiving some contribution. The traditional north-south and centre-periphery pattern is being replaced by a more complicated situation, with beneficiary regions emerging in the Netherlands (Frisia), Belgium (Hainaut), France and the whole of Eastern Germany. Nevertheless, the Community stopped short of taking the final federative step and accepting the Delors proposal for an increased budget which would have represented 1.37% of Community GDP. The agonizing agreement reached at the Edinburgh Council fixed a ceiling of 1.27% for 1997. It is curious that the reasoning of the banker Issing on this point coincides with that of President Delors: if we want a united and social Europe, we need a federal Europe.

Of course, currency will be managed on an increasingly federal basis and a high degree of skill will be required to sail through heavy seas with few navigational charts or known routes. This is why it is so important to concentrate our efforts on making the objective visible and attractive. At the moment, public opinion perceives it as obscure and remote. The man in the street is not familiar with the use of the EURO, has never carried it in his wallet and has never seen it cross the counter. He has not even used it in the form of traveller's cheques. Meanwhile, all the upsets and bad news are presented as necessary sacrifices in order to achieve something whose final shape is unknown.

The great financial storm of 1992–93 demonstrated clearly that history is not at an end, nor is it written in advance. Ratification of the Treaty was delayed by a further ten months, in circumstances which differed from those envisaged and beset by new problems. The best criterion to follow is perhaps that of President Lamfalussy, who considers it essential to 'return to stability without becoming prisoners of a system which it would be difficult to maintain'[14]. This is good advice for a journey which will last for at least a further two parliamentary terms, with all the consequences this entails in a democracy. Eight years is an extremely long period of gestation. Even though the aim is shared by the main political families, we are seeing the emergence of internal tensions (growing unemployment, cuts in the welfare state), social threats (radicalization and polarization, outbreaks of racism and xenophobia, marginalization and exclusion), and growing demands for membership (in spite of everything) from a substantial part of the Continent, reinforced by the risk of being flooded by economic migrants, circumstances which are adding to the already complicated constituent process now underway.

In sailing towards convergence, the helmsmen therefore need much skill, nerves of steel and broad agreement if they are to reach a safe harbour. Finally, a clear political will is also needed, which should be shared by the public. Economists may contribute their knowledge and technical judgement, but in the debate on economic and monetary union they ultimately put their signatures to collective manifestos in which they all emphasize the political nature of the option. The North American economist Lester Thurow, who sees Europe as a superpower of the 21st century, advocates resolute integration (in line with the advice given to Macbeth: 'If it were done when 'tis done, 'twere well it were done quickly'), making use of the argument *a sensu contrario* that there will be a European currency in the year 2000 in any case, and if it is not the ECU, then French, Danish and Italian undertakings will be obliged to carry out their transactions in marks. According to Thurow, a decision must be taken; political integration will follow economic integration, but the latter inevitably entails the former[15].

8 Do Employment and Welfare Have a Future?

> The nineteenth century is remembered as the century of Great Britain. It was the dominant economic power. The twentieth century will be remembered as the century of the United States. It was, and is, the dominant economic power. In terms of the calendar, the twenty-first century has not yet quite begun, but a future economic historian looking backward will date the end of the twentieth century slightly early. Just as the fall of the Berlin Wall in November of 1989 marked the end of the old contest between capitalism and communism, so the integration of the European Common Market, on Jan. 1, 1993 will mark the beginning of a new economic contest in a new century at the start of the third millennium.
>
> Lester Thurow
> *Head to Head*

So far we have concentrated our attention mainly on the institutional aspects of the drafting and application of the TEU. Nevertheless, the most original aspect of the European enterprise is its dimension of 'social revolution'. The decisive steps taken by the Community were the *de facto* dismantling of borders and customs and tariff barriers and also the psychological and cultural barriers which the peoples of western Europe had built up over the centuries. The method used consisted not in removing boundaries from maps but rather in eliminating their effects, making the four fundamental freedoms a reality: freedom of establishment and movement for citizens and the freedom of movement of goods, services and capital. This decisively broadened the field of action of employers and workers, both individuals and businesses, thereby setting in motion a vast process of reallocation of resources and tasks both geographically and sectorally.

The deadline of 1 January 1993 for the completion of the internal market mobilized Community business during the second half of the 1980s. It was a goal which had been set in the Treaty of Rome, but repeatedly postponed.

However, we have not reached our final destination. It has opened up a new phase of profound changes in which the process of socio-economic integration will continue by means of both 'real' integration, i.e. by means of the actions and adaptation of individuals, and 'official' integration, i.e. in accordance with the formulation of active policies, such as agricultural and social policy or funding from the social, structural or cohesion funds.

In any event, it is a phase of modernization with both positive and negative aspects. On the one hand there is the progressive internationalization of socio-economic life, with a greater innovative force, which requires greater flexibility and mobility, as well as more division of labour inside and outside the Community, generating a greater demand for education and training whilst offering new opportunities. On the other hand, pressure from the market, the constant increase in productivity and the need for growth are destroying jobs as a result of rationalization and the collapse of whole industrial sectors, the closure of non-competitive plants, the decline of certain regions and the rise of others, as well as growing pressure on the social security system – all this against a background of an ageing European population.

If we also take into account the political upheavals in Europe and the crisis in the welfare state, the sudden change of scenario is easier to explain. The entry of Austria, Sweden and Finland has led to the creation and consolidation of the leading trading power in the world, with 380 million Europeans enjoying democracy, peace and prosperity. Almost all the countries of Central and Eastern Europe are knocking on the door, asking for admission. Paradoxically, the feeling of prosperity cannot be said to have increased similarly. Now that the objective has been achieved, although not fully, the prevailing feeling is one of uncertainty and anxiety rather than joy or satisfaction. Despite the promises of new horizons there is clearly a risk that the European Union will be identified with the end of prosperity and stable employment.

In fact, the entry into force of the Treaty did coincide with the deepest crisis since the war. The evolution of capitalism and the economy is said, with good reason, to be cyclical. What has happened, however, is a sudden pause following a period of brilliant growth in the second half of the 1980s, which makes the situation stand out in striking contrast. After a phase of self-perpetuating development which saw a continuous strengthening of the Community, we are living now in a phase of bewilderment and reassessment, not only in economic but also in political and social terms, and it must be remembered that economics is at least 50% psychology. From 'Euro-optimism' we have reached a phase of 'Euro-hope', tinged with 'Euro-pessimism'.

A symptom of this is what has happened to the theory that the Community occupies the best position in the three-cornered competition between the United States, Japan and the Community. This theory was not only the result of Commission propaganda, but was backed by convincing arguments offered by people as different from one another as Michel Albert, who in his book 'Capitalism versus Capitalism', advocates the West German model with its mixture of efficiency and equity, or Lester Thurow, who claims in 'Head to Head' that Europe is in the best position. These two books are essential reading, as is the interesting essay 'Post-Capitalist Society' by the Austro-American author Peter F. Drucker, in order to see the European Union in context and the challenges it faces[1].

Since 1992 these brilliant prophecies seem to have faded away. Instead of progress and creative dynamism, all that is left are difficulties and problems. In the final analysis, is the crisis the result of maturing or of stagnation? Europe seems all the more vulnerable because it has not been consolidated: it progresses much better and is strengthened in periods of growth, but seems to be in agony in periods of recession, when it is on the defensive. The renowned journalist Jean Boissonat expressed this idea clearly when he said that 'the European construction will convince the European peoples only if they can measure its effects. In politics words are becoming increasingly less convincing. Only actions can change minds, and unfortunately at the moment the Community is fighting the crisis by avoiding additional disasters – which cannot be seen – rather than launching successful counter-offensives'.

On the other hand, the radiant dawns which used to mobilize our societies (for example, 1992 as a symbol of the internal market) are, when they arrive, the end of a phase, and instead of generating stability and gratitude they have negative effects. For example, concern is now centred on passport controls or on restrictions on freedom of movement, and no comparisons are made with the time when a passport was a treasured possession and a visa was a triumph.

Crises are important and decisive moments of change, in both living creatures and societies. In the current debate on the crisis and the response to it there are three separated interlinked issues:

1 The continuing dilemma of the choice between a free trade area and a common economic and social area.
2 What policies need to be formulated to overcome the present economic crisis and, above all, to generate jobs. This involves reconsidering the future of the welfare state and the culture of stability.
3 The relations between the Community and the rest of the world in a context of economic and commercial universalization, in which regulated regional trade organizations are being extended in the framework of the new World Trade Organization.

The quest for ways out must be approached with two fundamental ideas in mind: the system is alive and it is cyclical, which means that it experiences periodic crises: there are fat years and thin years. Furthermore, the pace of change and internationalization is constantly speeding up, which increases its destabilizing effects on society, since the process of change does not benefit all social strata and regions equally. This is not even perceived realistically. For example, in the French referendum on the TEU in September 1992 most of the votes against came from the categories and regions which benefit most from the Community (farmers and people in the countryside) whilst most of the votes in favour came from city-dwellers and professional people. How to manage society's capacity for adaptation and flexibility whilst maintaining its cohesion in a process of such rapid change will be the fundamental test of political skill. There is a clear risk of a world with global economics and tribal politics.

Duty-Free Versus a Common Area

The first subject of an ongoing debate originates in a view of the Community as an alliance of states sharing a free trade area, a fundamentally Thatcherite conception of Europe. A set of beliefs based on a free market, deregulation and monetarism, seen as universal values, was therefore applied to it. These beliefs dominated the scene in the second half of the 1980s and became the panacea advocated by conventional wisdom and prescribed in equal doses to former Communist 'apparatchiks' or African leaders who hardly have anything to deregulate.

The Community was never designed to be a mere free trade area. On the basis of the principles stated in the Treaty of Rome, policies such as the regional and social policies were drawn up, and the relevant funds (the ERDF and the ESF) were created. When President Mitterrand proposed a 'social Europe' in 1982, he found his best ally in the Danish Government, a centre-right coalition at the time, which proposed the introduction of health protection for workers at the workplace and environmental protection in the Single Act in 1985. The underlying reason for this was the fact that the 'welfare state' is a deeply rooted concept in the Nordic countries, mainly on the basis of the Danish and Swedish experiences, although the theories originated in the ideas of Lord Beveridge after the Second World War. The Danes have had and still have many reservations and criticisms about the state of progress of European construction (as regards citizenship, defence and currency), but in the social sphere their fear has always been the opposite: that of unfair competition through social dumping.

On this basis the Social Charter was drawn up and adopted by eleven countries in the Strasbourg European Council, with the sole opposition of the British Conservative government. The Charter became Community law in the Maastricht Treaty. The issue is important because the 'social dimension' concerns personal and collective economic and social rights enshrined in practically all the constitutions of the member states of the Community, to which it gives a new dimension, connected with the recognition of Community citizenship. It is not only a question of whether labour is more or less expensive, or whether wages are rising excessively, but rather of principles which are part of the foundations of European civilization and hallowed rights not only for industrial workers belonging to trade unions but also for young people, women and retired people, etc. The existence of the Charter does not mean that social security and welfare policies have been

included in the Treaty as objectives, which is what creates the
obligation to devise a common policy. Nevertheless, the debate on the social dimension (and, by extension, on the future
of the welfare state) originated in this context for three reasons: the first was ideological, because of the revival of neo-
conservative thinking; the second, because of the problems of
survival and adaptation encountered by the welfare state in
trying to overcome the crisis and the third because of the need
to adapt to the radical changes in the production system and
society.

Since the beginning of the Thatcherite age at the end of the
1970s, the British Conservative government has based its policy
on dismantling the welfare state and destroying the power of
the unions. Its action has been more constant and effective in
the second of these fields than in the first, although it has
maintained an enormously aggressive rhetoric of total opposition to any type of social measure in the Community, which
resulted in Great Britain's exclusion from social policy in the
TEU. In particular, there is dogged resistance to the adoption
of directives such as the one on maternity leave (in which the
Council trebled the number of articles proposed by the Commission) and Britain's self-exclusion from the directive on night
work for young people.

Even after the ratification of the Maastricht Treaty, the debate
continues, mainly because the Conservatives will not give in,
seeing their traditional ideas as the only reasonable and possible solution to the exclusion of all others, with the conviction
typical of conservatives (described by Lauren Bacall when she
speaks of the attitude of American Republicans who attacked
Humphrey Bogart and other liberal actors at the time of the
McCarthy witch-hunts, as if they were the only thing between
God and chaos[2]).

The argument is therefore not restricted to a simple choice,
but rather, if it is accepted, what it was intended to prove is
demonstrated, thereby solving the dilemma. Obviously the
contrary cannot possibly be right. The clearest example of this
is the article published on the eve of the Conservative Party
conference by the British Prime Minister (*The Economist*, 25
September 1993). Under the biblical headline 'Raise your eyes,
there is a land beyond' John Major says that he believes the time
has come to 'put away the old slogans, dreams and prejudices'

and he hopes that his fellow heads of government 'will resist the temptation to recite the mantra of full economic and monetary union as if nothing had changed. If they do recite it, it will have all the quaintness of a rain dance and about the same potency.'

In view of this, it is useful to remember that markets are not the result of a spontaneous or miraculous process. History shows that the market does not exist in nature – the noble savage did not enjoy its advantages – but rather its creation is an essential element in the formation of the nation state. Sometimes their histories even coincide, as in the case of the United States, Germany or Italy (with resulting problems in the latter that still exist today). It is formed and consolidated via a monopoly of power and finance held by the political authorities, with the systematic creation of transport and communications networks and of external barriers. Once power as such has been consolidated, in the case of both states and their colonial empires (which were designed to be a captive market) the tendency from the end of the 18th century was to advocate free trade if one was in a dominant position. Two notable exceptions to this rules are Germany and Japan, which after their respective defeats in the Second World War opted for freedom of trade as a fundamental principle, with an enormous degree of discipline and judicious organization of their internal markets. As far as the Community is concerned, the task of the 1980s basically consisted in creating and organizing the common and internal market by defining and harmonising the rules of the game. The mainstays of this economic sphere are the 300 directives which led to the Single Act.

This demonstrates the limits of belief in the infallibility of the free market theory seen as a sort of 'machine for producing perpetual motion in economic growth', as it was called by John Gray, a former theorist and proponent of Thatcherism and now one of its critics. To raise an economic instrument for allocating resources to the level of an absolute principle for the organization of society is a grave mistake and reduces human beings to one-dimensional phenomena, ignoring their identity as citizens and their two fundamental spheres of action, the private and the public. It reduces human society to the level of a beehive or a lunatic asylum.

The Social Dimension and the Welfare State

The second dispute about the social dimension and the welfare state arises from its increasing cost, combined with a degree of stagnation and its lack of adaptability in the current context of profound change.

In this sense the formula of the welfare state cannot be considered as the exclusive achievement of the reformist moves of the historical European Left. Even some of its main characteristics were the consequence of conservative responses to the emergence of the labour movement and social democracy (for example, the laws creating sickness insurance introduced by Bismarck or as part of Franco's legacy). The first elements of a welfare state actually appeared in the German empire, immediately after political unification and the creation of its internal market. In 1871 a law was passed establishing the limited liability of companies, in the event of bankruptcy, in respect of industrial accidents, and ten years later a system of compulsory insurance was introduced. Bismarck used this policy as a means of compensating for his repression of the Social Democratic Party. In his memoirs he wrote that advocates for democracy would have no success if the people realized that their princes were concerned about their welfare. Rather than voluntary mutualism, the purpose was to set up a system of compulsory protection to include all workers. It did not have the expected results, since it decisively strengthened social democracy and the trade union movement.

The idea of the welfare state as such was formulated by Sir William Beveridge, who had been secretary to the Webbs before becoming a Liberal Member of Parliament. In 1941 he was instructed to draw up a report on organizing a British social security system. His report, entitled 'Social Insurance and Allied Services', reviewed the most notable examples, including the German system, those of the Scandinavian social democrats and Roosevelt's system in the United States (the Social Security Act of 1935 was the first to introduce the term), which went a step further, going beyond the industrial and mutualist system. It is based on a new concept of social risk and the role of the State. The objective of social security is to relieve people of need, guaranteeing them security of income to accompany them from the cradle to the grave. 'Social risk' is anything which threatens the regular income of individuals: illness, industrial accidents, bankruptcy, old age, motherhood and unemployment, and the innovative nature of the proposal lay in the introduction of a global and coherent system with four main characteristics:

1 a generalized system covering the whole population, whatever their employment status or income
2 a unified and simple system, with a single contribution covering all the risks involved in loss of income
3 a uniform system with similar benefits, irrespective of the incomes of the recipients
4 a centralized system, based on a single public service.

At the same time Beveridge proposed a state social policy with three objectives: help for the family, the improvement of public health through the creation of a National Health Service, and the organization of employment, which were to be financed by additional taxation. In his view, this policy only made sense if it was closely linked to a policy of full employment, and he defended these ideas in his book 'Full Employment in a Free Society' published in 1944, in which he considered unemployment as a major social risk. At the time the concept of 'full employment' included heads of household only.

Considered in retrospect, the welfare state as such does not only consist in the establishment of various forms of universal and fundamental insurance cover for all citizens, although this alone would have justified its existence. In Western Europe, its greatest significance consisted in enabling most of the population to exercise basic democratic rights. That only landowners had the right to vote was the norm throughout most of the 19th century and when, for example, universal suffrage – for men only – was introduced in Restoration Spain, it took the form of election-rigging, i.e. a generalized system of fraud under the control of party bosses and people of influence.

The extension of voting rights to the other half of the population – women – was achieved much more recently, in this century. For this reason there is a close link between the achievement of political and social democracy – involving the majority of the population, since access is given to industrial workers, farmers and women – and what is known as the 'welfare state', which established as a right measures to cover the most basic needs of education, health and protection in old age and sickness. We can see the link in the reluctant attitude of Nordic women in the Danish, Swedish and Finnish referenda, fearing a loosening of their conquests in the Community.

In this sense the welfare state is the essence of what since the Weimar Republic has been called the 'social constitutional state'. It is based on the elimination of insuperable risks for individuals, taking recognition of their equality as the starting-point. Hitherto, throughout history, the problem had been solved by means of asylums, hospices and charity – islands of paternalism in an ocean of misery. Conservatives and reactionary liberals who furiously attack the very roots of the welfare state should say what the alternative is, especially for weak and marginalized people, since not all of society consists of hardened supermen prepared for battle.

The generalization of these rights and of the policies which introduced them helped to shape modern states and to establish a secure place in them for the organized labour movement. The government is no longer the 'Central Committee of the bourgeoisie', the classic Marxist definition, but has become the administrator which is able to provide better guarantees for the recognition and participation of the classes and sectors which were previously marginalized. This is undoubtedly the reason why for a long time, even during the early stages of the construction of the Community, the political Left and the trade unions preferred the national framework.

These events are engraved on the historical memory of the European countries and are part of their shared heritage, especially in places, such as the Benelux countries, Germany or Italy, where, in addition to strong political and trade union movements, cooperatives and social democratic organizations, there is a history of movements of religious origin which have also created or participate in mass organizations (for example, the trade unions in Germany). Both types of movement have consolidated democracy in the countries of Western Europe in the last 150 years and still dominate the European scene. Significantly, the force of circumstance has meant that parties which were originally poles apart have joined these families. For example, the European People's Party (EPP) has been joined by the Spanish Conservatives and, even more surprisingly, by the British Conservatives. These conversions to Christian Democracy are as remarkable as Saul's conversion on the road to Damascus . . . or the Italian former Communists joining the Party of European Socialists.

The welfare state is thus an undeniable achievement, one of the greatest in the history of humanity, and its problems are caused to some extent by its very success. As universal rights have been recognized and have brought about generalized benefits, so costs have increased, whilst revenue has decreased. The links between industry, with its growing productivity, and the welfare state have meant that expenditure on health has risen from 0.5% to 8–12% of GNP and on education from 2 to 10%. Most of this increase has been received by the workers, – i.e. by Marx's proletariat, as Drucker has rightly pointed out[3]. In this sense the workers' struggle has been one of the most powerful elements in renewing capitalism and making it more dynamic. Expenditure is tending to increase systematically, in view of the ageing population, as a result of the combined impact of the falling birthrate and increased life expectancy. Since an old-age pension has become a generalized right, this will place a growing burden on the working population.

At the same time the costs are constantly increasing, especially in the case of the shared system, which leads to the burden being borne increasingly by state budgets, via taxation – or to the growth of pension funds, which are well on the way to being the major institutional investment in a form of 'capitalism without capitalists', to quote Peter F. Drucker, given the degree of importance which this kind of fund is acquiring in advanced capitalist economies. It should also be noted that, as in any human activity, deception and fraud help increase social costs.

For these reasons a heroic defence of the welfare state should not be attempted without moves to update its organization, cover and financing methods. No institution has lasted without changing and adapting to external changes. The guilds of the old regime could not withstand the rise of commercial freedom and modern industry.

We are now witnessing the decline of not only the major industries of the 19th century – the iron and steel industry, coal mining and shipbuilding – but also of the large-scale multinationals which seemed to be impregnable fortresses. What has happened to the world's leading computer manufacturer, IBM, or companies in the 20th century's leading industrial sector, the automobile industry, offers examples of the profound changes caused by the increase in global productivity. At a time when there is so much talk of the Jurassic age, it is salutary to remember that the only animal surviving from that age is the mosquito.

At the same time, our societies require more and better services which tend to be 'static', as William J. Baumol said, because productivity increases very slowly: health, education, legal services, welfare programmes, the postal service, sanitation, repairs and maintenance services, the fine arts and restaurants belong to this category. For example, whilst since the time of Cervantes productivity in wheat production has increased more than tenfold, to write 'Don Quixote' would require a similar length of time and effort, irrespective of the skill of the author. This means that as the cost of products falls, an increasingly large proportion of resources can be devoted to services without reducing the consumption of industrial products, whilst the cost of services will grow, irrespective of whether they are provided by private or public entitites or by a combination of the two.

This point is worth making, because cultural factors and traditions limit the pressure of the market to what is socially tolerable. Thus, during the last few years it has once again been dogmatically asserted that if wages are lower more people will be employed, or that a lowering of interest rates automatically generates investment, but it should not be forgotten that you can take a horse to water but you cannot make it drink. Many years ago Keynes questioned the absolute validity of the theory that a reduction in production automatically reduces income and a reduction in wages reduces purchasing power, which perpetuates a recession.

The most recent experiment in neo-Keynesianism is that being carried out by the Clinton administration. It started with a package in which he defended before Congress the virtues of public expenditure as an investment in the future, with particular emphasis on education, infrastructure and the creation of a national health system. Its determination to defend American industry was evident not only in the GATT negotiations but also in the 'managed trade' policy, or the incredible announcement made by the White House in February 1993 about the introduction of an ecological car produced by the peaceful use of the ceramics obtained through military research in collaboration with USCAR[4]. One can imagine the outcry if an announcement of this kind were made in Brussels! Clinton's emphasis on job creation – 'jobs, jobs, jobs!' as the great challenge for the future – is, in any case, highly relevant.

In conclusion, it is clear that the creation of the European Union, in addition to its institutional dimension and its political values, such as citizenship and its ultimate goal of a single currency, also creates space for people. It cannot be claimed that this space is reserved for businessmen or tourists; students, professionals, and workers are all entitled to live in it. Furthermore, it is natural for people to want to improve their situation when they see that of their neighbours; emulation and envy are democratic values. For this reason it is quite right to develop social policy, even if one opts out. Joint plans for job creation and the improvement of living and working conditions, guaranteed adequate social protection, the promotion of dialogue between the social partners in order to develop human resources and achieve a high level of employment are an essential part of the creation of the Union.

GATT is Not Trade Alone

The same applies to measures to combat marginalization and social exclusion, since part of the population is weaker and more vulnerable than the rest and the dynamics of creative destruction abandon the people, communities and groups which must be helped. Progress is not a straight path, but a process which benefits some whilst harming and marginalizing others, the so-called 'society of the two-thirds', and for this reason there must be corrective factors to re-establish a balance and maintain the basis of the social fabric. In the European Union there are more than 40 million poor people.

Social cohesion, which seemed like an afterthought tagged on to economic cohesion, understood in a narrow sense as a transfer mechanism to reduce national inequalities, takes on a dramatic new meaning when we consider the situation of many districts on the edges or in the suburbs of cities, or in the dormitory towns in many Community countries, or the examples of social or xenophobic violence or gang warfare originating in feelings as varied as hostility towards immigrants and fanatical enthusiasm for sport. The situation is much more dramatic in places as far apart as American cities where curfews are imposed and Algerian cities where fundamentalism has a social role. For this reason, whilst respecting different traditions, systems and levels of development, there is no doubt that the social dimension is not a separate compartment or a relic to be done away with.

Returning to the original question, the creation of the internal market and the subsequent steps which are being taken undoubtedly entail profound changes in the very foundations of society and production. What is the best response? Should the welfare state be dismantled or should it be streamlined and rejuvenated?

The welfare state was originally modelled on the concept of the state as the direct and centralized administrator of essential public services, utilities such as postal and telecommunications services or the railways. Technological developments, combined with stagnation and rising costs, mean that the advantages of these models must once again be taken seriously, on the basis of integrated networks, with liberalized and more flexible final services. As far as the welfare state is concerned, a distinction must also be made between the recognition of fundamental rights – in this case the elimination of social risks for all citizens, as an issue of basic solidarity to be financed via taxation – and the adaptation of other aspects, such as uniformity, globality and centralization of the system. In addition to mutual benefit societies, investment funds and pension funds are promising formulae. The distinction between the recognition of rights, with universal basic benefits, and the differentiated management of benefit schemes or saving schemes for the future via voluntary systems constitutes the approach to be followed. It is therefore significant that in the last few years the formula of a guaranteed minimum income has been extended, with a national system in France (the RMI or *Revenu Minimal d'Insertion*), a traditional municipal system for the homeless (*Hochdachloss*) in Germany, or the system devised for the autonomous regions in Spain.

One of the major challenges facing the European Union is that the recognition of citizenship, combined with the removal of barriers, puts the issues of welfare and the social dimension on the immediate political agenda. Social security and social protection are included in the Social Chapter adopted by the eleven, as an issue on which the Council decides by unanimity. It is no mere hypothesis, since it has immediate effect for the more than five million Community citizens residing in a state other than their country of origin. These include not only traditional immigrants, whose rights cannot be guaranteed solely by bilateral agreements, but also many retired people from the north of the Community who use social security hospital and intensive care units the Mediterranean costs of Spain, for example.

Obviously, the solution does not consist in creating a gigantic centralized welfare system at Community level. Whilst respecting the historical and cultural diversity of the existing systems, and on the basis of rights already defined in the Treaties, there are significant opportunities for collaboration, ranging from regulation by the Community of investment and pension funds – a controversial project which is already under way – to the establishment of Community reinsurance systems in the field of social protection or measures to combat unemployment. In any event, this is an issue which must be tackled as real and immediate, since it is difficult to claim that shared citizenship and a single currency are possible without social protection and welfare being relevant.

Europe cannot live in a bell-jar or surround itself with walls like a fortress. This fact confronts the world's leading trading power with the question as to whether its policy is compatible with the political, economic and social values which it proclaims, at a time when democratic values, which once seemed a luxury reserved for a select club of Western capitalist developed countries, are becoming the major mobilizing force of the end of the century. At world level, the European negotiations in Brussels will automatically become a new Bretton-Woods conference, in Thurow's opinion[5].

In fact, the main purpose of the multilateral system established by the Bretton-Woods agreements in the monetary field and by GATT in the trade field was to put an end to the division of the world into separate trading blocks (the Japanese sphere of influence, the British Empire, the French Union, Germany and Eastern Europe and the America of the Monroe doctrine), a world in which joint pressure to limit imports multiplied the depressive effects. The golden rule of the new system was that each country should treat all the others in the same way and automatically extend the most-favoured nation clause to them. In actual fact, the system has not worked like this, because regional trading blocks have been formed, the most advanced example of which is the European Community. In the meantime the world situation has changed profoundly, the most significant aspects being, firstly, that the United States is no longer the undisputed leading world economic power; secondly, not only are captive markets disappearing but a sizeable number of former Third World countries are also emerging and having success in international trade.

The Third World, as conceived in the non-aligned movement, with Nehru's India, Tito's Yugoslavia or Castro's Cuba as leaders, has been consigned to history. Now above all it is the People's Republic of China, the 'dragons' of South-East Asia and Latin American countries such as Mexico and Chile which are asserting themselves, and many of them are playing a growing role in international trade. In agriculture the Cairns Group, a union of farming countries with an export tradition (Australia, Argentina, New Zealand or Uruguay), or the emerging Asian rice-exporting countries are making their presence felt. These countries are joining multinational fora and actively working to protect their interests. In the meantime, countries which are not taking off, such as those in sub-Saharan Africa, are being relegated to a 'Fourth World', which is increasingly marginalized and poor. This new situation makes negotiations more complex and difficult but also more important, since in the agricultural sphere the main industrial powers are being called to account and, in general, because all industrial activities and services have to be considered as a whole.

In the present tense situation, dominated by the crisis and growing unemployment, self-righteousness about free trade does not receive such a good press and has been replaced by conflicting and often contradictory statements and actions.

The Clinton's administration's aggressive rhetoric is symptomatic of a trade policy based on market access, especially in the field of high technology, which operates simultaneously in multilateral, regional and bilateral frameworks, applying the principle of managed trade. This is not a new concept, since the Reagan administration applied it in the 1986 bilateral agreement with Japan on semiconductors, which specified that 20% of the Japanese trade should be in American hands by the end of 1992, the date when the miracle happened. In response to Japanese criticisms that agreements dependent on results in the form of quantified objectives laid down on the basis of macroeconomic data violate the principle of free trade, the chairman of Clinton's Council of Economic Advisors, the Berkeley Professor Laura Tyson, answered that in a situation where the United States no longer occupies a dominant technological position and has lost part of its markets and skilled jobs, it is necessary to defend the systematic policy of access to foreign markets which it considers closed to competition. The method used consists in trying to achieve specific objectives with the partner in negotiations, threatening to impose sanctions if they are not achieved.

This policy is part of the philosophy of unilateralism, deeply rooted in the American mentality and legislation, which is based on the definition of behaviour considered as offensive on the part of natural or legal persons or countries against the United States. The unfairness of these actions is judged unilaterally by the Administration without reference to (or often in open conflict with) the rules of multilateral trade.

Current US legislation in the field of trade takes this philosophy further. In fact, the main aim of the 1974 Trade Act, partially modified by the Omnibus Trade and Competitiveness Act of 1988, is to open up outside markets to US goods and services and to devise effective unilateral sanctions against countries which are considered to be competing unfairly with the United States. The most audacious weapon is contained in Section 301, which allows unilateral action against other countries. The United States has carried out reprisals against the Community in accordance with Section 301 on two occasions (the hormonoe dispute and oilseed subsidies) and has threatened to use them in the case of tinned fruit, shipbuilding and the Airbus.

The problem of access to the Japanese market goes beyond the customs tariff context, since in the last few years it has lowered its rates in response to criticism. The greatest difficulty lies in Japan's enormous skill in setting up non-tariff barriers, such as restrictions of access to distribution, agreements, administrative barriers, etc.

The coalition governments formed after the political upheavals of spring 1993 announced measures to deregulate these kinds of barriers.

It should be remembered that the Community is the world's leading exporter and that, despite internal tensions, it maintains a coherent policy of openness. Recently, the seriousness of the crisis in the Community has generated sectoral protectionist reactions, and even a degree of withdrawal and suggestions that the Community preference should be increased. It is difficult to justify a more protectionist attitude in view of the facts. The EU has an impressive trade surplus with the countries of Eastern Europe, and the Asian tigers have captured only 3% of the Community market, compared with 8% for the USA. It should be remembered that Japan is the country which is most actively diversifying activities and still has the lowest rate of unemployment.

The positive outcome of the negotiations has led to the formation of a system organized in an increasingly stable way, the World Trade Organization, that must be accompanied by a system of guarantees for the observance of workers' human and social rights and a system of environmental protection with more binding force than the ILO conventions, recommendations on equality of sexes of the Cairo and Copenhagen Conferences or the Rio agreements, a system that was conceived at the end of Second World War and failed.

Just as the denunciation of violations of human rights and the use of demands for their observance as a political weapon are superseding the rationale of *realpolitik*, which has always prevailed in international relations in the form on 'noninterference in internal affairs' – as if citizens were the property of countries – the exercise of social rights is becoming a basic requirement of humanity. The struggle of workers for better and more decent working conditions is not a characteristic of developed countries alone. Nowadays the highest incidence of strikes and industrial action is in countries such as Korea or in Latin America. One indication of this is that in the United States demands for clauses covering trade union rights or environmental protection have become essential conditions for membership of the North America Free Trade Agreement between the United States, Canada and Mexico. The ratification and application of ILO Conventions and the recognition of the social dimension of human rights must become an important future weapon not only in the political field but also in the economic field.

In the environmental sphere, issues such as the effects of CFC gases on the ozone layer or the destruction of virgin forests highlight the need to include the 'green' dimension in world trade, since it is already a part of social policy and life. The Rio summit demonstrated political sensitivity to the problem, now it must be integrated as a permanent and operational element.

Ultimately, what is envisaged, as Peter Sutherland rightly said, is the construction of a world order in which the UN, the IMF and the WTO are fundamental and cohesive pillars.

The Creation of Jobs

The third major issue raised when the Maastricht Treaty was ratified was the need to respond to the crisis by generating jobs.

The situation has been complicated by the radical change in economic trends: a generalized recession, the most pessimistic forecasts of the post-war period, a spectacular growth in unemployment, worsening budget deficits and global debt and, above all, two worrying weaknesses – a fall in competitiveness and a diminishing capacity to generate jobs (although nine million jobs were created in the period 1985–1990).

The economic crisis has centred, above all, on the world's three major trading partners – the Community, the United States and Japan – which, with 16% of the world's population, account for 75% of GDP. What is needed is a growth model, not mere compliance with the indicators defined in the Treaty as convergence criteria. In addition to positive and official integration, i.e. that proposed in Brussels and negotiated among the member states, emphasis must be placed on real integration, that is to say integration in society, by promoting an increasing number of initiatives. For this reason it is important to be able to overcome the crisis of confidence through mobilizing factors.

Finally, the breakdown in the convergence strategy must be overcome, not only in order to comply with the criteria laid down in the Treaty, but also in order to help economies recover and give them strong currencies.

What is needed is a uniform economic outlook geared to stability, which requires important changes in the consideration of variables such as inflation, debt and taxation, but above all a shared vision of the nature of the current crisis and the way out of it. In essence there are two different reactions to the crisis: one is the tendency of economies to turn in upon themselves, trying to protect themselves from the increasing competitiveness of the newly industrialized countries and defending declining industries at all costs; the other is the desire to take advantage of the opportunity to prepare the next leap forward.

The 'capitalism versus capitalism' debate is still open, with various solutions ranging from the deregulating British model, Germany's liberalism tempered by the social market economy or the combination of monetary orthodoxy and protectionist tendencies which is found in France.

Initially, the data showing the weaknesses of the European economy can be summarized as follows: the loss of international competitiveness, which is reflected in shares of the world market (−3.7% in the 1980s, compared with +2.2% for the United States and +0.5% for Japan); a relative weakness in fast-growing and future products, and less investment and training for high qualifications (39% in Europe, 75% in the United States and 76% in Japan). To this is added the new international pattern of division of labour, with the globalization of markets and the swift emergence of the newly industrialized countries (the 'tigers' of ASEAN, China, Mexico, Chile, etc.), all of which leads to the universalization of business strategy and of transfers, subcontracting and relocation.

Over the long term, the Community is the least dynamic of the three trading partners. Between 1970 and 1990 the United States created 28.8 million jobs, Japan 11.7 million and the Community 8.8 million. Worse still is the pattern of unemployment: 16 out of 100 unemployed people are under 25; 45% of the unemployed have been out of work for more than a year and 28% for more than two years. In addition to the waste of human resources, it should be borne in mind that the policy of early retirement has practically been exploited to the full and the birth rate is making it necessary to reconsider the retirement age. The creation of jobs has therefore become the first priority.

The European Council in Brussels of 1993 approved the White Paper on Growth, Competitiveness and Employment, which contains the guidelines for entering the 21st century with a programme of economic recovery and investment in infrastructure.

An improvement in the relationship between growth and employment has at present become the greatest priority. If we carry out a classic study based on the four basic elements of a nation's wealth – the active population, natural resources, financial capital and invisible assets – we can see that in a situation where the population is ageing significantly and natural resources are scarce, the fundamental factor we must work with is invisible: human knowledge, to be precise.

The combination of these factors – the 'mix', to use economic jargon – provides conditions for competitiveness, which include macroeconomic and monetary conditions, the business acumen of companies, the judicious use of technological advances and labour costs. As Paul Krugman remarks: 'Most if not all the time, the proper role of government is simply one of providing the right environment – the skilled labour force, the infrastructure, the tolerable regulations and taxes that allow industrial success to happen'.

If jobs are to be created, growth must return. It is a necessary (but not a sufficient) condition. One of the most important areas in which steps can be taken to promote job creation is a reduction in the indirect costs of labour, which entails reconsidering the social protection system. This means that a distinction must be made between basic rights, the importance of which increases as marginalization and social exclusion increase, and supplementary schemes, which can be financed by voluntary contributions.

Technological progress is another fundamental element in job creation. Although in an industrial world, especially one in a state of crisis, the negative elements of creative destruction prevails, in particular because of the reduction in the number of jobs in major industries or because factories and production are transferred to other regions or countries, technological progress is closely linked to continuous training and the organization of labour. On the one hand, this means that production becomes increasingly capital-intensive, which makes greater flexibility and adaptability necessary and, in some cases, makes automation a likely prospect – that is to say, complete automation with production feedback in certain sectors. On the other hand, the structure of the world economy as a whole entails the relocation and transformation of certain activities and the conversion of others. At any event, a Europe structured on the basis of a high level of income and standard of living must increasingly choose to concentrate on sectors with a high technological value, in R & D, for which the very existence of the internal market is an essential condition. In addition to electronics, biotechnology or genetics, the major industry of the future will comprise informatics, telecommunications, television and information.

The final element is the formulation of active policies in the labour market based on continuous education, involving training throughout one's working life.

The integration of women in the labour market is a decisive factor in making it dynamic, with all that this implies as regards equality of opportunity and the need to create the relevant social services.

The role of the social partners in negotiations covering the issues of training, apprenticeship and retraining and their participation in the active policy of organisations responsible for employment, with the regulated participation of negotiating bodies, are essential elements in this process of increasing the flexibility of the system rather than dismantling it. Other essential elements are the development of flexible for part-time work and the social aspects of labour.

At any event, public services will become increasingly expensive and their financing will be a permanent cause of concern. How to do so will be the subject of a major political debate, since it will have to be achieved by budgetary means, which will make the tax on energy consumption all the more relevant. The tax on the consumption of hydrocarbons is being debated in the Community and makes increasing financial and ecological sense.

However, the solution is not to be found by means of diagnostics alone, although if the diagnosis is good it can be half the battle. The key is to turn the task of overcoming and recovering from the crisis into sustained action, placing it in relation to the final objective: a single currency as the symbol of a solvent and prosperous economic power, with a high standard of living and social protection. Its achievement may be a plan which covers the next legislature and takes the form of a large-scale European pact. In the political, economic and monetary spheres, it is inconceivable that the plan for the second and third stages can be achieved without extending the consensus of heads of government to the main European political families. It is a constituent programme which requires the active collaboration of the socio-economic partners starting with a determined move to relaunch the European economy.

The scale of the problem requires a commensurate and determined response, a 'new deal' to use the time-honoured phrase – a compromise which will allow us to cover the decisive remaining distance by 1999. Its basic elements are a vast programme of public investment, an idea adopted at the Edinburgh Summit with the European initiative for growth, and developed on a much more ambitious scale in the White Paper on trans-European networks so as to provide the nervous system and circulation which Europe needs (trans-European road and high-speed train networks, and an integrated services digital telecommunications network), in plans for environmental saving and regeneration (for example the Spanish water plan, the recycling of waste, the elimination of pollution, etc.), and a vast programme of urban renewal and rehabilitation. Such a programme makes more sense if account is taken of the fact that public investment in general in Northern Europe is less than half what it was at the beginning of the 1970s.

The financing of a programme of this kind should not raise serious problems in a situation characterized by excessive savings and insufficient investment, and hence the proposed ECU 250 000 million by the end of the century, based on appeals to private savers by the issue of bonds, makes sense. A reduction in basic interest rates would be the necessary accompaniment to this.

As far as employment is concerned, a plan of this kind would make it possible to tackle decisively the main problem, which is the more marked rise in unemployment among unskilled workers. Solutions must be devised which make it possible to maintain criteria of social solidarity with a degree of flexibility. Thus, for example, in response to the call for the abolition of a minimum wage, it would be more sensible to explore possible solutions which allow for partial or total exemption from social security contributions or tax up to a certain level; this would mean financing job creation through subsidies rather than interest rates.

Such initiatives also have the advantage of spelling out the fact that the European Union is something tangible for the people and not merely a combination of natural forces and uncontrollable phenomena which leads to withdrawal and the growth of problems such as rejection, breakdown and social exclusion.

Towards the Knowledge Society

Any policy with aspirations for the future and a long-term perspective must start with this overall vision, the keystone being the enhancement of education seen as a process which may provide a response to the reality of a knowledge society. It requires a new concept of schooling, with a qualitative leap forward similar to that provided in medieval education by the Czech Comenius when he created his textbook. This school of the future should, as Drucker says when he talks about the knowledge society, 'provide universal literacy of a high order; imbue students on all levels and of all ages with the motivation to learn and with the discipline of continuing learning; it has to be open to both, already highly educated people and to people who, for whatever reason, did not gain access to advanced education in their early years; it has to impart knowledge both as substance and as process; finally, schooling can no longer be a monopoly of the schools. Education in the post-capitalist society has to permeate the entire society, with employing organizations of all kinds – businessmen, government agencies, non-profits – becoming learning and teaching institutions and with schools increasingly working in partnership with employers and employing organizations[6].

These are not Utopian visions belonging to science fiction. I, for myself, can say that most of the instruction I received, during my education from primary school to university, on

Europe, law or economics can be considered as obsolete, and I have already retrained four times up to the present.

I have also witnessed events as different and significant as the creation of the 'universidades populares' in various Spanish cities, along the lines of German *Volksschulen* following the return of democracy, in which thousands of adults have undergone additional training or have discovered a new dimension to their lives. The experience of the University Institute Euroforum, attached to the Complutense University and associated with INSEAD, with its dual role of research centre and residential college for continuing education, convinces me of the rightness of Drucker's proposals, the roots of which can be found in Ancient Greece. Strangely enough, the countries which in the last few decades have shown a great capacity for organizing society, business and industry – Germany and Japan – both attach great importance to training, believe in continuing education, and do not have business schools, paradoxical though this may seem.

Without wishing to be chiliastic, I would say that we are witnessing the birth of a new age, a time of radical change in which, in the space of a few decades, society is reshaping its vision of the world, its basic values, its political and social structures, its arts and its key institutions. Fifty years on there will be a new world and the people born then will be unable to imagine the world in which their grandparents lived and into which their own parents were born – as Drucker says[7]. Accordingly to him, the post-capitalist society is coming into being. Others, such as Alain Touraine, talk about the 'post-industrial society' and Alvin Toffler talks about the 'third wave'. The fact is that the Community has already radically changed the Europe that existed until 50 years ago and even more so the Europe which Drucker, who was born in Vienna in 1909, knew in his childhood. At the same time, the production system has developed to such an extent, because of technological progress and economic globalization, that it is conceivable for us to find a way out of the present crisis simply by using the classic therapies. The most interesting and creative way undoubtedly lies in transition to a knowledge society.

9 Europe and the World

As for Europe, it seems nobody knows where it got its name from, nor who gave it this name, unless we grant that it took it from Europa of Tyre, because in earlier days, just like the other two parts of the world, it did not have a name. Europa was most definitely an Asiatic, and never came to the country which the Greeks now call Europe; she merely travelled from Phoenicia to Crete and from Crete to Lycia.

Herodotus

It is commonplace to say that the continent of Europe has a universal vocation. This has certainly been the case since the Renaissance, when the states of Europe were involved in a permanent struggle for hegemony, conquering the world and carving out colonial empires in their image, seeking to make them a part of themselves. For better or worse, Europe shaped the globe, mapping out a Eurocentric vision of the world extending no further than the Sublime Porte. This was true until the present century, when the combined effects of power and discord led to repeated self-destruction.

It is significant that the Community was founded after the last major failed attempt by two European powers, France and Britain, to impose their will by force in the Suez crisis of 1956. In recent times, the countries which once ruled the world through their colonial adventures have behaved like emigrants, returning after many years to the family home, living off their memories and nostalgia at times, but preoccupied by their daily domestic problems. They have attempted to bring together many of their former colonies in an original grouping known as the ACP (grouping together a continent, Africa; an archipelago, the Caribbean; and an ocean, the Pacific) under the Lomé Convention.

During the cold war and the division of the continent, the overriding concern from the outset was to protect and stand firm against the expansionist threat of Stalin. The most notable feature of the world created after the Second World War, based on the leading role of the United States in the reconstruction of Europe, was the establishment of multilateral structures and alliances. For the first time since the Holy Alliance, all the states of Western Europe, with the exception of the dictatorships at its periphery, were linked together in a network of cooperation, where they became accustomed to jointly planing their economic, political and defence strategies. Given the scale of the task of reconstruction, mutual aid and continuing dialogue were essential, encouraged by effective pressure from the United States. There was a determination not to repeat the tragic error of the surrender of Versailles and to ensure that Germany was not left on the sidelines. So, through the creation of institutions (which began with Bretton-Woods and GATT, followed by the United Nations, the IMF, the World Bank and the OECD), a transatlantic structure was built up and consolidated, supplemented by the security and defence arrangements under the Atlantic Alliance and its military arm NATO, while the Paris and Brussels agreements laid the foundations for the establishment of the Council of Europe, the ECSC and the WEU. The early stages were based on a practical approach geared to economic integration. The lack of political will was exposed in 1954 with the failure of the European Defence Community (EDC). The Treaty of Rome contained no provision for powers in the field of foreign policy and security. In 1970, the Community ministers adopted the Davignon report, which helped to lay the foundations for Community cooperation in the field of foreign policy. Not having been given general powers, the European Community developed its own specific powers in the areas laid down by the Treaties.

Increasingly the Community took the place of its members in commercial and economic affairs at the international level, concluding a growing number of agreements with third countries, opening delegations and taking part and negotiating in international fora.

In the political field, it was not until the first meeting of the CSCE in Helsinki in 1975 that the Community was able to express itself with a single voice. As efforts progressed to establish a common philosophy, the declaration of the Venice European Council in 1981 offered a notable precedent, both by dealing with an issue as delicate as the Middle East peace process and by putting forward a then controversial view which was subsequently vindicated by the Israel/PLO peace agreement twelve years later. European political cooperation (EPC), which was institutionalized by Title III of the Single Act, was seen as an activity to be pursued through intergovernmental cooperation.

The long process of gestation and construction occurred in a climate which, for all its shortcomings, produced a genuine greenhouse effect, shaped by the coexistence of two nuclear superpowers, one of which, the United States, played the role of guardian and protector.

At the end of the last decade the European Community came of age, both of its own volition and under the influence of surrounding events.

The thaw of 1989 led to the fall of the Berlin Wall, prompted by *perestroika* in the Soviet Union and the democratic revolutions in Central and Eastern Europe. The USSR disintegrated, the Warsaw Pact disappeared and NATO found itself besieged as its former enemies became orphans seeking asylum. The Gulf War broke out, the former Yugoslavia was in flames, the Middle East peace conference opened and the Czech and Slovak peoples achieved a peaceful divorce. After standing still for decades, history was frenetically on the move.

This new situation meant that the Community had to come of age. The disappearance of the bi-polar world as well as its own growing strength warrants that it takes in hand its own destiny and responsibilities. The umbrella which had offered it comfortable protection and, to some extent, an excuse for inaction, no longer exists. The truth is that the European Union has to find its place on the world map, where different Europes are attempting to forge relations in a process of movement and redefinition. The situation is a flexible and shifting one where the European Union seems to be the only stable pillar of the continent, whilst a complex process of crystallization is occurring in the centre and the future in the East remains unpredictable.

Against this background, the European Union is exercising a genuine magnetic pull. Its growing strength has created a pole, an island of prosperity that is not only material, but also has a veneer of security and stability more visible from the outside than from within. For the first time, Europe is expanding without being expansionist.

As this process takes place, the democracy of ideas and information is becoming universal. However, this is not a linear process, since no sooner has fear been banished than other frustrations which have been buried for many years rise up. The world is made up of light and shade and Europe cannot escape this harsh law, which Braudel rightly defined as 'paradise and hell'. Paradoxically, the trend towards the universal coexists with a trend towards fragmentation and withdrawal into the self, threatening the continent with a return to the worst excesses of the past in the form of intolerance, racism and nationalism.

Regional conflicts, local wars, the proliferation of nuclear capacity, regional powers seeking local supremacy, potential environmental and nuclear disasters, terrorism – in some cases state-sponsored – and unrestrained migration all represent direct or indirect threats to the future of the European Community.

The security dimension goes beyond purely military considerations. The Union should not overlook any of the instruments at its disposal. As the leading economic and trade power, a model of integration and prosperity based on the democratic values set out at Helsinki, enshrined in the Charter of Paris, and today accepted by all European states, the European Union must continue to develop its cooperation and development aid policy decisively, and help to establish a more just world order by strengthening the United Nations and the regional groupings capable of protecting the rights of citizens and encouraging mutual respect.

In the immediate future, the success of this policy will depend on Europe's ability to resolve regional conflicts, provide the economic aid needed for the new democracies to consolidate their position and move to a market economy, and encourage international trade.

In the medium to long term, the challenge is equally formidable. We must establish a European security system, formulate crisis management mechanisms for the peaceful and negotiated settlement of disputes, and resolve the problems posed by migration and the environment.

The CFSP

The European Union has at its disposal a vital instrument, the common foreign and security policy (CFSP), the characteristics and legal provisions of which are laid down in Title V of the Treaty on European Union. The CFSP inherited the legacy of European Political Cooperation, but represented a qualitative step forward in that it set out objectives (Article J1) and provided the means for achieving them (Articles J2 and J3).

In view of the aims of the European enterprise and its international context, the Union clearly needs to develop a foreign policy characterized by a higher level of cohesion, greater capacity for action and appropriate control by the democratically elected authorities.

The globalization of the economic, cultural, social and political activities of the Member States means that they and the Union – in view of its high level of integration – need to pursue their own objectives whilst increasingly taking into account the international aspects which are likely to influence the outcome of policies adopted exclusively for internal purposes.

The objectives of the CFSP are at present as follows: to safeguard the fundamental interests and security of the Union and its member states, to maintain peace and international security, to strengthen democracy, and to safeguard human rights and fundamental freedoms. Effective action by the Union at international level therefore assists the achievement of internal objectives and, by the same token, ineffective action in the international context directly jeopardizes internal objectives.

The strengthening of the CFSP is a fundamental requirement. The member states can no longer act in isolation, since their action would not have the degree of effectiveness needed. None of them separately has the 'critical mass' needed to enable it to implement an autonomous foreign policy: in view of the high level of integration achieved within the Union, any attempt in this direction is doomed to failure. On the other hand, the interests of the individual member states are better protected and safeguarded in a Community dimension, in which the solidarity of the other member states provides the support needed to ensure the safeguarding of individual and common interests which are playing an increasingly predominant role.

Although the decision of creating the CFSP was a major one, its implementation can hardly be considered as a quick and overwhelming success, especially if compared with public opinion expectations and apprehensions.

The present system is based on an intergovernmental structure and operational procedures which are difficult to reconcile with the supranational concept of the Community pillar. The need for unanimity in decision-making, the limited role of the Commission, the hardly existent role of Parliament, the exclusion of the Court of Justice's jurisdiction are all factors which prevent the Union from carrying out fully its role in international relations. The Council's action is too often paralysed by vetoes and reciprocal opposition, which reduce the effectiveness of common actions and render the taking of positions a declarative activity. Agreement therefore has to be reached on the basis of a very low common denominator at a time when dramatic developments on the international scene require rapid and decisive action.

The few decisions actually taken are in any case beyond the control of the national parliaments, without this being adequately offset by the European Parliament, which is relegated to the role of spectator. Admittedly, the role which national parliaments play in foreign relations depends to a great extent on the nature of such relations, which rarely result in legislative acts. In actual fact they more often consist of diplomatic activities which, if they result in the drawing-up of an international agreement, merely allow the parliamentary authority to approve or reject as a whole the text submitted for ratification.

Furthermore, shortcomings in the functioning of the CFSP are likely to worsen, for obvious reasons, with the entry of new member states. The planned accession of countries in Central and Eastern Europe and the Mediterranean also show that it is an illusion that the foreign policy of a Union with 25 or more member states might function in accordance with the current rules or, at least, without abandoning the principle of unanimity.

The reforms to be carried out in the context of the 1996 Conference must represent a qualitative leap forward. The European Council has to give the vision through consensus, and the rule by which the Council of Ministers takes decisions has to be the majority.

In addition to ensuring that its own basic interests and security are safeguarded, the Union must play an active role in promoting international peace and security by participating in action undertaken under the aegis of the United Nations

Security Council. As the world's leading trading power, the main provider of humanitarian aid and the entity which has two permanent members on the Security Council, it must accept its responsibilities at this stage in history, which is marked by the end of the cold war and the creation of a new balance of power in the world. This objective must be pursued by a permanent common strategy of the Union and the members states within all the international organisations.

Furthermore, insofar as foreign policy cannot exist without a 'security' dimension, the safeguarding of the Union's security must include the 'defence' dimension of the Union's policy. This implies abandoning the ambiguous formulations of the current Treaty and considering that the time has arrived to implement this policy. Anomalies such as the WEU, considered to be the Union's military body, although it has a separate institutional structure, are no longer tolerable.

This policy must have definite objectives an specific procedures. In this context, common defence policy should guarantee that the borders of the Union and its Member States are safeguarded, and enable the Union to carry its responsibilities for maintaining and restoring the rule of law internationally, ensuring that the Union absorbs the WEU's power.

It should be possible for a qualified majority of member states to undertake humanitarian, diplomatic or military action which would qualify as a 'joint action', with guarantees that no member state should be forced to take part if it does not wish to do so, while at the same time such a state should not be able to prevent the majority from taking such action.

This would greatly increase the coherence of European integration and strengthen solidarity among the member states. It would mean extending, over the whole Union, the provisions of Article 5 of the WEU Treaty, according to which if a member state is attacked the other member states are automatically obliged to come to its assistance.

The multi-pillar structure cannot be considered satisfactory. Rather than increasing its effectiveness, the bridges between the pillars show up its contradictions. In many cases it is not easy to define the nature of an act in order to establish to what extent it belongs to the CFSP pillar of the Community pillar, with their respective procedures. There should be a more effective EU foreign policy within the framework of the Community pillar, integrating the common commercial policy, development cooperation policy, humanitarian aid and CFSP matters.

The Commission should be fully integrated in the definition and elaboration of the CFSP, with a right of initiative. It should be given implementing power. In order to rectify difficulties that have emerged in the field of policy design and formulation, a joint Commission-Council planing and analysis until should be established.

In order to improve parliamentary control, the obligation to consult Parliament must be strengthened and made effective. Obviously, in order to take into account the special requirements of foreign policy (confidentiality and rapidity), it is conceivable that in certain specific cases consultation may be of an ad hoc nature or carried out after the event.

To the same end it should be ensured that the Court of Justice is able to guarantee respect for the law in the interpretation and application of the provisions concerning external relations and foreign and defence policy. This would imply extending to this sector the rules governing preliminary rulings and proceedings for annulment or for failure to act.

The Community's reluctance to tackle the security and defence dimension is one of its most surprising characteristics. Now that we have decided to unite our destinies, the most appropriate comparison is that of a marriage where two people have decided to live together, share their wealth, labour and money, but encounter difficulties and distrust when it comes to defending the house and the peace. This may be understandable when there is a guardian to protect them, but it is hard to justify once the decisive step has been taken. It is increasingly untenable for 240 million Americans to have to guarantee the security of 340 million Europeans as part of a plan designed to deal with an enemy that no longer exists, at a high cost per capita and with an increasingly expensive and declining presence.

Perhaps the most striking picture of the current contradiction for the EU is the image on TV of the sacks of humanitarian aid to the former Yugoslavia bearing the common logo, while the peacekeeping troops keep their national symbols – although there are troops from eight countries of the EU – apart from the blue helmet and each one burying its own dead.

The Different Europes

A new situation is taking shape, which could be described as a transition from the magmatic stage to that of molecular aggregation. This is because everyone now aspires to the common title of European, in the face of the monopoly imposed by the Community, which had taken the name of the continent for itself. This is why there has been much talk of a 'return to Europe' on some circles, while others have insisted on the importance of the centre of the continent. Just as the navel of the ancient world was located at the temple of Delphi, several Central European countries are now claiming to be the centre of Europe.

It is possible to identify various sub-groups within the continent in relation to the European Union:

1 The first block consists of the remaining countries of the European Free Trade Association (EFTA), which was set up in 1957 as an alternative to the newly-emerging Common Market. Together with these countries, the Community has established the European Economic Area. After the entry of three leading EFTA members, Austria, Sweden and Finland, the remaining members are Norway, Iceland and Liechtenstein. Following the referendum rejecting ratification of the EEA, Switzerland has cautiously decided to postpone accession negotiations.

2 The second is the Central European group, also known as the Visegrad Group, in honour of the Hungarian city where it was founded. It consists of Poland, Hungary and, after their divorce, the Czech and Slovak Republics. European association agreements have been signed with these countries establishing cooperation not only in the commercial and economic sectors but also in areas such as education, the environment and at the political level (with the inclusion of a human rights clause). The preamble to these agreements explicitly refers to the desire of these countries to become members of the Community.

3 The Mediterranean group, consisting essentially of Malta and Cyprus. The Commission has drawn up reports favourable in principle to their accession. Apart from its

specific problems, the accession of Malta raises the additional complication of how micro-states can be accommodated in the institutional set-up. In the case of Cyprus, the partition of the island and the Turkish occupation are problems which are being dealt with in the framework of the United Nations. The agreement reached is to begin negotiations after the end of the IGC.

4   Turkey, a Eurasian country, applied for membership of the Community most recently in April 1987. Recently, a Customs Union treaty has been signed, and ratified by the EP after a bitter debate because of the situation of human rights in the country.

5   Various situations existing in Eastern Europe and the Balkans can be categorized as follows:
    – Romania and Bulgaria have concluded association agreements with the European Community
    – The Baltic States – Lithuania, Latvia and Estonia – with which Association treaties have been signed
    – Albania, with trade and cooperation agreements
    – The Republics of Slovenia and Croatia.

Some of the Republics belonging to the CIS, such as Belarus and Kazakhstan, have declared their intention of joining, although this cannot be seen as a serious possibility. Elsewhere, Morocco has made a similar declaration of intent. The Community's response has been to conclude partnership agreements, with the aim of establishing free trade areas.

This brief description assumes that the European Union is an open process, after its enlargement to include fifteen members in 1995. By the beginning of the next millenium, the Union could have twenty members and, in a foreseeable future, bearing in mind the number of applications made, its numbers could increase to thirty.

At the same time, a new architecture is emerging on the continent embracing various new structures. Among these is the Organization for Security and Cooperation in Europe (OSCE), an organization that is not strictly European, given the presence of the United States, Canada, Russia and Turkey. A product of the Helsinki Conference, whose great historic task was to secure the recognition of human rights as the supreme value as set out in the Madrid Declaration, the OSCE had devastating ripple effects on the Communitt block and went on to achieve the historic triumph represented by the 1990 Charter of Paris. It was in Paris where, for the first time in history, all the countries of the continent agreed to the fundamental values of a freely-elected parliament, a government with democratic legitimacy, respect for human rights and individual freedoms, the rule of law based on a constitutional order within an independent system of justice, free trade and a market economy. Since that time, the OSCE, whose membership extends to the very centre of Asia, has faced the difficult task of consolidating its role and its image, overwhelmed as it is by urgent tasks for which it has neither the cohesion nor the infrastructures (rapid intervention in conflict areas, protection of minorities, conciliation and arbitration machinery).

At the same time, the Council of Europe, the institution which has defined democracy on the Continent since 1949, is entering a new phase marked by the accession of the new democracies of Central and Eastern Europe. With its vast store of experience and knowledge, the Council is making a vital contribution to improving constitutional and legal provisions so as to promote respect for human and minority rights, as well as the training of political, legal and administrative leaders. The main event in 1996 has been the entry of Russia, although its current legislation and record of human rights have received a critical evaluation.

By so doing, the Council is consolidating its position as the major political assembly of Europe. The 1993 Vienna Summit marked a positive step forward with the line being taken by leaders such as President Mitterrand. In April 1990, I suggested to him that he should base his proposed confederation on the Council of Europe. By virtue of its structure and history, the Council of Europe has always seemed the ideal political framework for dialogue and stability in Europe.

Because it must operate as a political community and because of its economic character, the European Union cannot embrace all states of Europe, nor should that be its role. Furthermore, it would be wrong to overlook the existence of Russia and the CIS, for which the Union is hardly a subsitute.

The search for bodies and fora which can provide the continent with stability is therefore a fundamental political task for the Union. The positive results of the stability pact are a first step that demonstrates that the method of multilateral meetings on concrete proposals under the patronage of the EU and its member states is a fruitful one.

At the same time, our horizon is not covered merely by looking eastwards, however important that may be. The common home has four walls, of which only the western one is secure. In the south the situation is even more complex, since the Mare Nostrum is in reality, as Braudel rightly said, 'a complex of seas'. A meeting place and a frontier between civilizations, it is now experiencing a fresh encounter between the three religions of the book where clashes and conflicts occur and where demographic, economic and political differences mean that a clear priority must be given to efforts to create multilateral, political and economic institutions for the area. A model along the lines of the Conference on Security and Cooperation established in Helsinki would mark a decisive step forward. This is another historic challenge for the newly-created CFSP.

The Essen Summit of December 1994 has made a clear step forward, accepting the Mediterranean as an are of clear priority. From one side, the decision has been taken of launching a Conference on Security and Cooperation along the lines established in Helsinki, and at the same time a reinforcement of economic cooperation on a multilateral basis. The Euro-Mediterranean Conference that took place in Barcelona in November 1995 has defined a framework and a program for developping cooperation with financial support.

Reinforcement or Enlargement?

Since the beginning, the process of the Union has been seen as an open process, to countries both European and democratic. At each one of the four enlargements, the debate on reinforcing or enlarging has returned. The present task of the EU is not to deepen – we are not talking of the Channel Tunnel or a buried treasure – but rather to reinforce a construction that is under way in order to consolidate it. Moveover, the change in every enlargement has not been purely mechanical but dialectical, in the sense of producing transformations unexpected at the time the process was begun.

In the current situation, there is a consensus on the fact that the Union cannot proceed to a mechanical enlargement once again. In the last round, made by an emergency procedure that the push of history could justify, the debate was already very heated. Now, we must take advantage of the appointment of the 1996 IGC for adapting our structures, making them more capable to include new members. The Union may have twenty members at the turn of the millenium and thirty in a not-too-distant future. It must avoid being destroyed by its own success.

Everyone has taken stock of the situation and proposed models of how the enlarged Union might function, causing many of the problems that were papered over when the Treaty was negotiated to resurface. Examples of these are the Council blocking minority allowing two large states to combine with a small state in order to veto measures, the introduction of double majorities in the Council (including weighted voting in accordance with population size) and, most of all, the replacement of unanimity by the qualified majority.

Central and Eastern Europe

In the case of the countries of Central and Eastern Europe, despite all the difficulties facing them, the present situation in Europe offers them a unique historical opportunity. In the past, their destiny had always been defined by the great powers, the Austro-Hungarian Empire, Germany or Russia, and in the present century by the victors of the two World Wars. After the First World War, it was the decision of President Wilson and Clemenceau to encourage the growth of national identities and the dismantlement of the Austro-Hungarian Empire that shaped their destiny, while after the Second World War it was the deliberate redrawing of the map of Central Europe by Stalin. Now they can be the masters of their own destiny and thus of their own successes or failures.

The Community must now face up to the challenges represented by the return of the countries of Central and Eastern Europe to democracy and to Europe itself. As they emerge from a long period of political isolation, these countries are facing a triple challenge: to consolidate democracy, to restructure their economies and to learn the value of co-existence. These are the same tasks which faced the Community countries in the post-war years.

One generally encouraging aspect of the process is that, with certain exceptions (Romania and Albania initially and, above all, the former Yugoslavia), the political transitions have been achieved peacefully, with parliamentary democracy serving as a model for the organization of political society.

Despite their deep differences, these countries have one general feature in common, namely was disturbing fragmentation of political forces combined with inadequate social infrastructures, failings which are part of the disastrous legacy of the Communist dictatorships.

An indication of the speed with which events have unfolded is the fact that the first recognition of the European Community by Comecon occurred with the Luxembourg Declaration of 1988. One year later the Community was seeking to devise a new approach to relations under the influence of events in Poland and Hungary. Subsequently, the domino effect worked spectacularly with devastating results and the Soviet Union and Comecon were consigned to history. Elections were held even in Albania. Most of the countries concerned are by now members or observers at the Council of Europe or are thinking about joining. The Community has concluded economic and cooperation agreements with virtually all the countries in the area and is upgrading them through association agreements, which include aspects of political cooperation as well as fields such as education, the environment and technology transfer.

All these measures have served as an emergency response and have been like a sip of fresh water for peoples who have suffered a fifty-year drought; although their thirst is far from quenched. It is still curious that when so many were expecting Germany's concerns to shift eastwards, all eyes are now turning towards the West.

While acknowledging that the premarital formalities will take some time, it is nevertheless vital to move firmly ahead in order to strengthen the democratic process, consolidate economic development and encourage good neighbourliness.

As far as the first goal is concerned, stepping up the political dialogue will require a framework that clearly must move from the bilateral to the multilateral stage, a structure which must apply equally to the countries of Central and Eastern Europe, where arrangements must be developed to protect minorities and to deal with border conflicts or environmental disputes. The Stability Pact, a French initiative that has become a joint action, has provided an agreement between Hungary and Slovakia and impelled the negotiations between Hungary and Romania.

Of particular importance is the need for security and protection, a fact reflected in the applications of Central European countries for NATO membership. Partnership for Peace is the first platform for stabilizing the heart of the continent. The greatest contribution the European Union can and must make in this field is to strengthen the WEU and to help develop association arrangements. The situation in Europe has changed radically and the threat no longer comes from a possibility of a direct invasion or occupation by a nuclear superpower such as the Soviet Union, but rather from the tension and instability generated by ethnic and tribal conflicts or by the desire of certain middle-ranking countries to rule the roost in their own region. In any case, it will be a long and hard road, since civil society in these countries needs to acquire greater strength and maturity.

The second main challenge is in the economic field where goals which have been set as principles, such as improving access to the Community market, are encountering difficulties in practice against vested interests in agriculture and industry.

The experience acquired by the PHARE programme as an instrument for providing technical and economic assistance for structural reforms and adjustment has made a useful contribution to laying the foundations for a properly structured society with a market economy and a modern administration. Investment in trans-European transport and telecommunications networks, as well as urgent measures in sectors such as energy (particularly nuclear security) and the environment, will be of benefit to all.

In future, the PHARE programme could continue to embrace sectoral and regional development programmes, through the creation of structural funds similar to those established by the Community. This begs for radical reforms for the EU budget. With the current spending patterns, the entry of the Visegrad countries would mean almost the doubling of agricultural spending and a substantial increase in the structural funds, almost doubling the Community's current budget. On the other hand, deep cuts in these spendings represent a political gamble in each one of the member states.

The Tragedy of Yugoslavia

No review of the situation in Central Europe can afford to overlook that thorn in the Community's side, the terrible war in the former Yugoslavia, which has progressed from a civil war to an international conflict.

By one of history's cruel ironies, the conflict broke out in the only country to have liberated itself by its own efforts from the Nazi invasion without undergoing Soviet occupation. This autonomy was to rebound against it when the thaw came and a large part of the Serbian Communist *nomenklatura* converted to pan-nationalism, with the romantic and suicidal impulse inherent in the aspiration to a greater Serbia. The former President of the remains of the Yugoslav Federation, Cosic, who was appointed and sacked by Milosevic, has written a wide-ranging account with the eloquent title *Vreme Smrti* ('The time of death') in which he defends the tragic and solitary destiny of his people with a dramatic call to the Serbs who, in his view, have won the wars yet lost the peace.

The situation in Yugoslavia demonstrates in exemplary manner the tragic consequences of collective madness and the absurdities produced by hatred of one's neighbour and the refusal to recognize ethnic, religious or linguistic differences, real or imaginary. Once again, we are forced to acknowledge the truth of the words of Ibn Hazam de Córdoba that 'civil war is a flower that does not bloom'.

Criticism has been levelled at the impotence and divisions of the Community in the face of the Yugoslav crisis. Certainly there is a feeling of shared frustration at the barbaric nature of a conflict between Siamese twins who, in trying to separate, are killing each other. It is right to criticize the vacillations and tensions within a Council divided by historical memories and allegiances shaped by the pattern of alliances that emerged from two World Wars. There is no shortage of grievances and it was in Sarajevo itself that the first World War began, with the assassination of the Crown Prince of the Austro-Hungarian Empire. During the Second World War, the Croatian Ustashi were allies of the Nazis and were largely responsible for large-scale massacres of Serbs. The principle of 'an eye for an eye' goes back a long way in the history of a land that lay at the frontier between the Austro-Hungarian and Ottoman empires, between the Orthodox and Roman churches and whose fierce inhabitants were forever locked in the absurd conflicts that were commonplace throughout Europe throughout the centuries.

If the Community has made a mistake, it was its failure to foresee that the situation could reach such extremes of internal strife and destruction, and its reluctance to believe that the chronicle of a war foretold could come true. Germany's insistence that the independence of Slovenia and Croatia be recognized has been heavily criticized. The fact in isolation probably did help to trigger the fratricidal conflict, although the more important question was knowing when the time was right to sign the death certificate of the Federation. Perhaps nerve was lacking at a vital moment, such as the Serbian bombing of Dubrovnik, which should have served as adequate warning.

The basic fact remains that the divorce was not achieved by consensus or mutual agreement, as the Czechs and Slovaks were later able to do. The historical reasons are many but undoubtedly the most serious was the emergence of ideas such as ethnic cleansing and homogeneity between brother peoples whose destinies are intertwined. It is the modern version of purity of blood, which is fundamentally at odds with all the values on which the United Europe has been built. Significantly, most of the sympathy has been for the Republic of Bosnia, wrongly described as Muslim at its outset, in that it represents the civic values embodied in Sarajevo – a prime example of peaceful coexistence between peoples and religions, including the descendants of the Sephardic Jews who were expelled 500 years ago by the Catholic monarchs of Spain and later persecuted by the Nazis.

Europe's position from the outset has been that a political solution must be found within the framework of the United Nations. With this in view, the Community has concentrated on three main areas: active participation, including bringing pressure to bear (the sanctions against Serbia and Montenegro);

mediation between parties who have persistently defied the rules of war right from the time of the Vance-Owen and Owen-Stoltenberg plans; humanitarian aid, which is substantially a Community effort; and the provision of a network of monitors and a large proportion of the peace-keeping troops. The Community has not resorted to arms except in cases of legitimate defence and has suffered human losses in these territories.

Having led and participated in countless debates between Members of Parliament and Community leaders, between doves and hawks, and having listened to representatives of the parties to the conflict, I believe that there are few alternatives to this policy, which was launched before the CSFP came into force with binding effect. The most absurd criticism has been that the war in former Yugoslavia represents a failure of the Treaty, as if we should stop building our own house because the one next door is on fire. The hardest task is the need to continue combining political pressure with humanitarian aid and protection of the civilian population, even where there is the risk that this merely provides an easy source of supplies for the warring parties. Above all, we need to create firebreaks to prevent the spread of the conflict, which directly affects two Community countries, Greece and Italy, and is constantly in danger of spreading to the Balkan region as a whole. In fact, this is the first occasion when the Community countries have jointly sent troops outside their own frontiers to perform a peace-keeping role under a higher mandate – that of the UN – rather than imposing their will by force through a military invasion, the usual reflex of the old alliances. Although belated, the entry into the arena of the United States and Russia has added a new international dimension to the conflict.

The involvement of the United States, marked by the first act of war by NATO in its history, has made possible a negotiated peace settlement between Bosnia, Croatia, and Serbia in the Dayton agreements. Although it is the European Union which has made the greatest efforts, it has been unable to achieve the desired results.

The pathetic conflict in Yugoslavia is the clearest example of the disparity existing between the processes occurring on the continent: on the one hand a union is being built by free consent among the countries which invented the nation-state – in its most absolute form in the 19th century – while on the other exclusive nationalist movements are emerging (in a Europe where peoples, ethnic groups and cultures are part of a never-ending mosaic) with the aim of each creating their own state, currency and frontiers.

Meanwhile, at least 95% of the collective efforts of the European Community and its institutions are devoted to the de facto abolition of frontiers without actually touching them, and to establishing common rules for goods, foodstuffs and capital. We are now in the process of creating joint citizenship, a common currency and a common foreign and security policy. Ironically, the only point in common among Serbs, Croats, Bosnians and others is that they accept the German mark as being the only currency with real value.

The Future of Russia and the Collapse of the Empire

Although complex, the crisis in the former Yugoslavia looks like a laboratory experiment compared to the situation in the former Soviet Union, where we are seeing the disintegration of the greatest multi-ethnic empire since Roman times. Given the size and scale of what is happening, at best this will be a long process, full of vicissitudes.

A first noticeable characteristic of the transition taking place in the Soviet Union is that, as a general rule, it is occurring peacefully for the first time in history. The three Baltic Republics have been able to recover their identity and begin the transition to democracy, re-establishing the Baltic Sea as a Common European area together with their Scandinavian neighbours, while at the same time seeking to redefine their *modus vivendi* with their colossal neighbour. The improvement in civil rights legislation for the population of Russian origin in these countries – under the influence of the Council of Europe and the Union – is a step in the right direction. It should not be forgotten that Russia is the European state with most citizens living outside its frontiers, and that it continues to have an idea of itself as a great power, with genuine interests over its own zone of influence.

Nevertheless, it is impossible to overlook the existence of a series of bitter and bloody conflicts in the former Soviet Union, mainly in the Caucasus (war in Chechenia, civil war in

Georgia, conflict in Nagorno Karabak between Armenia and Azerbaijan) and in Central Asia (Tajikistan). However, the main question is the future of the Russian Federation, which represents 75% of the population and wealth of the former Soviet Union and which continues to maintain the essential nucleus of its armed forces and its claim to the role of a great power, particularly in neighbouring regions. This is a complex and Byzantine process dominated by the paradoxical and impetuous character of Boris Yeltsin, the first Russian President in history to be elected by universal suffrage, a man who acted in defence of Parliament initially yet two years later gave the order to destroy it. The West is in the uncomfortable and difficult position of supporting the most democratically-elected representative, while seeking to ensure that the democratic process takes root in this vast region.

The elections of December 1993 were acceptable more from the point of view of the electoral process than any equality of opportunity offered during the campaign. A sufficient majority was achieved in the constitutional referendum, which is a sign of greater political stability. However, the result of the legislative elections was much less clear and shows a disturbing trend towards radical nationalism, together with a suicidal division among reformers and a proliferation of individual candidates which seems to portend a climate of parliamentary and political instability.

The European Union is attempting to define its relations with the independent states and with the CIS as a whole. This is a particularly complex process, given the fluidity of the situation and the speed with which events occur. At present the Community and its Member States provide four-fifths of the emergency aid given to the CIS, although a considerable part of this aid is facing supply problems. A partnership agreement has been negotiated, but its ratification has been postponed.

The Community's approach is determined by its willingness to assist these states in reaching common agreement on their future economic and financial relations, to encourage their membership in international financial institutions and launch exploratory talks for the conclusion of cooperation agreements, while at the same time closely monitoring the destruction of nuclear weapons. All this should be achieved on the basis of respect for the principles of the Charter of Paris, which are far from being observed at present.

Behind this brief description lies an extremely complicated picture, full of uncertainty and shadows, where the European Union must play a vital role as a stabilizing and guiding element.

A Common Market in the Middle East

The Middle East is more closely related to Europe than is normally thought, not only because of the latter's undeniable historical and moral responsibilities in the region. The impact on the region of the political transformations in Europe is palpable, not only because of the waves of Jewish immigration from Europe to Israel (most recently from Russia), but also because the European Union is the main trading partner and principal aid donor for the entire region. In addition, one of the main objectives of Israeli foreign policy is to achieve a similar status to that of the EFTA countries. Although military assistance and the crucial guarantees are provided by the United States, it is Europe which is vital to the country's survival. It was Shimon Peres who rightly pointed out that 'no solution can be found to the national problems of any country outside a regional framework[1]. This remark that sums up the current situation of the world by a man whose life has been identified with the struggle for self-determination and the creation of the State of Israel, including the building-up of its defence system, and who is today the great architect of peace.

Developments have vindicated the approach taken by the Community initially and later by the Union. The most important historical forerunner of the CFSP was the Venice Declaration of 1981 on the Middle East. Since that time, the Community has pursued a coherent line, advocating a just and lasting peace. The negotiating process began in Madrid. The Community was present without being one of the leading players, although the Israel/PLO peace agreement was in line with the approach that it upheld.

The European Union's great opportunity will come with efforts to give genuine form to the peace process. It can now use all its experience and expertise in bringing together irreconcilable enemies on concrete issues, of which there is no shortage in a region racked by border disputes, where resources need to be managed in common (water, agriculture, efforts to combat desertification). Infrastructure must also be built through a major transfer of the resources made available as a peace dividend in the region of the world where most money is spent on arms and where vast pockets of wealth can be found side by side with poverty and a rapidly expanding population.

Regional Developments

The Community represents a significant precedent for what has become a major historical trend, the need felt by states to group together in regional organizations. While the most striking phenomenon of the period after the Second World War was the process of emancipation from the colonial yoke, together with self-determination and the creation of new states (which often sought to imitate the colonial states), in recent years efforts to establish regional organizations have been on the increase in many parts of the world.

In Latin America, where there is a shared aspiration to achieve the ideals embodied by Bolívar, various steps are being taken in this direction including the Andean Pact, the renewed efforts to relaunch the embryonic Central American common market of the 1970s, now being established as part of the peace process, and the most recent initiative known as Mercosur involving Argentina, Brazil, Paraguay and Uruguay. However, the process that really marks a turning point in the history of the continent and which is being established with giant strides is that launched by the North American Free Trade Agreement (NAFTA) between the United States, Mexico and Canada, which is already negotiating with Chile and is a growing attraction for the countries of Central America, Colombia and Venezuela, among others.

The Mexican crisis is a good example of the importance of a careful and balanced approach. The difference between NAFTA and the European Union process is that the first limits itself to a free trade area and the fact that it was implemented without transition periods. In addition to the claim made in the US Congress about the necessity of clauses on the rights of workers and the environment, the importance of the monetary dimension has appeared in the worst and more unpredictable way.

In the Far East, the Asia-Pacific Economic Conference (APEC) has been set up.

In Africa, the Arab-Maghreb Union (AMU) has been established by Morocco, Algeria, Tunisia, Mauritania and Libya. Arrangements for regional organizations involving the Lomé countries are at various stages of development.

Clearly, none of the associations mentioned is comparable to the Community in size or influence, but all are evidence of an increasingly marked historical trend.

Transatlantic Relationship

Although the challenges facing the European Union in its own continent and elsewhere are many and complex, there is one fundamental link which the Union must reconsider to update, namely its relationship with the United States, its protector and staunchest partner.

This relationship cannot be taken for granted indefinitely. Like all lasting unions, it needs to be updated every so often. The 1990 Transatlantic Declaration laid the foundations for this process, and the Madrid Declaration of December 1995 represents a wide-ranging review and a relaunching of the relation taking into account the changes which have occurred – in the first place, because the decision to establish the European Union and to initiate the CFSP means that the European pillar advocated by Kennedy in the early 1960s will become a reality. It is also important in the economic and trade sector because, as was pointed out in connection with GATT, clashes between objective interests are occurring at a time when a restructuring of the world regional blocks is under way.

Although it continues to dominate in the military field, the United States does not enjoy unchallenged hegemony in all sectors. The priority accorded to the ratification of NAFTA is a clear illustration of this. For the first time in history the Monroe doctrine can become a reality for all Americans, and America will no longer be for the North Americans alone. In addition, the growing focus that needs to be given to the Pacific basin, as shown by the APEC Summit in Seattle in 1993, is indicative of fundamental changes. Although the most important world trading relationship is between the United States and the European Community, the Pacific basin as a whole accounts for twice the volume of trade. Moreover, we should not forget some of the historical reasons which were at the root of the creation of the United States as a new world in contrast to the old Europe and which were reflected in the recommendation from Washington concerning non-entanglement in the Babylonian affairs of Europe. Twice in this century the United States has had to make a massive and crucial intervention in order to save order and democracy in Europe. We are now experiencing the third profound upheaval, which will be the acid test for the solidity of what has been created in Europe and the desire for change on the part of Europeans.

With the decline of the American presence in Europe – numbers have fallen from 300 000 to 100 000 soldiers and the process has accelerated since the Gulf War – the continuing debate on burden-sharing and President Clinton's electoral victory, won on the basis of an 'America First' programme focusing on the urgent need to cut the deficit, modernize industry, rebuild infrastructures and introduce solidarity and social justice, there are an increasing number of signs that the Transatlantic Declaration needs to open the way for a new kind of relationship.

While the Bush administration took a rather distant approach to European integration, Clinton has expressed his full support, saying in Brussels that the new security system must be based on European integration, integration of security forces, market economies and national democracies[2]. As the Secretary General of NATO, the late Mr Wörner, pointed out, this is a process in which transatlantic solidarity and European integration are not alternatives, let alone opposites. Europe must enhance its unity and strength in order to take on its share of responsibility. As David Calleo has rightly pointed out, 'Over the years three grand rival ideals for European order have come forward to shape policies and institutions: from the outset, the building of Europe was based on a complex mixture of Atlanticist, European and pan-European[3]'. In a veiled manner, these ideals were able to survive under the protection given by the unclear umbrella and the presence of United States troops in the face of the Soviet threat. However, the collapse of this world meant that Europe had to opt for its own defence policy, albeit in the highly cautious and intricate terms used in the Treaty on European Union. The underlying problem is that there are fewer shared ideas in this field than in others. Thinking on these matters is relatively less well-developed and established than in other areas covered by the Treaty. Of the two partners of the Franco-German axis, it is France, where the EDC foundered, that is a staunch supporter of a European defence.

For its part, Germany has been totally dependent on NATO. While the country's vision is clear on the political and above all economic and monetary aspects of the European Union, efforts to alter the post-war status quo in the field of security and defence have been encountering strong resistence and failing to secure consent among the political forces. However, the ruling of the Constitutional Court in 1994 allowing the participation of German troops in peacemaking operations with the approval of Bundestag is a breakthrough.

This situation has emerged at a time when Germany is being persuaded to make a contribution that goes further than financial assistance and the taking in of refugees from the conflicts in Eastern Europe, particularly in Yugoslavia (although in this case there was additional resistance for historical reasons). For its part, Great Britain has maintained a defence posture based on the status quo with an extreme Atlantic bias, a position shared by large sections of public opinion in the Netherlands and by a large proportion of European military commands. In the case of Spain, the decision to enter NATO marked a break with traditional arrangements which led to the agonizing political struggle over the 1985 referendum and the clear decision to revitalize the WEU as a pillar of European defence, reflected in the ten-point porgramme drawn up by the Spanish government.

The renewal of the transatlantic relationship is a vital interest for Europe. Recently, this statement has been made by different government representatives and has been included as a proposal in the investiture speech of the new Commission President, Mr Santer. The question is how to proceed, and the Transatlantic Policy Network (TPN) has made an effort of two years of intensive reflection, bringing together political, industrial and government leaders across Europe. I served as joint

Chairman of the project, and I share its views. The report sets out a step-by-step European strategy for building a balanced political partnership between the EU and the USA, able to advance the global interests of both partners in this period of dynamic geo-political and economic change.

The core recommendation of this report is to create much stronger linkages between the political, economic and security interests of Europe and America. To achieve this goal by the end of the century, the report recommends three intermediate steps of historic scope:

1   The transformation of the present Transatlantic Declaration into an economic and political treaty between the European Union and the United States through confidence building on specific issues.
2   The restructuring of NATO around a partnership between the United States and an integrated European defence pillar.
3   The linking of both these treaty-based partnership structures to a single transatlantic presidential summit process (whereas today there are two separate and distinct summits, one linked to NATO and the other to the mechanisms established under the Transatlantic Declaration).

To ensure pragmatic progress toward these objectives as rapidly as possible, the report calls for immediate expanded cooperation between the European Union and the United States on a range of specific common political, economic and security interests, both bilateral and multilateral.

The report goes on to stress the 'window of opportunity' now clearly open in Washington for real power-sharing with the European Union. This puts the ball squarely in the court of the EU member states to develop common external Union policies, and to take steps during the 1996 Intergovernmental Conference to further integrate political economic and security policies within the European Union.

The development of the common foreign and security policy has meant wiping the slate clean with regard to foreign policy as practised and understood by every European state since the Renaissance. The Venice Declaration on the Middle East was symbolic in this connection, since its proposals were inspired by UN resolutions and it placed the emphasis on seeking common interests in order to end the conflict. The origins of this conflict go back to the time of Abraham (or Ibrahim, depending on the point of view), in other words more than 5000 years. The first step towards this pragmatic approach, which was greeted with a certain amount of scepticism at the time, has been the long road form the Conference on Peace and Security in Europe.

Since then, the patient work of trying to arrange multi-lateral meetings and conferences, seeking to diffuse open conflicts, bringing pressure to bear, cajoling, proposing formulas to secure ceasefires, cooperation and recognition of mutual interests, like a spider's web in which the opposing sides become entangled, in a practice which has led to common action becoming the fundamental intrument of the CFSP. Its essence lies not only in the fact that it is adopted by vote, and thus the minority accepts the will of the majority, but especially in the ability to reach joint solutions.

Calleo has rightly pointed out that 'European Security may now be moving from what might be called an age of Hobbes to an age of Hegel. In a Hobbesian age, conflict are not so much reconciled as deterred by force. In a Hegelian era, conflicts are not so much deterred as overcome'[4].

This is a clean break with the long history of struggle for hegemony through wars, battles, invasions and destruction; but at its root is the desire to go beyond Von Clausewitz's classic maxim that 'war is the continuation of politics by other means' an effort to move beyond these means and replace them once again by politics.

Against this new background, it is important to reconsider the value of Atlanticism, not with a view to rejecting it, since there are sufficient reasons to justify its continuance, as reflected in the Charter of Paris. Reaffirming the fundamental nature of pluralist democracy and respect for the human rights of individuals and minorities represents a triumph over the invocation of reasons of state as the *ultima ratio*.

In addition to reaffirming our common values, not only as shared principles, but also because they correspond to the desires of a growing majority of mankind, the two sides of the Atlantic Alliance must make major efforts to strengthen and develop the United Nations and its philosophy (Japan should play a role in keeping considering the crucial economic influence it wields). We must move beyond the narrow commercial concerns of the existing relationship. The face that a system of regional cooperation is increasingly taking shape in America is not an obstacle to this process. In Asia no such cooperation exists and one of the great unknown quantities is how relations with Japan can be built up against the background of the growing strength of China. Security policy and thinking must also be adapted to the changing situation in the world, where a balance of opposing forces is no longer the rule.

Nevertheless, we should not overlook the difficulties of consolidating democracy in Russia (and in the CIS in general), nor should we neglect the military uncertainties of a system where the Red Army behaves more and more as a pretorian guard. The most likely scenario is an increase in small-scale bitter conflicts of the kind occurring in the former Yugoslavia, the Caucasus or Algeria, with complex civil, tribal or religious origins, and made highly acrimonious by the presence of radical nationalism (Sudan, Somalia, Haiti). These conflicts may be accompanied by efforts to secure regional hegemony by medium-sized powers with easy access to the international arms market, including the nuclear sector, where sales are booming following the disappearance of the Soviet Union. In this connection, two regimes with clear expansionist aspirations can be singled out, Iraq and Iran. After the long and exhausting struggle between the countries, the Gulf War represented a new kind of conflict. Here the UN played a role in offering a framework and legitimacy for the operation and ensuring the multinational composition of the forces under its command. The most striking features of the action taken by the Community were the immediate provision of humanitarian aid on the ground – not as widely reported as the fighting but crucial in terms of saving human lives – and the efforts to coordinate measures to monitor the sanctions. Whatever happens, this part of the Middle East will continue to be a highly sensitive area for the foreseeable future.

The philosophy of overcoming conflicts through cooperation requires a new approach calling for a perseverance that can be achieved by combining the infinite patience of Job with the idealism of Don Quixote in order to gradually change the harsh reality surrounding us. This task is not the monopoly of the great powers of the world. Small and active neighbours can make a vital contribution as has been apparent in the case of Nicaragua and El Salvador and the San José conference in Central America, the role of the countries of West Africa in the civil war in Liberia, and the contribution of the OAU countries, particularly those of black Africa, in securing the independence of Namibia, and defeat apartheid in South Africa, and now in Angola.

Now that the European Union has decided to embark on the CFSP, its new foreign policy must be more Hegelian than Hobbesian, aiming to settle conflicts by persevering in the difficult task of eliminating their causes rather than seeking to impose a solution by force.

Epilogue

It is difficult to bring to a close a study such as this, whose subject is a work under construction, before the deadline for completion has expired. I hope, however, that I have fulfilled the original purpose of this book: to advocate a federal Europe as the most balanced solution, to help explain what our project involves and to highlight some of the main challenges facing us.

It is not merely a case of completing a technocratic or architectural agenda. Politicians are not simply engineers ensuring that social operations run smoothly, as Monsignor Lustiger has rightly said; reflection also needs to be given to values, now that values such as democracy, tolerance and civil peace appear firmly established in this part of Europe, a victory which is not and never can be definitive and irreversible. The defence of values acquires particular significance at a time of far-reaching change in the way in which politics are conducted.

The historic thaw in Europe is also sweeping away many of the balances which have held sway in political life since the end of the Second World War. A growing unpredictability is making public response to political leaders and traditional political parties more fickle. This phenomenon can be most clearly observed in Italy, which is experiencing a peaceful change of Republic after a long period in which the political majority was perpetuated by the deadlock arising from the existence of the largest Communist party in Western Europe. We are witnessing a grass-roots revolution in which the power of the courts and the media is becoming decisive; a process which should be followed attentively since Italy, though it is often denigrated, tends to be in the vanguard in many areas – and not only in art or fashion – and, moreover, because events are unfolding in the *piazza*, in public view. *Tangentopoli* provides an illustration of the growing phenomenon of the adoration of the 'golden calf' as the supreme divine being of the age. 'The increase in the number of financial "scandals" in the major democracies is not so much an anomaly' – as Géhenno has written – 'as the logical consequence of the triumph of the sole remaining universality; money'[1]. This is a provocative vision which reflects the great challenge of the coming years, to generate collective enthusiasm for the noble task of politics and give it a soul. This has implications for public and political virtues. Victoria Camps has approached the problem in an intelligent way, starting with the negative side, the corresponding 'vices', summing up those of the public as indifference, intolerance and lack of public spirit compared with those 'more specific to politicians', which she lists as the corporate spirit of party politics, lack of transparency and unstoppable corruption as the 'most prevalent, well-known and ancient political vice'[2].

In the North American constitutional debate at the end of the 18th century, Hamilton declared that a covetous man who attains public office, when reflecting upon the time when he would be forced to forgo his emoluments, might easily be tempted to take advantage of his office while he could, making unscrupulous use of the most corrupt practices in order to reap a harvest as abundant as it was ephemeral. Faced with different prospects, on the other hand, the same man would probably be content with the normal privileges of his post and would be able to resist any benefits he might gain from abusing his position.

This notion is highly relevant to present-day Europe, where an intense and welcome debate is taking place on the relationship between ethics and politics. A basic feature of democracy is the ability to provide an appropriate counterweight for self-interest and personal weaknesses through a system of checks and balances designed to have a deterrent effect on the human beings who make up society. It should be based on the assumption that we are liable to be tempted to help ourselves where we can. Rules governing political behaviour and control over our own self-interest and weaknesses are therefore essential components of democracy.

This is a new dimension of the fledging European Union. The Community's functionalist approach has had major advantages as well as some matching disadvantages, one example being that, for many years, Community life was reduced to a process of bargaining between the various interests involved. The practice of lobbying in Brussels to achieve a specific objective was considered the most convenient one and openly defended. The Community's image has long been dominated by rival interests and influence-peddling as the most visible and tangible aspects of a process of association which has gradually replaced the classic struggle for continental hegemony among the European states.

As a result, we should not be over-alarmed at the reactions of some sections of the public during the debate on the ratification of the Maastricht Treaty, in which the fundamental values of political life have been incorporated into the texts for the first time. History offers few examples of such a noble cause being so badly promoted. Despite this, it has succeeded in overcoming serious challenges.

Democracy, transparency and subsidiarity form a triptych to which European leaders have been forced by events to attach the greatest priority. The aim is to make proceedings clear and transparent on the basis that their influence plays a part in all human relations, whether in the public or in the private sphere. The role of influence is typified in a number of classic examples which are inherent to life in any society, ranging from courtship to unexpected presents. In principle, telephone calls and requests for interviews with members of Parliament, ministers or leaders of councils are not illegitimate. This is simply the form which lobbying takes.

Its results can be seen in odd phrases during the debate on any piece of legislation. When considering amendments to a draft budget, tax law or regulation fixing farm prices – whether in the Spanish or the European Parliament – there is no need to launch a detailed investigation in order to ascertain who or what has succeeded in attracting support. Influence-peddling needs to be regulated because human behaviour – which is not always pure and altruistic – itself needs to be regulated. The Americans refer to this with their usual frankness as pork-barrel legislation, which plays an even more important role in a system of individual constituencies. The parliamentary process is more transparent and open than the mere practice of lobbying. It should also be borne in mind that NGOs with altruistic rather than egoistic motives, such as Amnesty International and Médecins Sans Frontières, also count as interest groups.

For all these reasons, it is more positive to adopt an approach which recognizes the fallibility of human nature and endeavours to perfect the controls which are necessary to make our behaviour transparent. This restoration of the necessarily ethical character of public activity must be based on transparency and self-control, both among politicians themselves and those who carry out public responsibilities such as judges, officials and journalists.

At the same time, the European Union might provide an inspiring model of a community, particularly for young people. This is not an unthinking appeal to the values of youth, which should be upheld by the efforts of young people themselves, but because we are succeeding in overcoming the Europe which, in the words of Paul Valéry, was a 'paradoxical system which achieved the greatest possible degree of intellectual union with the greatest possible degree of disunion as regards intentions'. This is a curse which should be borne in mind in order to ensure that it is finally consigned to the past.

This new page of history is being written at a time when the societies which make up the European Union are clearly moving from the *realm of necessity* to the *realm of freedom*. The possibility of transcending the subjection and servitude which have constituted the history of mankind thanks to the spectacular and liberating development propelled by continued technological progress is opening up infinite horizons. The alternatives are either to withdraw among ourselves, surrounded by barriers to prevent contamination by poverty, or to play an active and cooperative part in a better future for humanity. Europe has always fulfilled its true destiny when it has opened up to the world.

How can we best define the European democracy of the future? The best definition is doubtless that provided by Pericles two and a half thousand years ago in his famous *Funeral Oration* to the Athenians who had fallen in the Pelopponesian War:

> Let me say that our system of government does not copy the institutions of our neighbours; it is more the case of our being a model to others, than of our imitating anyone else. Our constitution is called a democracy because power is in the hands not of a minority but of the whole people. When it is a question of putting one person before another in positions of public responsibility, what counts is not membership of a particular class, but the actual ability which the

man possesses. No one, so long as he has in it to be of service to the city, is kept in political obscurity because of poverty. . . . Thanks to the greatness of our city, all kinds of goods from all over the world come to us, so that to us it seems just as natural to enjoy foreign goods as our own local products. . . . Our city is open to all. . . .

Our love of what is beautiful does not lead to extravagance; our love of the things of the mind does not make us soft; we regard wealth as something to be properly used rather than as something to boast about. As for poverty, no one needs to be ashamed to admit it: the real shame is in not taking practical measures to escape from it.

Here each individual is interested not only in his own affairs but in the affairs of the state as well; even those who are mostly occupied with their own business are extremely well informed on general policy; this is a peculiarity of ours; we do not say that a man who takes no interests in politics is a man who minds his own business; we say that he has no business here at all. We, Athenians, in our own persons, take our decisions on policy or submit them to proper discussions; for we do not think that there is an incompatibility between words and deeds. The worst thing is to rush into action before consequences have been properly debated.

In a world which is fascinated by any prediction of the future which has a scientific gloss (so-called 'futurology'), and which is unconsciously overawed by the close of the current and the dawn of the coming millennium, the validity and freshness of this definition is instructive. For those who will live in and lead Europe and the world in the next millennium, it is useful to remember that, despite enormous upheavals and technological progress, the human soul is still similar at its best and its worst aspects to that of the classical Athenians: with resolve and boldness, it can change its course. The proof is the European Union.

Glossary

A

Acquis communautaire
The whole body of principles and laws which a country has to accept *en bloc* in order to become a member of the European Union.

ASEAN
The Association of the Nations of South-East Asia was set up in 1967 by the Bangkok Declaration. Its member states are Brunei, Indonesia, Malaysia, the Philippines and Singapore. The objective is to establish a tariff-preference zone and to foment the economic growth and social progress of the member states.

Association Agreement
'Association' establishes a contractual agreement with third countries guaranteeing close economic cooperation, political dialogue and financial support over and above the rules governing Community trade policy. Its objective is to prepare the country in question for possible EC/EU accession.

The Association Agreements recently reached with the countries of Central and Eastern Europe link the granting of association status with respect on the part of the countries concerned for democratic principles, human rights, and the principles of market economy.

The EC signed Association Agreements with Turkey in 1964, Malta in 1971, Cyprus in 1971, Hungary in 1992 and Poland in 1992. Agreements are currently being ratified with the Czech Republic, Slovakia, Bulgaria and Romanania.

B

Benelux
On 3 February 1958, Belgium, Holland and Luxembourg signed the Treaty of the Hague which officially established economic union, the final stage in the integration process which these countries had initiated with the Monetary Convention of 1943.

Blocking Minority
A 'coalition' of member states who together have sufficient votes (26 out of 87) to force the rejection of a decision requiring a qualified minority for its adoption.

Bretton Woods Agreements
Signed in July 1944, they established the mechanisms for a new worldwide monetary system, with a fixed reference currency for monetary exchanges,

the dollar and that linked to gold; its institutions are the IMF and the World Bank. The dollar/gold link ended during the Nixon Presidency in the USA.

Bundesbank
Central Bank of the Federal Republic of Germany.

C

Caprice des Dieux
Nickname of the EP building in Brussels, due to its resemblance to a well-known French cheese.

Central Bank
Institution holding a national monopoly to print bank notes and mint coins.

Cohesion Fund
The TEU establishes a new Cohesion Fund financed by the Community to provide financial support for Member States with a per capita GNP of less than 90% of the Community average (currently Spain, Ireland, Portugal and Greece). Financial support will be given to investment projects in the field of transport infrastructure (trans-European networks) and to environmental projects.

Commission
It comprises 20 Commissioners responsible for specific portfolios, including a President and two Vice-Presidents. The Commissioners are appointed by the member states, although they must swear to carry out their functions entirely independently and in the general interest of the Community. Their decisions are collegiate, i.e. they express the overall will of the Institution, even when they are the result of internal vote which must represent at least a simple majority of the 20 Commissioners. The Commission's headquarters are in Brussels.

The Commission is the driving force of Community policy, that it has the power to initiate legislation. It is the guardian of the Treaties and ensures that they are applied, implemented and complied with.

The Commission is an executive body which manages the Community's policies and the implementation of the budget. It represents the Community in numerous international bodies and, on a mandate from the Council, negotiates agreements with third countries.

The TEU, by extendindg the powers of the Community, has increased the Commission's role by the investiture vote. At the same time, the Commission is now more subject to political and financial controls by the EP, and its members, once they have been appointed by the Member States, must submit as a collegiate body to approval by the EP. The Commission has to resign if the EP adopts a motion of censure by a two-thirds majority of its Members.

Committee of the Regions
An advisory body set up by the TEU, it represents an important step towards taking account at Community level of the interests and viewpoints of the

various regional and local bodies. It will have 189 Members. It shares its organizational structures with the ECOSOC.

Common Agricultural Policy (CAP)
Its objectives are laid down in the Treaty of Rome: to increase agricultural productivity, to ensure a fair standard of living for producers, to stabilize markets, to ensure the availability of supplies, to ensure supplies reach consumers at reasonable prices. In order to attain these objectives, three fundamental principles are taken into account: the unity of the market, community preference and financial solidarity.

After almost 30 years of CAP, on 21 May 1992, the Council of Ministers of Agriculture adopted a decision on the reform of the CAP (based on the McSharry report of the Commission) decided on at the Maastricht Council. The objectives of the reform are to reduce the enormous subsidised surpluses of European agriculture and cattle production, to prevent the 'rural exodus', to safeguard the purchasing power of producers and to protect the environment.

Community of Independent States (CIS)
Set up by the Minsk and Alma Ata Agreements, December 1991. Initially announced as the successor of the Soviet Union, it is currently a statement of intent to uphold economic, political and military cooperation between the former Soviet Republics which it comprises.

Competitiveness
Capacity of a country to compete on the international market. It depends on the different elements in play: quality of products or services, prices, costs, technology, deadlines, etc.

Convergence
The process bringing the economic policies and the economies of the Member States closer together in order to achieve Economic and Monetary Union.

COREPER
The Committee of Permanent Representatives, mandated by Council to coordinate the preparatory work for Community decisions. It is involved in all areas of Community activity.

The meetings of Coreper I deal with technical issues; the Member States are represented by their deputy permanent representatives.

Coreper II comprises the Ambassadors and deals with political issues. It carries out whatever tasks the Council entrusts it with.

COSAC
The coordinating body of the national parliaments and the EP on issues of a Community nature.

Council of Europe
The Council of Europe was established on 5 May 1949. It has 34 members and several applicants. Its headquarters are in Strasbourg. Its objectives are

to bring about a closer union between its members with the purpose of safeguarding and developing the ideals and principles which constitute their common heritage, and encourage their economic and social progress. The Council is active in all areas except defence. One of its greatest achievements is the European Convention on Human Rights, signed in Rome in 1950, which came into force in 1953. This Convention set up a European Human Rights Commission and Court, which may be appealed to directly by the citizens of those Member States which have accepted this possibility.

Council of Ministers
This is composed of a representative, of ministerial rank, from each of the fifteen Governments. Although, legally, there is only a single Council, in reality there are 20, bringing together all the national ministers in a given field (Agriculture Council, Transport Council, etc.). It exercises legislative power and manages the EU's foreign relations.

In the Community set-up, it represents the interests of member states. It adopts its decisions by unanimity or a qualified majority (54/62/87/76 of the weighted votes) according to the nature of the decision being taken. Its headquarters are in Brussels, and it occasionally meets in Luxembourg.

It is assisted by the Coreper in preparing its decisions.

Council of the European Union
The new name of the Council of Ministers following the coming into force of the TEU.

Court of Auditors
Set up at the instigation of the European Parliament, the Court of Auditors assumed its functions in October 1977. It consists of fifteen members appointed for six years by the Council (after consulting the European Parliament). Its task is to examine the revenue and expenditure of the Community and to ensure the correct administration of the budget. It was accorded the rank of Community Institution by the TEU.

Court of First Instance
On 24 October 1988, the Council adopted a decision establishing the Court. It has fifteen members and deals with statutory matters and with the law on competition, antidumping and the contentious areas of coal and steel.

Court of Justice
Comprises fifteen judges elected by the Member States who are assisted by six Advocates-General. They serve for a six-year term. The Court has its seat in Luxembourg.

The function of the Court of Justice is fundamental: it guarantees the rule of law in the application and interpretation of the Treaties and of the provisions of secondary legislation.

The TEU allows the Court of Justice to impose economic sanctions on any member state which fails to comply with a second judgement against it on any one case.

D

Decision
A community legal measure. Decisions are binding on those to whom they are addressed (e.g. governments, businesses, etc.).

Delors II (package)
A Commission report establishing the forecast of the Union's revenue and expenditure for the period from 1993 to 1997.

Devaluation
The reduction of the rate at which one currency is exchanged for another. Strictly speaking, the term 'devaluation' (and 'revaluation') applies only to fixed-rate systems. In systems with floating rates of exchange the terms used are *currency appreciation* and *depreciation.*

Directive
A Community legal act binding on the member states as regards the objectives of the directive, leaving the member state free to choose the form and the means of its implementation.

Dumping
The sale of a product on a foreign market at a lower price than on the domestic market in order to increase the market share or eliminate competition. The term covers a multitude of phenomena. The term 'social dumping' is used when an enterprise seeks to use cheap, non-unionized labour in developing countries. Similarly, the term 'ecological dumping' has been coined to describe the activities of enterprises which have low production costs as a result of their countries' lack of environmental controls similar to those which exist in more developed countries.

E

ECHO (European Community Humanitarian Office)
A Commission service whose task it is to centralize and coordinate Community emergency aid to third countries.

ECOFIN
The Economic and Financial Affairs Council. Its principal task is to implement EMU.

Economic and Monetary Union (EMU)
EMU is the logical complement of the completion of the internal market. An age-old aspiration of the Community, it was first mentioned at the summit in The Hague in 1969. In 1970, the Werner Report proposed the creation of the EMU in three stages over a period of ten years. A number of initiatives were taken before the European Council of Madrid decided to initiate the first stage of EMU on 1 July 1990. This set in motion the process which was to be further elaborated in the TEU and through which the EMU

would be attained in three stages with the deadline of 1 January 1999 (cf. the timetable for these stages on page 125).

Economic and Social Committee (ESC)
An economic advisory body of the Council and the Commission, comprising 229 representatives of the various categories of economic and social activity, in particular representatives of employers, farmers, employees, workers, dealers and and professional occupations (Article 2193 of the EEC Treaty). Its headquarters are in Brussels. Its make-up and its purpose, which is both political and technical, mean that it exercises a significant influence over the Community's decision-making process. It establishes a link between politics and the different sectors of professional life.

ECU
The European Currency Unit, introduced on 1 January 1979. It is based on a composite of the currencies of the Member States weighted in proportion to their economic power. It is used within the Community (the budget was set in Ecus) and in the international market. The Madrid Summit of December 1995 has changed its name, that has become the EURO.

Enlargement
The EC has admitted new members on four occasions:
- 1 January 1973: accession of Ireland, Denmark and the United Kingdom
- 1 January 1981: Greece
- 1 January 1986: Spain and Portugal
- 1 January 1995: Austria, Finland and Sweden.

EURO
The new name of the ECU, that is set to become the single currency of the European Union.

Eurobarometer
A periodical Commission publication on public opinion within the EU on Community issues, on the basis of opinion polls.

Eurocorps
Embryo of the European Army whose creation was decided on by F. Mitterrand and H. Kohl in May 1992. The Franco-German nucleus has been joined by forces from Belgium, Spain and Luxembourg. Its headquarters are in Strasbourg.

European Agreement (see *Association Agreement*)

European Bank for Reconstruction and Development (EBRD)
An institution inaugurated on 15 April 1991 with the purpose of contributing to the development and economic reconstruction of those countries of Central and Eastern Europe which undertake to respect and apply the principles of democracy and pluralism and the market economy.

The EBRD has both a financial and political role, since it is designed to encourage both the market economy and democracy in the former Communist bloc. It has 41 shareholders: the 39 founding states, the Commission of the European Union and the EIB. Its headquarters are in London and its operations are divided between the private sector (60%) and the public sector (400%).

European citizenship
European citizenship comprises all those political, social and economic rights of citizens guaranteed by the Union (TEU Article 8), over and above those enjoyed by citizens as nationals of one of the member states. By virtue of European citizenship, the TEU recognizes the right of citizens to freedom of movement and residence and their right to vote and to stand for election in municipal elections and European elections, and their right to petition the EP; it also establishes a European Union ombudsman, and offers diplomatic or consular protection to Community nationals in third countries through the good offices of the embassies and consulates of all the Union's member states.

European Coal and Steel Community (ECSC)
This was born with the Schuman Declaration of 19 May 1950 proposing to all the countries of Europe the idea of setting up a 'coal and steel Europe' under the direction of a supranational High Authority. On 18 April 1951, six countries – the three Benelux countries, Germany, France and Italy – signed the Treaty setting up the ECSC in Paris, founded upon a common market, common objectives and common institutions (Article 1). The common market in steel and coal has been operating since May 1953.

European Council (or Summit)
A meeting of the heads of states and governments of the member states, accompanied by their respective General Affairs Ministers and the President of the Commission.
Set up in 1974 as a talking shop, the European Council has been incorporated into the Treaties by the TEU, which establishes it as the highest political body of the Union. It meets at least twice a year, normally at the end of each six-monthly Presidency of the Council. Its function is to encourage the development of the Union and establish its general guidelines. Its decisions have no juridical value.

European Defence Community (EDC)
A draft European Defence Community which provided for the integration of the armed forces of the six ECSC Member States into a single European army. It was submitted as the first stage in creating a European federation. In May 1952, this took concrete shape with the signing of the Treaty in Paris. The Treaty was rejected by the French Assembly in August 1954.

European Development Fund (EDF)
Multilateral aid financed by all the member states of the European Union.

European Economic Area (EEA)
The EEA is the world's biggest common market, comprising 380 million consumers. It consists of the fifteen EU member states and three of the EFTA countries (Switzerland rejected the agreement in a referendum on 6 December 1992). The EEA Agreement guarantees the free movement of persons, goods, services and capital and the abolition of non-tariff trade barriers. To this end, the EFTA countries adopted a section of Community Law.

It provides for a Cohesion Fund to help the less developed Member States of the European Community and widens the scope of cooperation between its members in the areas of education, research and development as well as consumer and environmental protection. The EEA sets up a series of common political and administrative bodies and was to have entered into force on 1 January 1993 at the same time as the EC Single Market. The Agreement is in force only with regard to Norway, Iceland and Liechtenstein.

European Economic Community
Set up by the Treaty of Rome on 25 March 1957. Also called the Common Market, the Twelve and the Community.

European growth initiative
A Programme of public investment to promote economic recovery in Europe, adopted in December 1992 at the Edinburgh Summit.

European Investment Bank (EIB)
Established by the Treaty of Rome (Rule 129), the EIB is the EU's financial institution. Its purpose is to fund investment which contributes to the Union's development and to reinforce its economic and social cohesion. Its objectives are to encourage the development of less favoured regions, the conversion or modernization of businesses, the establishment of a European transport and telecommunications infrastructure network, etc.

The EIB also funds industrial and agricultural infrastructures and projects which contribute to the development of the Mediterranean countries or the ACP.

Its seat is in Luxembourg and the shareholders are the member states. It is endowed with its own legal personality.

European Investment Fund
At the Edinburgh Summit, the European Council called on the ECOFIN and the EIB to establish the European Investment Fund, whose capital could total ECU 20 000 million. It is a key instrument in the financing of the European growth initiative.

European Monetary Institute (EMI)
The EMI is a centre for decision-making and for the assumption of responsibilities. It is the body responsible for preparing the transition to the third stage of EMU. Its tasks are to prepare a single monetary policy, the creation of a single currency, the establishment of the ESCB and the ECB. The EMI is an independent body and its president is Alexander Lamfalussy.

European Monetary System
Its principles were laid down at the Bremen Council of July 1978. It was approved by the Council in Brussels in November 1978 and put into practice by means of an agreement between the central banks of the member states of the EC. It has been in operation since March 1979 and its objective is to enable closer monetary cooperation between member states in order to create an area of monetary stability in Europe.

It is based on a grid of parities between the currencies and in relation to the ECU. Exchange rate fluctuations are confined to a margin of ±2.25% (6% for the Peseta and the Pound Sterling) in relation to the central bilateral parities established in the grid. The EMS has been destabilized by a number of monetary upheavals in the past two years. The bilateral parities have been modified on a number of occasions. The Pound Sterling and the Italian Lira provisionally left the system (September 1992). The maximum margin of fluctuation was increased to 15% in August 1993.

European Parliament (EP)
The Parliament currently has 626 Members who since 1979 have been elected through universal suffrage.

Since it is an institution working for Community integration, Members are grouped according to political group rather than nationality. It has one President and fourteen Vice-Presidents. Plenary sittings are held in Strasbourg and additional sittings in Brussels.

Its nineteen Committees prepare the work for these sittings in Brussels. The General Secretariat is based in Luxembourg.

The European Parliament has powers in a number of fields: budgetary powers, legislative powers with regard to the internal market, the power of assent concerning the accession of new members and certain international treaties as well as supervisory powers over the Council and the Commission.

The TEU grants the European Parliament greater powers as regards legislation and the control of the executive, particularly due to the new co-decision procedure, its practical involvement in the appointment of the President of the Commission, the creation of the office of Ombudsman and the ability to appoint committees of inquiry.

European Political Cooperation (EPC)
Institutionalized by Title III of the Single Act, EPC is a system of inter-governmental consultations and coordination; it possesses no legal or institutional apparatus. Its decisions are taken unanimously.

G

G7
The 'Group of 7' are the seven most industrialized nations in the World (Canada, France, Germany, Japan, Italy, the United Kingdom and the USA).

The Presidents of the Commission and the Council take part in the meetings.

The G5 are Germany, France, Japan, the United Kingdom and the USA. The G3 are Germany, Japan and the USA.

General Affairs Council
Meeting of the Council of Foreign Ministers of the Member States. The General Affairs Council deals with the Community's current affairs and co-ordinates the work of the other Council of Ministers. It also coordinates the Intergovernmental Conferences (EMU, Political Union, AGC 1991, IGC 1996).

Government Deficit
Situation where a government's revenue is lower than the expenditure. The opposite situation is one of government surplus.

Gross Domestic Product
A measure of the economic activity of a country in a given period (normally a year).
    The total flow of final goods and services produced in a country. The word 'gross' means that no deduction for the value of expenditure on capital goods used in production has been made.

Gross National Product (GNP)
The GNP is equivalent to the GDP plus the income due to national factors (labour and capital) abroad minus the income of foreign factors earned in the country.

I

Inflation
The increase in the general level of prices in an economy. The retail price index (RPI) is the most commonly used indicator used to measure the rate of inflation.

International Monetary Fund (IMF)
A specialized United Nations body established on 22 July 1944 by the Bretton Woods agreements. Its task is to promote international cooperation in monetary matters and the development of world trade, granting low interest loans to countries facing balance of payments difficulties.
    Its headquarters are in Washington and it has 150 member states. The CEC takes part in its activities.

L

Languages
The EC/EU has eleven working languages: Danish, Dutch, English, French, Finnish, German, Greek, Italian, Portuguese, Spanish and Swedish. There are thus 110 language combinations for simultaneous interpretation. Two countries, Ireland and Luxembourg, have forgone the use of their official languages as official languages of the Community (Gaelic and Luxembourgish).

Lomé Convention
Since its birth, the Community has been involved in organized cooperation for development with the ACP countries of Africa, the Caribbean and the

Pacific. Various conventions have been drawn up (Yaoundé I and II, Lomé I, II, III and IV) establishing objectives and development activities following the negotiations held by the Member States. Lomé IV was signed in 1989 and currently affects 460 million people in 69 countries. It makes provision for EDF funding of various programmes and projects within the framework of the sectoral development policy of the ACP countries for the period 1990–1995.

Luxembourg Compromise
On 29 January 1966, this compromise brought an end to the institutional crisis which had paralysed the Community for six months. On 30 June 1965, France, fearing the funding of the CAP would affect its vital interests, blocked the decision-making procedure (by qualified majority by implementing the 'empty chair policy').

The compromise stated that when decisions affected very important interests of one or more Member States, the Council of Ministers should reach a unanimous agreement (rejection of the principle of the majority decision).

M

Maastricht Treaty
The usual way of referring to the Treaty on European Union (TEU).

MERCOSUR
The common market formed by Argentina, Brazil, Paraguay and Uruguay.

The EEC signed a 'third generation' cooperation agreement on 29 May 1992 with the Mercosur.

Monetary Committee
Set up by article 105 of the Treaty of Rome, the Monetary Committee is an advisory committee comprising the Deputy Governors of the member states' central banks, who meet every month in Brussels to coordinate monetary policy.

N

NAFTA (North American Free Trade Agreement)
Establishes a free trade area of 358 million consumers between Canada, the USA and Mexico. The Agreement was signed by the Heads of Government of the three countries on 17 December 1992. It was ratified by the US Congress on 17 November 1993 and is scheduled to come into force on 1 January 1994.

NATO
The North Atlantic Treaty Organization, established in 1949, is a regional defence organization whose aim is to safeguard the collective security of its members. Any act of aggression directed at any member is considered as an act of aggression against all members of the organization. In the event of conflict, the states are bound to help the member state(s) under attack.

It has sixteen members (the EU member states except Ireland, plus Canada, Iceland, Norway, Turkey and the USA) and its headquarters are in Brussels.

The policy of the alliance is laid down by the North Atlantic Council consisting of representatives of the sixteen governments.

Non-tariff barriers

National regulations and technical standards on goods, verification procedures, inspection arrangements prior to dispatch and regulations on the origin of products can all act as trade barriers in the same way as quotas and quantitative restrictions on imports, without there having to be a tariff, customs duty or levy to increase costs. The GATT also aims to limit or eliminate these barriers.

O

Ombudsman

The European Ombudsman's office has been set up by the TEU, to deal with claims concerning 'cases of maladministration' on the part of Community institutions or bodies. The Ombudsman is appointed after each EP election. His mandate runs concurrently with the life of Parliament.

Organization for Economic Co-operation and Development (OECD)

The OECD was established on 14 December 1960 as a successor of the OEEC. It comprises 24 countries (the fifteen EU states, the EFTA countries with the exception of Liechtenstein, Australia, Canada, the USA, Japan, New Zealand and Turkey). Its headquarters are in Paris. Its aim is to coordinate the economic and social policies of its member states in order to increase economic wealth and contribute to a balanced functioning of the world economy.

The Commission of the EU participates in the work of the OECD.

P

Pact of Stability

A pact on stability in Europe adopted at the Copenhagen Summit of June 1993. It entails the pursuit of preventive diplomacy capable of defusing potential border or ethnic disputes in Central and Eastern Europe. Following a phase for the identification of such conflicts, the EU shall put itself forward as mediator between the parties to enable them to negotiate and to reach agreements which will be included in a broad pact on European stability and security. Thenceforward, the rights of minorities shall be recognized and borders shall be final and inviolable.

Paris Charter

A charter signed on 21 November 1991 by the member states of the CSCE. In it they proclaim their wish to cooperate for the purpose of ensuring respect for human rights, establishing democracy and the rule of law, economic freedom, friendly relations between states and security in Europe and the world.

PHARE
A programme established by the G7 in July 1989 to support and promote the process of economic restructuring and reconstruction in Hungary and Poland.

It was later expanded to include other countries in Eastern and Central Europe and the Baltic republics. The Community plays a fundamental role since, through the EBRD, it supplies the majority of the G24 aid to the former Eastern Europe.

Primary Law
The constitutional framework of the Community, consisting of the treaties establishing the Community, the treaties on the accession of new member states and the treaties introducing reforms such as the SEA and the TEU.

Q

Qualified majority
Following the adopting of the Single Act, the Council stopped the practice of systematically aiming for unanimity, observed since 1966. A large proportion of Council decisions are adopted by a qualified majority. Article 148(2) of the Treaty of Rome lays down that for their adoption, acts of the Council shall require at least 62 votes in favour out of a total of 87 where they are adopted on a proposal by the Commission and 62 votes in favour cast by at least 10 members in other cases. The votes are weighted as follows: France, Germany, Italy and the United Kingdom, 10; Spain, 8; Belgium, Greece, the Netherlands and Portugal, 5; Sweden and Austria, 4; Denmark, Ireland and Finland, 3; Luxembourg, 2.

Since the Single Act, decisions have been taken by qualified majority on matters pertaining to the establishment and functioning of the Internal Market, to the area of research and development and to public health.

The TEU extended the scope of the qualified majority decision-making procedure to encompass sectors such as agriculture, transport, the environment, vocational training etc.

R

Regulation (161 TEU)
A generally applicable Community legal act. It is binding in its entirety and directly applicable in all member states.

Rio Group
Established in 1986 as a Permanent Mechanism for Consultation and Political Conciliation, the Rio Group is the most important Latin American political forum for dialogue and the practical promotion of integration. It has eleven members: Argentina, Bolivia, Brazil, Chile, Colombia, Ecuador, Mexico, Paraguay, Peru, Uruguay and Venezuela. In addition, a Central American country chosen by the counties of the isthmus and the country holding the Presidency of the Caribbean Community (CARICOM) have observer status.

The group maintains institutionalized relations with the EC/EU, ministerial conferences being held annually. These meetings involve the national

Ministers for Foreign Affairs of both integration programmes. On 20 December 1990, they signed the Rome Declaration which provides for a broad programme of mutual consultation and cooperation.

S

Safeguard
A measure to protect a production sector or branch against any serious damage due to an unforseen increase in imports.

Schengen (Agreement and Convention)
An agreement signed between Germany, the Benelux countries and France with the aim of abolishing internal border controls and establishing free movement of persons without discrimination on the basis of nationality. On 19 July 1990, the five countries signed a convention providing for common regulations with regard to the fight against terrorism, drug trafficking and crime as well as immigration, political asylum and visa policies.

Italy joined the group in 1990, Spain and Portugal in 1991 and Greece in November 1992.

Seats of European bodies and institutions
EP .... Strasbourg
(Secretariat in Luxembourg and Brussels as place of work)
CEC .... Brussels
Council .... Brussels
Court of Justice .... Luxembourg
Court of Auditors .... Luxembourg

ESC .... Brussels
EIB .... Luxembourg
EBRD .... London
WEU .... Brussels

Council of Europe .... Strasbourg
OECD .... Paris
NATO .... Brussels

Decision adopted by common agreement by the
Twelve at the Brussels summit of 29 October 1993:

Agency for Health and Safety at Work .... Bilbao
Centre for Development of Vocational Training .... Thessaloniki
EC Translation Centre .... Luxembourg
EMI and the future ECB .... Frankfurt
European Agency for the Evaluation of Medical Products .... London
European Environment Agency .... Copenhagen
European Monitoring Centre for Drugs and Drug Addiction .... Lisbon
European Training Foundation .... Turin
Europol and the Europol Drugs Unit .... The Hague
Office for Harmonization in the Internal Market
(trade marks, designs and models, including its
    Board of Appeals) .... Alicante

Office for Veterinary and Plant Health Inspection and
Control, ...Dublin

Secondary legislation
All the measures adopted by Community institutions to implement and
develop the principles and objectives of the Treaties (Regulations, Directives, Decisions, Recommendations, Opinions).

Single European Act
The treaty which came into force on 1 July 1987, amending the Treaty of
Rome and extending its objectives. It incorporates provision for the completion of a true internal market with full freedom of movement for persons,
goods, services and capital. It improved the Community decision-making
procedure, by increasing the number of laws to be adopted in Council by
a qualified majority and giving the EP a larger role in European integration
(cooperation procedureà. The Single Act extended the Community's powers
to environmental and research and technological development policy and
encouraged the harmonious development of the Community by creating the
Structural Funds (ERDF, ESF, EAGGF) for the less-favoured regions, social
groups and sectors, as a necessary counterweight to the internal market.
  The Single Act laid the foundations for a nascent common foreign policy
(European Political Cooperation) of an intergovernmental type.

Social Charter
Adopted in Strasbourg in December 1989 by eleven Member States (the
exception being the UK), the Social Charter establishes the basic social
rights of workers. It was subsequently integrated into the TEU. The UK, in
a protocol, agreed that the other Member States should develop social policy
within the institutions, procedures and mechanisms of the Community.

Structural Funds
The Structural Funds comprise the EAGGF, the ESF and the ERDF. The
Community uses these funds to help bring about the economic and social
cohesion of different regions and layers of society within the EC.

Subsidiarity
The principle according to which the European Union must only assume
those tasks which can thus be better fulfilled than if the Member States act
individually. This principle is defined in Article 3B of the TEU. Its objective
is to ensure that decisions are taken as close to the citizens as possible.

T

TACIS
A technical support programme established to promote the process of economic reform in the CIS and Georgia. It was adopted by the European
Council at Rome in Decembe 1990 and ratified by the Community and the
then USSR in 1991. It was later revised in February 1992 due to the break-
up of the Soviet Union.

Third Generation Agreement
Following the first generation agreements, which were commercial in nature, and the second generation agreements, which cover financial and economic aspects, third generation agreements include technology, training, the environment and non-institutionalized political aspects.

Tomb of the Pharaohs
In Community slang, a nickname for the new Council building in Brussels.

Treaties of Rome
Treaties establishing the European Economic Community (EEC) and the European Atomic Energy Community (EAEC or Euratom). They were signed in Rome on 25 March 1957 and came into force on 1 January 1958.

V

Value Added Tax (VAT)
VAT represents one of the Community's own resources, accounting for approximately 60% of revenue, and is derived from the levying of a uniform percentage from each Member State's revenue from VAT.

Visegrad Treaty
A treaty signed in 1991 by Poland, Hungary and the former Czechoslovakia with the aim of creating a free trade area between these countries for a period of ten years.

W

Western European Union (WEU)
The origins of the WEU lie in the Treaty of 1948, revised in 1954. At present, it has ten Members: Germany, Belgium, France, Italy, Luxembourg, the Netherlands, Portugal, the United Kingdom, Spain and Greece Denmark and Ireland have observer status. Norway, Turkey and Iceland are associate members. The WEU has its seat in Brussels.

The TEU incorporates the WEU in the development of the European Union and accords it a key role in future common defence.

White Paper on Growth, Competitiveness and Employment (1993)
A working document approved by the European Council of December 1993 to stimulate fresh thinking and cooperation in the taking of decisions leading to greater sustainable development in the European economies, allowing them to face challenges posed by international competition whilst at the same time creating millions of jobs.

It contains plans for trans-European transport and communication networks, research and technological development, education for life, and changes in the vocational training and educational systems.

Notes

Introduction

1. The plural of cow, *Kühe* in German, sounds phonetically very similar.
2. A. Spinelli: *Diario Europeo 1976/86*. Il Mulino, 1992, p. 320.
3. 1898 was the date of the Spanish-American war, with the end of the colonial Empire and a deep cultural change.
4. *The Federalist Papers*, introduction by Gary Mills. Bantam Books, 1982.

Chapter 1   A Ramble Round Historic Maastricht

1. José Ortega y Gasset: *La Rebelión de las masas*. Colección austral, Espasa Calpe, 1986, p. 197.
2. E.L. Jones: *El Milagro europeo*. Alianza Editorial, p. 136.
3. Data taken from Mary McLure & Derek Blyth: *A walk through Maastricht*. Stichting, Historische Reeks Maastricht, 1990.
4. Vide. G. Duby: *Les Foires de Champagne*. Geoffrey Parker: *The Spanish Way*.
5. Angus Macab: *España bajo la media luna*. J. Olañeta, 1988, p. 28.
6. Duroselle: *Historia de los europeos*. Aguilar, p. 106.
7. The 'Battle of the Spurs of Gold' (1302) is the Flemish epic narrated in romantic literature in *Le Lion de Flandre*, by Henri Conscience.
8. Fernand Braudel: *La Méditerranée à l'époque de Philippe II*. Vol. II p. 21.
9. Ramón Carande: *Carlos V y sus banqueros*. Ed. Crítica, 1987, Tomo I, p. 1.
10. Roy Strong: *Arte y poder: las Fiestas del Renacimiento*. Alianza Editorial.
11. Op. cit.
12. Martin Rady: *Carlos V*. Alianza Editorial.
13. '*CESARIS POTENTIA PRO REGIS PRUDENTIA ISTE EXCELSIUS MONS ET ARGENTUS ORBEM DEBELARE VALENT UNIVERSUM*'
14. Paul Kennedy: *The Rise and fall of the great powers*. Unwin & Heyman, London, 1988, p. 31.
15. R. Carande: Prólogo, op. cit. p. 14.
16. P. Kennedy, op. cit. p. 71
17. Jean Bodin: *Méthodes*, p. 9.
18. Pieter Geyl: *The Revolt of the Netherlands*. Cassell History, pp. 60 and 66.
19. *Historia de los europeos*, p. 273.
20. The *Sedanfeste* commemorated the German victory in 1870 over France at the Battle of Sedan. The *Heroenkult* is the cult of heroes.
21. Maurizio Serra: *La ferita de la modernità*. Il Mulino, 1992, pp. 35–6.
22. P. Kennedy: *The rise and fall*, op. cit. p. 48.
23. *La Naissance*, op. cit. pp. 137–39

Chapter 2   An Open-Ended Constitutional Process

1. *La Naissance d'un continent nouveau.* Fondation J. Monnet pour l'Europe. Centre de Recherche européenne, Lausanne, 1990, p. 121.
2. *La Naissance d'un continent . . .* p. 41.
3. It comprises the French Council for a United Europe, the Independent League for Economic Cooperation, the New International Teams, the European Union of Federalists, the European Parliamentary Union and the United Europe Movement.
4. *La Naissance d'un continent . . .* p. 45.
5. Federico Mancini: *La Corte di Giustizia: uno strumento per la democrazia nella Communità Europea.* Il Mulino, 3/93, p. 595; *Democracy and the European Court of Justice*, Mancini & Keeling, Skimizu Lecture, London School of Economics, April 1993.
6. Laurent Cohen-Tanugi: *L'Europe est en danger.* Fayard, p. 119.
7. Vid. Gil Carlos Rodríguez Iglesias: *Tribunales Constitucionales y Derecho Comunitario 1993.*

Chapter 3   The Community Labyrinth

1. Emile Noël: *L'Acte Unique européen et le Développement de la CE.* Actas del XIV Congreso Mundial de Ciencia Política. Washington, 1988.
2. General Affairs and Foreign Affairs, Agriculture, Ecofin, Social Affairs, Transport, Energy, Internal Market, Consumers, Environment, Development, Research, Education, Culture, Health, Budgets, Fisheries, Telecommunications, Justice, Industry, Immigration.
3. The jungle of Community acronyms is an inextricable labyrinth. There are specialized Commission officials responsible for the virtuosic devising of acronyms for Community programmes, seeking to produce a Latin word on the basis of the initial letters in English.
4. The troika, formed by three ministers, representing the previous, current and next Presidency respectively, helps ensure continuity of action.
5. In fact, there are two COREPERs:
    COREPER 1 comprises, despite its numeral, the assistant permanent representatives. It deals with budget, fisheries, agriculture, social affairs, internal market, transport, environment, culture, education etc.
    COREPER 2 comprises the ambassadors, and deals with external relations, association agreements, cooperation and development, finance and economics, the preparation for European Councils, and has achieved control of CSFP. Of course it is entitled to tackle any subject.
6. Le Monde, 25.9.1983.
7. This is the new name following the Treaty; previously it was called the Commission of the European Communities.
8. *Mémoires de l'espoir.*
9. S. Mansholt: *La crisis de nuestra civilización.* EUROS, p. 45.

10. Greens v. EP, 23.4.1986; Comitology: EP v. Council, 27.9.1988; Chernobyl ruling, 22.5.1990.

11. The acronyms represent the following political groups: PSE, Group of the Party of European Socialists; PPE, Group of the European People's Party (Christian Democrats); LDR, Group of the European Liberal, Democratic and Reformist Party; V, Green Group in the European Parliament; ADE or RDE, Group of the European Democratic Alliance; ARC, Rainbow Group; DR, Technical Group of the European Right; NI, Non-attached Members.

   The countries are: B, Belgium; DK, Denmark, D, Germany, GR, Greece, E, Spain; F, France; IRL, Ireland; I, Italy; L, Luxembourg; NL, Netherlands; P, Portugal; UK, United Kingdom.

12. The 1993 Brussels Council also fixed the number of seats for the countries seeking accession: 21 for Sweden, 20 for Austria, 16 for Finland and 15 for Norway.

13. La Constitución de la CE. Noticias CEE (5/93).

Chapter 4   The Gestation of the TEU

1. J. Habermas: *Conciencia histórica e identidad postradicional.* Letra Internacional, n°9.

2. With reference to this issue, the Agreement reached at the Edinburgh Council is substantially what was agreed by the Bureau of Parliament, unaided, a good two years earlier.

3. A battle which was won in 1066 by William the Conqueror and the invading Normans. As a result, French was the language of the English court until the fifteenth century.

Chapter 5   The Treaty on European Union (TEU)

1. J.V. Louis: *El Ordenamiento jurídico comunitario.* EEC Commission, Fourth edition, pp. 111–140.

2. J. Habermas: *Ponencia base de un encuentro en el Instituto de Filosofía del CSIC,* Madrid, pp. 10 and 11.

3. Jean Monnet, *Mémoires,* Fayard, p. 460.

4. J. Delors's speech at the opening of the ESC Conference on a Citizen's Europe. Brussels, 27.9.1993.

5. Addressing the round table on regulation/deregulation, Encuentro España en la Unión Europea. Instituto Euroforum.

6. Eleazar: *Exploring Federalism,* University of Alabama, 1987.

7. El País, 30.09.1993.

8. Eleazar: op. cit. p. 239.

9. J. O*Toole and W. Bennis: *Our Federalist future: the leadership imperative.* California Management Review, Summer 1992, Vol.34, n°4.

10. Eleazar, op. cit. p. 197.

11. Eleazar, op. cit. p. 43.

Chapter 6   From The ECU, Illegitimate Child, To The Euro, Sole Heir

1. See Giscard d'Estaing: *Le pouvoir et la vie.* Vol. 1.
2. Interview with Angelo Bolaffi. L'Espresso, 24.5.92.
3. F. Braudel: *Les Jeux de l'Echange.* Arnaud Colin, pp. 169–170; *Les structures du quotidien,* p. 407.
4. P. Kenen: *'Speaking up for EMU'.* Financial Times, 28.7.92.
5. M. Emerson and C. Huhne: *The ECU Report.* Pan Books, 1991.
6. Philippe Jurgensen: *Naissance d'une monnaie.* J.C. Lattès, p. 114.
7. Klaus Reeh: *L'Allemagne, la loi et l'après-Maastricht,* 11.8.93.

Chapter 7   Sailing Towards Convergence

1. M. Emerson: *The ECU Report,* p. 196.
2. M. Emerson: *The ECU Report,* pp. 54–55.
3. C. Tugenhadt. *Alianza,* p. 66.
4. Padoa-Schioppa and other experts: reports to the Commission on efficiency, stability and equity. 1988.
5. T. Padoa-Schioppa: *L'Europa verso l'Unione Monetaria.* Einaudi paperbacks, 1992, p. 11.
6. Financial Times, 22.10.1993.
7. Peter F. Drucker: *Post-capitalist Society,* Butterworth-Heinemann, Oxford, 1993, p. 69.
8. M. Matthes: *Europäische Wirtschaft und Währungsintegration.* Goethe Univ., Frankfurt, 1987.
9. Michel Albert: *Capitalismo contra capitalismo.* Paidós, 1992.
10. Ph. Jurgenssen. op. cit. p. 110.
11. The Economist. 13.6.1992.
12. Ch. Bean, London School Economics; D. Cohen, Ecole Normale Supérieure (Paris); F. Giavazzi, Un. Bocconi (Milán); A. Giovannini, Columbia University (New York); J. Von Hagen (Mannheim); D. Neves (Liège); X. Vives, Un. Autónoma de Barcelona; Ch. Wypolez (INSEAD): *L'Union monétaire face à ses critiques.*
13. Speech in Madrid on 26.10.92. Le Monde 13.11.1992.
14. Addressing the EP Subcommittee on Monetary Affairs. 6.10.1993.
15. Lester Thurow, interviewed in *L'Express.* 11.9.1992.

Chapter 8   Do Employment and Welfare Have a Future?

1. Peter F. Drucker: *Postcapitalist society,* op. cit.
2. Lauren Bacall: *By myself.*
3. Financial Times, 23.10.1993.
4. Peter F. Drucker: op. cit. p. 35.
5. Thurow: op. cit. p. 75
6. Peter F. Drucker: op. cit. p. 180.
7. Peter F. Drucker: op. cit. p. 1.

Chapter 9 Europe and the World

1. Le Monde, 11.09.93.
2. Speech in the Salle Gothique of the Town Hall, 9.1.1994.
3. David Calleo: *The US and Security in the New Europe.* Art. in Colectiva *Global responsibilities: Europe in tomorrow's world.* Bertelsman Foundation, p. 164.
4. Calleo, op. cit. 182.

Epilogue

1. Jean Guéhenno: *La Fin de la démocratie.* Flammarion, p. 146.
2. Victoria Camps: *Virtudes públicas.* Espasa Calpe, Colección Austral. Epilogue to the paperback edition.

Index